FRED HALLIDAY

POLITICAL JOURNEYS

The openDemocracy Essays

Edited by David Hayes

SAQI

ISBN 978-0-86356-461-1

First published by Saqi Books in 2011

A full CIP record for this book is available from the British Library.

A full CIP record for this book is available from the Library of Congress.

Printed and bound by CPI Mackays, Chatham, ME5 8TD

SAQI
26 Westbourne Grove, London W2 5RH
www.saqibooks.com

POLITICAL JOURNEYS

Contents

Introduction

by STEPHEN HOWE

The essays collected here, written for openDemocracy between the start of 2004 and the end of 2009, explore many of Fred Halliday's abiding preoccupations. He comes to them always with fresh knowledge and insights. They demonstrate how his range of interests, passions and enthusiasms continued always to broaden. And they delve into matters, like Halliday's intense sense of place and his diverse literary loves, which his previous writing – for all its extraordinary range – had rarely touched upon. Those who come new to him with the present collection will find an ideal introduction to his brilliance in all its diversity. Beginning here, at the last stage of his journey in politics and thought, they will – one hopes – be stimulated to go back to its start and to follow all the intervening twists and turns. There is something to be learnt from every phase in his travels, just as Halliday himself was always learning even as, simultaneously, he taught the rest of us so much.

In September 2005, in an essay republished here ('Maxime Rodinson: In Praise of a "Marginal Man"'), Halliday paid tribute to one of the writers who, for decades, he had most admired, the French Marxist Maxime Rodinson. Rodinson was, he suggested, not only the greatest of all French writers on the Middle East, 'arguably the greatest *tout court*', but an inspirational model of intellectual integrity in wider ways – in his 'unceasing belief in universal values, in the need for intellectual aspiration beyond what one is actually capable of, and for an enduring, unyielding scepticism towards the values and myths of one's own community.' He praised Rodinson's committed secularism, his life-long refusal to indulge the iconic claims of 'identity', 'community' or 'tradition', as well as the remarkable breadth of his knowledge and sympathies, and the unrelenting rigour of his scholarship. Halliday could, had he been a less modest man, have been writing about himself. The qualities he praised in Rodinson were those he himself possessed, perhaps in greater measure than any other writer of his generation or any other commentator on Middle East or wider international affairs.

Halliday's academic specialism, the field in which he taught and held his professorships, was International Relations. 'IR' is sometimes seen by critics as a rather self-enclosing scholarly ghetto, not to mention being in the main an ideologically conservative one. Halliday's relation to it was thus always and inevitably a healthily sceptical and critical one; his position consciously that of an inside-outsider. Yet his contribution to it was huge. If the academic IR mainstream often seemed to emphasise, even fetishise, continuity – proclaiming the undying relevance of seventeenth-century and earlier thinkers like Hobbes, Grotius or Machiavelli – Halliday's great enthusiasm was for exploring radical change.

If the dominant current in North Atlantic IR theory, that rather question-beggingly dubbed 'realism', appeared to think that states were the only important actors in the global system, Halliday always recognised the significance both of supra-state economic and political structures (here the lessons learnt from Marxist thought remained productively present in his work) and of sub-state or non-state actors, especially social movements including, crucially, those fighting for women's rights.

He thus brought to bear an understanding both of structure and of agency – especially that of people and movements in the Global South – far richer and more complex than that available to many IR specialists. He intervened both sharply and thoughtfully in the heated debates over method and approach that marked the study of IR, after the end of the Cold War had seemingly made many of the discipline's old assumptions obsolete. But equally, he had suitably little patience with the claims, both vague and hubristic, advanced by some in IR as elsewhere that everything had suddenly changed beyond recognition, all older theories and methods been made redundant. Such claims, usually loosely labelled 'postmodernist' (does anyone still remember postmodernism?), were the objects of some of Halliday's most vigorous and frankly impatient negative polemics. Echoes of these can be found in this book, as can salutary doses of the irreverence, even mockery, he rightly brought to bear on so many received ideas about global politics and on the pomposities and the dishonesties of the powerful – as in the essays 'The World's Twelve Worst Ideas' and 'The Attorney General Comes to Town'.

Ever since the 1970s, Halliday brought together, both imaginatively and systematically, the 'East–West' and 'North–South' conflicts that have shaped our world, in a way which almost no other contemporary commentator from the Left or Right has done. He always saw the Cold War as involving a genuine and profound clash of ideologies and social systems, and as having a huge, abiding legacy. (He explores one facet of this in 'Cold War Assassinations: Solved and Unsolved', included here.) But the global picture, and the possibilities for illuminating transnational comparison to which he was always so alert – this collection includes many brilliant examples of that – never obscured for him a keen recognition of the distinctiveness and importance of particular places, of local conflicts and loyalties. His Irish childhood, where travelling just a few miles from his hometown of Dundalk took one not just across an international frontier but into utterly different, often antagonistic, cultural and political worlds, no doubt taught him that at an early age. (See the very first essay here, 'Lessons from Ireland'.) Subsequently, and helped by his astonishing flair for languages, he had an almost uncanny ability to catch the political atmosphere of diverse places and spaces; one articulated in the many wonderful political travel reports collected here, as in so much of his earlier writing – read his tales from Cuba and Yemen, from Madrid, New York, Beirut, Jerusalem, and perhaps above all, those from Tehran.

And his sharp eye for change did not mean that either of the twin concepts so massively shaping Halliday's earlier work, imperialism and revolution, had lost their relevance in the twenty-first century. He insisted on the continuing 'pertinence of imperialism'. Sketching the history of radical thought on imperialism, he argued that it encompassed five broad themes: the 'inexorable expansion of capitalism as a socio-economic system on a world scale'; the inevitably competitive, expansionist and warlike character of capitalist states; the global reproduction of socio economic inequalities; the creation, also on a world scale, of inequities, which were not only economic, but also social, political, legal and cultural; and that through the very process of capitalist expansion, movements of anti-imperialist resistance would inevitably be generated.

All of these claims, Halliday argued, retained force in the world of the twenty-first century. Ironically, and of course uncomfortably for Leftists, it was the last of them – the fate of anti-imperialism, and of what are often now termed 'anti-systemic' and 'anti-globalisation' movements – which had been most thoroughly transformed.

Across the twentieth century, massive struggles against imperialism and capitalism, whether revolutionary or reformist and usually calling themselves socialist, had convulsed the world. But all had seemingly failed. More, we have witnessed 'the deformation of anti-imperialism itself.' Anti-imperialism had classically involved a set of shared, universalist, goals including democracy, economic development, equality of men and women, and secularism, and a belief in a potential historical alternative. Today, all this had seemingly been replaced in many quarters, around the globe, by movements of religious fundamentalism, ethnic chauvinism, romantic anti-modernism and other irrational ideologies. This historic regression, as Halliday saw it, was the most disturbing and depressing of all contemporary global developments. Militant political Islam was just one of its manifestations, though the one to which in his later writings he devoted most attention.

Imperialism, then, was alive and well, but anti-imperialism in its previous progressive forms was direly sick. This, though, did not imply that the idea of revolution, anti-imperialist or other, was defunct. Indeed Halliday devoted one of his most lastingly important works to analysing this idea: *Revolution and World Politics: The Rise and Fall of the Sixth Great Power* (Palgrave Macmillan, 1999). This was a bold attempt to compare all the world's major revolutions of the past few centuries, and evaluate the continuing significance of the whole phenomenon of revolution. As he often pointed out, International Relations as an academic subject has neglected the importance of revolutions in reshaping the world system. The most influential modern studies of revolutions, meanwhile, have usually been inspired by historical sociology, and have been very weak on their international dimensions.

Straddling academic specialisms as sure-footedly as he does centuries and continents, Halliday's work corrects both deficiencies. Essays in this book like '1968: The Global Legacy', 'The Lessons of Communism' and 'Terrorism in Historical Perspective' superbly exemplify those skills.

Halliday believed that the political utopianism that drove Communist dreams – or such latterday successors as faith in a morally perfect world order based on Islam – has a never-ending capacity to renew itself. We live in a world that is more unequal than ever before; and global communications ensure that more people are bitterly aware of that inequality than in any past age. For all the complacency that may reign among the world's richer and more stable societies – a complacency, Halliday also notes, disconcertingly like that which prevailed a century ago – we have almost certainly not seen the end of the age of revolutions. What is far more doubtful is whether future revolution might hold out any rational hope of furthering the political ideals and humane values in which Halliday believed. (See, for instance, the essays here on 'The Vagaries of "Anti-Imperialism"' and 'Iran's Revolution in Global History'.)

If imperialism and revolution were two of the great overarching themes of Halliday's work, then surely the natural third pillar was the idea of internationalism with its close relative, that of solidarity. He published, or delivered as lectures, many different reflections on aspects of this – many of his openDemocracy columns were variations on that theme – and had planned a major book on it. His premature death must mean that such a work can never appear in the way he might have wished it, though apparently there are strong hopes of bringing together the work he had already done into book form. He believed that in the course of the later twentieth century something strange, and distorting, had happened to these concepts. In their true form they depended on one central principle, that of (as he put it in a lecture on 'The Fates of Solidarity', which to my knowledge remains unpublished):

> the shared moral and political value and equality of all human beings, and of the rights that attach to them. The concept of solidarity presupposes that of rights ... The reason to support others within our own society or in others is that they too have rights, by dint of the humanity we share.

The contemporary crisis derived from the way so many on the Left had abandoned that principle (the political Right had never really believed in it): denigrating the very language of universal human rights; attacking the international institutions and conventions that tried to implement it; disparaging the values of rationalism and the Enlightenment which are its necessary foundation.

Militant Islamism, and those Western Leftists who entered into a tactically foolish and morally repugnant alliance with it, were again just a particularly extreme expression of these very widespread and ominous tendencies. Many must share the blame for helping undermine the better ideals of internationalism and solidarity: the legacies of colonialism and of Communism were especially culpable, but numerous contemporary intellectual currents – including ones espoused by close friends and former comrades of Halliday's – had contributed to this moral and political disaster. (See the essays here: 'The Crisis of Universalism' and 'Looking Back on Saddam Hussein', among others.) Too many had succumbed to a regression, whereby membership of a particular community, or particularistic claims of ethnicity, nationality or religious adherence, were believed to confer special rights, or particular moral advantage. Such degenerate developments, Halliday felt – and exemplified in many detailed analyses – were especially prolific in relation to the Middle East and to the politics of Islam. He discussed them extensively in relation to the Israeli–Palestinian conflict, but also reflected on them several times in relation to the Ireland of his birth.

Halliday brought the same intellectual values and qualities to bear on his discussions of Political Islam, and of Islamophobia. (See his 'Anti-Muslimism and Contemporary Politics' in *Islam and the Myth of Confrontation* [IB Tauris, 1996], and several of the essays in his *Nation and Religion in the Middle East* [Saqi Books, 2000], as well as the Iranian and other Middle East-related pieces in this collection.) He carefully explored the way in which, in recent years, hatred of Muslims has evidently been politically salient in several far-flung places, including America, Britain and France, among right-wing Israelis and Russians, advocates of Hindutva in India and of Heavenly Serbia.

Each of these, however, is, as he insists, an antagonism with very specific, local political roots, and is best explained and challenged in terms of each of those specific circumstances. 'Anti-Muslimism' is, in his words, not one ideology but several. Islamists, however, are by definition committed to the view that there *is* a shared, invariant, essentially timeless Islamic character, and that by the same token, any manifestation of hatred towards Muslims, anywhere, must be directed against that character. Their ideology negates the possibility of any more local, contextually and historically specific explanations. Thus there is a very ironic twist here – maybe one of the few things that really *is* almost unique to Islamist thought and its enemies. Islamists do not react to 'Islamophobia' by criticising or deconstructing the stereotypes (as blacks or Jews or gays usually do), but by accepting them as badges of pride: 'Yes, you're right: we really are a deadly threat to all that you hold dear – and a good thing too!' So Halliday, writing in a spirit of sympathy and solidarity with the victims of anti-Muslim hatred, found himself under attack from those who proclaimed themselves spokespeople for a mythicised, homogenised 'Islam'.

All this and more was brought together with characteristic breadth, boldness and humour in a short essay written at the start of 2005 (and reproduced here), where in a kind of manifesto for what proved to be the last phase of his work, Halliday proposed a new key to the contemporary international system: the 'Three Dustbins Theory'.

The mid-1990s, he suggested, marked the end of the interregnum following the end of the Cold War, itself the third chapter, after the two world wars, in a great century-long European civil war. Today that European era is decisively finished: 'After five centuries when the Atlantic was the strategic and economic centre of the world, the focus has now shifted to East Asia and the Pacific.' Yet too much of our thinking remains prisoner to the Cold War's legacy and its enduring myths, contained in those three dustbins. Dustbin One holds the legacies of communism: unresolved ethnic conflicts; corrupt, authoritarian and inept post-Soviet elites and their regimes – 'a transition not to democracy but to post-Marxist kleptocracy'; and nuclear proliferation. The Second Dustbin, Halliday suggested:

> is that of the West, the USA in particular. One of the costs of winning the Cold War is that the West has failed to rethink its assumptions about the conduct of international relations. Instead, and above all with the Bush administration, we have seen the recycling of policies that were as wrong then as they are now.

Worst of all are a 'pervasive denial, compounded by self-righteous declamation' about the consequences of past policies, notably America's role in creating the 'terrorist threat' itself, and an imperial arrogance in the exercise of power over other peoples and instinctive resort to force. We shall now never know whether or not Fred would have seen the Obama administration as effectively breaking from those legacies, struggling out of that dustbin. The Third Dustbin, though, contains far too much of the international Left and its thinking. The contemporary global protest movement, Halliday charged, resembles 'a children's crusade of intellectual demagogues, dreamers and unreconstructed political manipulators.'

So, in his last years Fred Halliday was beginning to sketch a new map of the world, bringing together his multiple interests and spheres of expertise. The essays in this book, forty-five pieces written across the last six years of his life, represent perhaps the fullest flowering of that diversity – as David Hayes, his editor at openDemocracy, says:

> In subject-matter, the columns embrace the world – from Jerusalem to *jihadism*, Finland to Libya, Iraq to Fred's native Ireland, Cuba to his beloved Yemen and Iran; in style they combine sharp political assessment with rich personal memory and voice; in content they deploy years of concentrated learning and observation in the constant effort to understand, to *get inside* the reality under scrutiny. Everything in this collection exudes Fred's immense scholarship and range, his boundless intellectual curiosity – and not least his sheer love of life, which is so movingly conveyed in the last selection of this volume, his celebration of Barcelona.

Fred Halliday's illness, and then his heartbreakingly early death at the age of 64 in April 2010, cut short the continuing, ever-changing evolution of his thought. His was an intellectual journey that could have no 'natural' end, but deserved far better than so brutal, so total a break. Despite all their remarkable richness and variety, these essays can give only a taste of what would still have been to come. Those who knew Fred Halliday personally will read, or re-read, him here with sharp sorrow for all that might have been, as well as with enormous pleasure. Those who were acquainted with him only from his earlier published work will discover in this book many new, unfamiliar Hallidays. They may also catch a hint of how creative and important was the relationship between Fred and openDemocracy. He found, in his last period of active work, much to be disillusioned with, or disturbed by, in how the 'old forms', both of British academia and the mainstream media, were developing. The newer, more open communicative form of openDemocracy, and relations with his close comrades and collaborators there – Anthony Barnett, Tony Curzon Price, David Hayes and others – were a lifeline for him, as well as the setting for the last great flowering of his creativity.

Perhaps one might conclude by saluting Halliday's particular combination of mutability and steadfastness, his coupling of a willingness always to question and rethink with lifelong adherence to a set of core values. In one of openDemocracy's memorial tributes, it was recalled how he would joke (I recall him using very similar words to me): 'At my funeral the one thing no one must ever say is that "Comrade Halliday never wavered, never changed his mind."'

And of course no one, in all the thoughts and memories poured out since Halliday died, has dared say that. Yet he also wrote, with a characteristic hint of self-mockery:

> That is my tribe, the Bani Tanwir, or what might be called the descendants of Enlightenment rationality. And, as with most tribal affiliations, seeing what a dangerous world it is outside, I do not intend to forsake it.

And he never did.

Preface

For the past five years, I have had the great pleasure and stimulus of writing a column for the website journal openDemocracy. What began as a provisional and intermittent engagement on both sides has developed into one of the most extended and challenging writing commitments I have known. No subject, no country, no awkward view has been excluded; and the editors, if at times seeking to insert some editorial good sense while keeping me to the overall mission of that fine journalistic project which is openDemocracy itself, have ultimately given me the freedom to range over the countries and topics that have engaged me. The result has been over eighty columns, at times weekly, later monthly; a selection of which, supplemented by a few pieces written elsewhere at the same time and published in other journals, forms the present book.

If there is an underlying theme in this work, beyond the eccentricity of its author, it is that of the times in which these articles were written: the time of the aftermath of 9/11 in Europe, the USA and the Middle East; the growing involution of the Bush administration; and the tension evident in so many spheres of life across the world between the claims of unilateralism and power and those of diversity and respect, ideals that are understood as much in cultural as in political terms. Inevitably, a selective vision prevails: I wrote these articles against a background of working and teaching in Britain since the 1960s, but have spent much of the past five years teaching and researching in Barcelona. In this city, I have found a different vantage point from which to observe this world of ours, at once fascinating, tragic and, in the repeated outbursts of human hope and decency that mark it, hopeful.

None of this would have been possible without the support and sustained encouragement of my editors, first at openDemocracy and later at the Barcelona paper *La Vanguardia*, which ran many of these pieces on its 'Opinion' page. At openDemocracy, it was the publisher Anthony Barnett, a friend of over forty years, who first encouraged me to write regularly for them, while David Hayes has worked enthusiastically and helpfully on my articles over the years, with an editorial professionalism, commitment and discretion I have rarely met. It was David, too, who prepared the first version of this book, carefully constructing its sections and selections, and it is to him above all that my thanks are due for the continued relationship I have with the journal. That David and Tony Curzon Price, openDemocracy's editor-in-chief, should have proposed and encouraged this collection, to which they have shown such commitment, has been a source of great encouragement to me.

Fred Halliday
Barcelona, 1 November 2009

One

Points of Departure

I. LESSONS FROM IRELAND
26 May 2005

Dundalk, Republic of Ireland. In much of the world an optimistic, even romantic view of events in Ireland seems to prevail: a mixture of timeless mysticism around 'the Isle of St Brendan'; neo-liberal simplification of the Republic's recent economic record; and a naive if not opportunistic misrepresentation of what is inaccurately termed 'the Northern Ireland Peace Process'. If in the USA this is largely a matter of pro-Catholic exilic propaganda, in other countries it takes a different form, nowhere more so than in Spain, where in addition to their affection for *cerveza negra* ('black beer', i.e. Guinness), many involved in the Basque cause seek to draw comfort from the Irish case. There are certainly lessons for the Basques and the Madrid government to draw from Ireland, but these are not examples that should bring comfort to anyone except those committed to an enduring intimidation and brutalisation of democratic politics.

The British elections on 5 May 2005 may have confirmed Tony Blair and his Labour Party in their continued, mildly reformist, hold on power in the United Kingdom, but in Ireland they have marked a watershed –

welcome for some, ominous for many others – in confirming the dominance of intransigent parties within the two communities in Northern Ireland, Sinn Féin on the Catholic/nationalist side and the Democratic Unionist Party (DUP) on the Protestant/loyalist side, which promise years of confrontation to come. The DUP leader, the Reverand Ian Paisley, has called for the 1998 Belfast peace agreement to be 'buried'. Some would suggest that with the IRA refusing for seven years to disarm, and the persistence of violence and intimidation within the Catholic community, the funeral must have taken place long since; even if, as has happened before in these parts, it was in secret. Much of this is unseen by the outside world, whether through innocence or short-term reluctance. But if one holds to the dictum that those who cannot think straight about Ireland cannot think straight about anything, then there is no better place to start than the town of Dundalk, home to 40,000 and capital of the smallest county in Ireland. (County Louth lies along the east coast of Ireland, half-way between the twin political capitals, Belfast in the North and Dublin in the South.) The *Rough Guide to Ireland* warns, with a vague reference to menace, that tourists should stay away from Dundalk. It is easy enough now to speed through on the road bypass or train from Dublin to Belfast. In my case this is somewhat harder to do, as Dundalk is my home town, the place where I grew up and which has been, for some five decades or more, the source of many political emotions and insights.

Beyond taking the pulse of Ireland, North and South, Dundalk is a litmus against which to test broader claims about nation and religion, state and society, politics and economics – not to mention right and wrong, peace and violence, and, let us not forget, truth and lies. Recently, talking to a wise long-term observer of the town's affairs, I asked him if, over the past thirty years, anyone around there had changed their mind about anything. He looked at me a bit askance and replied curtly: 'Of course not.' That was all that needed to be said.

Against a backdrop of the ever-changing Cooley Mountains to the north, this is the quintessential frontier town, diverse in composition (including a district named after its Huguenot settlers): an uneasy but special vantage point for observing this island's politics. Dundalk is a town that has seen many of the vicissitudes of violence in the course of European history: the Irish poetic hero Cúchullain fought in the neighbouring mountains; the Vikings tried to settle here; in the seventeenth century Cromwell made it the outer limit of his stockaded colonial zone, 'the Pale'. In the nineteenth and early twentieth centuries it was integrated into the industrialising economies of Northern Ireland and north-west England, linked by regular shipping to Scotland and Lancashire and by rail to Ulster.

Modern Irish politics has severed it from its economic links to the industrial north. People here have long memories, going back to the British semi-criminal 'Black and Tans' racing around the main streets, the fighting of the civil war between pro- and anti-'Treaty' groups in the 1920s, and more recently, the first post-war bombing campaign, of 1956–8, during which IRA volunteers trained a few miles out of town. The war in the North, which broke out in 1969, led to many uneasy movements and sealed mouths. Yet for much of the past century it has been famous as the political and possibly more general centre of activities of the Irish Republican movement, the rear base of the IRA and, more recently, the breakaway 'Real IRA'. Ian Paisley oft denounced it as not 'Dundalk' but 'Gundalk', or 'El Paso'. In 1982 Margaret Thatcher famously told Ronald Reagan that if the Israelis were justified in invading southern Lebanon, she should be sending the RAF to bomb the town.

More recently, things have begun to look up. European and some US investment has brought jobs to the town; the road and rail links to Belfast and Dublin have been greatly improved; and a new Technical College – in effect a new university – with 7,000 students has just celebrated its first twenty-five years. In 2000 Bill Clinton came to town and addressed a huge crowd, citing his friendship with local pop group The Corrs in the main square. In a bid to break the image of sectarian hostility associated with its history, the local museum and the Technical College recently held a festival of Protestant culture, replete with a pipe band, drums and a visit from senior members of the Orange Lodge. One of the latter was photographed shaking hands with the Sinn Féin chair of the local council, a first indeed. The Belfast peace agreement of 1998 has certainly spawned all sorts of cross-border and commercial activities.

Yet as my wise companion's remark to me suggested, and the British general elections have shown all too clearly, all is not quite as rosy as it would seem in this part of Ireland – or indeed in the island as a whole. To see the emergence of this polarised politics solely in terms of Northern Ireland, and with implications only for this province, would be mistaken. As has been the case for a century or so, the conflict in

Northern Ireland has implications for the future of Ireland as a whole, in particular for Sinn Féin, the political wing of the IRA, which is now developing a strategy in both North and South of Ireland designed to secure its place in a future ruling coalition in the decades to come.

All of this has been accompanied by the largely successful publicity campaign carried out by Gerry Adams and his associates in recent years. Adams has presented himself as a man of peace, even, God help us, as a statesman, offering advice to the Basques about the prospects for peace in Spain and producing mawkish autobiographies that make him out to be some sort of neo-Celtic gentleman. His policy of weakening and overtaking the more moderate, anti-violence SDLP has been greatly helped by the passage of time: the younger generation has forgotten the killings, disappearances and tortures, and admires him for getting the kind of TV coverage that the more staid and responsible SDLP leaders John Hume and Seamus Mallon never got. Yet the IRA has not changed, and the professed difference between the IRA and Sinn Féin, whereby Adams issues 'appeals' to the IRA, is in fact no greater than that between a ventriloquist and his dummy. As the killing of the Belfast man Robert McCartney in January and of a Dublin man some time later showed, the republican movement continues to operate on the ground as a criminal organisation. In Dublin it is deeply involved in the drugs trade. Any social momentum created by the 1996 killing of the pioneer anti-drugs journalist Veronica Guerin, later recorded in a dramatic film, has been lost. The republican movement, as supremely contemptuous as it always was of democracy or the legitimacy of law or majorities, retains its weapons and its powers of intimidation: 'We still have the tool kit in the garage,' as they say. In the South there is growing awareness that whilst pursuing its criminal activities, the IRA has also been engaged in a sustained clandestine campaign to infiltrate the middle ranks of the Republic's administrative and security services.

Nor is this turn a purely Irish affair: the conflicts of Ireland may be insulated from Britain, a convenience that serves both sides quite well (and is eased by large subsidies of up to €10 billion a year for economic and security expenditures, from London to Belfast), but the polarisation in the North is very much of a piece with the rise of particularist, identity-based, nationalist politics elsewhere in Europe and indeed across the world. Like all nationalisms, Irish republicanism celebrates its difference and uniqueness, except when it suits some of its leaders to parade themselves as Nelson Mandela or Martin Luther King: but what is happening beneath all the posturing, smiling and self righteous indignation that marks Northern Irish politics is a tale of broader significance, one that will not go away. The same goes for the supposed economic success enjoyed by the Republic: the economy may have boomed, but as *The Celtic Tiger in Distress* (Palgrave Macmillan, 2001), a critical study by Dublin social scientist and journalist Peadar Kirby, documents so well, this has been at the cost of increased social polarisation and widespread poverty, all adding up to a neglect by the Irish state of much of its social responsibilities.

The polarisation in the North and social problems in the South provide a good recruiting ground for the republican movement. What Sinn Féin is aiming for is not just some entrenched blocking role in Northern Ireland, but a long-term partnership with the main ex-republican party in the South, Fianna Fáil. At the moment, the FF leadership under Bertie Ahern is critical of the IRA; its refusal to engage in visible and convincing disarmament, and its involvement in criminal activities relating to violence and drugs: but the resurgent nationalist mood in Ireland, fuelled in part by the economic boom of recent years, and the apparent domestication of Sinn Féin, the result of a sustained and mendacious public relations exercise by Adams and his friends, has shifted opinion quite substantially. Middle-ranking FF officials now talk quite openly of entering into a long-term alliance with Sinn Féin to hold power in Ireland for decades to come. This is the real significance and unstated strategic goal of the Sinn Féin strategy in Northern Ireland.

One longer-term lesson of these Irish events, which has broader significance for other developed countries, is that the consequences of European civil wars take many years to be overcome. In a marked reversal of the normal, themselves ideological, allocations of 'civilisation' and 'barbarism', it is noteworthy that Third World countries are often better able to overcome civil wars, and integrate the supporters of victor and defeated alike, than the supposedly more sophisticated states of Europe. The civil war in Nigeria in the 1960s, in Yemen and Oman in that and later decades, the war in Vietnam that ended thirty years ago in 1975, and the later civil wars in Central America all produced winners and losers: but these countries have, to a considerable degree, moved on. The Biafrans are very much part of Nigerian life; few among the young in today's Vietnam care for the bloody war between north and south.

Yet in the European countries that had civil wars in the last century – Ireland, Spain, Finland and Greece – not to mention the USA after 1865, the political differences endured. Irish politics is still split between the factions that fought what were, in effect, the two civil wars of the twentieth century: that in the South, over the Treaty, from 1922 to 1924; and that in the North, between Protestant and Catholic, from 1969 to 1998. If for whatever reason others seem to have forgotten this, we can rest assured that the leadership of Sinn Féin, their eyes set on power in a reunited Ireland, have not.

2. 1968: THE GLOBAL LEGACY
11 June 2008

'With the coming of the dawn, the promises of the night fade away'. In politics, as in love, the old Spanish saying sounds a pertinent warning; not least in regard to the memorialisation and assessment which the events of 1968 (and particularly the Paris uprising of May of that year) are receiving on their fortieth anniversary. Anyone who lived through those exhilarating and formative times – as I did at the age of twenty-two – can testify to the hurricane force of that year. Like every such phenomenon it carried multiple elements: in this case a generation's visceral rejection of the accumulated conformism of post-1945 Europe and North America; a heady encounter with new forms of music, art, thinking and debate; and a many-centred solidarity with global movements of protest and revolt – be they in Vietnam or Latin America, in Czechoslovakia or Russia, or in the United States among African-Americans and anti-war protesters.

As one of the editors of the newly founded radical weekly *Black Dwarf*, I well remember the day that we decided on the front-page affirmation that to me encapsulated the aspirations and enthusiasms of that time more than any other: 'Paris, London, Rome, Berlin. We shall fight, and we shall win!'

The problem is that in many ways, we lost. 1968 was a wonderful time. It shaped the intellectual and moral framework of my adult years. It does not deserve the sneering, partisan dismissal of some of its unacknowledged beneficiaries such as Tony Blair and Nicolas Sarkozy. But it is equally ill-served by the kind of one-dimensional and (in the true sense) uncritical celebration that contemporary media, publishing and intellectual cultures too often regurgitate.

A recollection of the larger political currents that contextualise the experience of 1968 exemplifies the point. The theatre of Paris in May '68 notwithstanding, the year did not alter the politics of any Western European country. France is the primary exhibit. A month after May, after all, came the mass rallies in favour of Charles de Gaulle in the Champs-Elysées; followed by the general elections of 23–30 June in which the French Right won a resounding victory. When de Gaulle resigned a year later, his successor was the loyal subordinate Georges Pompidou. It took until 1981 for a candidate of the Left, François Mitterrand, to be elected president – and this socialist was a former Vichy collaborator whose conspiratorial style of politics was the very opposite of the best of May '68. Such tainted political advances are characteristic of the year's ambiguous legacy.

In Britain, too, the anti-Vietnam War demonstrations of March and October 1968 (in both of which I was an enthusiastic participant) did not presage any wider change, either within or outside the parliamentary system. The protestors denounced the Labour Prime Minister Harold Wilson, but his replacement after the election of June 1970 was not a figure of the Left but a Conservative, Edward Heath. In the United States, 1968 marked the onset of a politically reactionary epoch rather than a progressive one. The election of Richard Nixon on 6 November, albeit narrowly won, was its augur; though it came to fruition only with Ronald Reagan's victory in 1980, after the insipid administration of Jimmy Carter in the late 1970s – just as the Labour governments of Wilson and James Callaghan in Britain were in retrospect an interlude in a long Conservative hegemony, confirmed by Margaret Thatcher's election in May 1979.

True, Germany did see a momentous and long-overdue political change with the victory of Willy Brandt's Social Democratic Party (SPD) in 1969 (marking, as Brandt's victory speech had it, the final defeat of Nazism). But this was self-evidently the work of an established party descended from the respectable Second International centre-left, not the 'extra-parliamentary opposition' of 1968. Rudi Dutschke, whose rhetorical and personal appeal had enthralled me at a conference on Vietnam in Berlin in January 1968, was permanently damaged by an assassination attempt in April that year, which forced his withdrawal from the scene.

But one polity in Western Europe that was irrevocably altered by 1968 was Northern Ireland, dominated since the 1920s by the representatives of the province's Protestant majority, the Ulster Unionist Party. The rise of a 'civil-rights movement' demanding equal voting, residence and employment rights for Catholics soon collided with the state's sectarian institutions and instincts. After serious inter-communal violence exploded in 1969 and the British army was deployed to guarantee order, leadership of the Catholic community was seized by the Provisional IRA, a murderous and itself sectarian body that owed little to May 1968 and far less to the non-violent civil rights movement in its American or Northern Ireland variants. I well recall, in an interview in Dublin in 1971 with the then Provisional leader Rory O'Brady (this was before he became Ruairí Ó Brádaigh), making an inquiry about the connections between his 'national liberation' movement and that of its putative equivalents in Vietnam and Cuba. His brisk reply was worthy in tone and content of the schoolmaster he was: 'Mr Halliday, in Ireland we have no need of your Che Guevaras and your Ho Chi Minhs.' The pattern of the three decades to come was being set, whereby militarised Catholic nationalism battled its enemies to a dead end over the bodies of hundreds of innocents, its struggle finessed or cheered by 'socialist' fellow travellers who strained to see a trace of the dreams of 1968 in the carnage.

That the political consequences of 1968 defied its combatants' ideas and hopes is not to our disgrace. The events were indeed extraordinary, and remain indelible. What is wrong in the memorialisation is the fetishism of the moment, and the associated loss of perspective and overall judgement, which leads to three kinds of distortion of focus. The first is that the glorification of what was and remains positive about 1968 obscures – and thus at some level perpetuates – the darker sides of the year. In retrospect, the most striking absence from the currents of the time was that of feminism: true, there was talk of 'sexual liberation', but the radical critique of gender came only with the 'second-generation feminism' of 1969 and later. (I recall attending the Dialectics of Liberation conference at London's Roundhouse in July 1967: among thirty prominent left-wing and radical speakers there was not one woman; equally, no one commented upon this absence.)

The second distortion of the 1968 events is the way that the indulgence of violence is filtered out of consideration. Much of the Left thought little about the ethics and politics of violence beyond regarding it as permissible (and even beyond criticism) as long as it was the weapon of the oppressed; but a small section of the movement in Europe and North America, intoxicated by self-glorifying rhetoric and unable to face the blockage of their own politics, opted for proclaimed 'urban guerrilla warfare'. The Rote Armee Fraktion (RAF) in Germany, the Brigate Rosse in Italy, the Black Panthers and Weather Underground in the United States were (as much as hippies, anarchists and proto-environmentalists, though with far more damaging effects) also the children of 1968.

The third distortion of judgement in regard to 1968 is the absence of political realism: the ability to match aspiration and imagination with a cool assessment of the balance of existing political forces. It was the political 'winners' who were to benefit from the events of the year (among them Georges Pompidou, Richard Nixon and Edward Heath) who in this respect showed a political capacity that their adversaries in the lecture halls or on the barricades more often lacked.

The inability of many leftist '68ers to anticipate or comprehend the conservative reaction to their own initiatives represented by these 'statesmen' is telling here; as is the unreflective tendency of those who espouse some variant of revolutionary Marxism to laud 1968 as a single moment of glorious resistance without looking too closely at its dynamics. This fatal lack of political realism, however, is only part of a wider absence of understanding of the whole period: in particular, the inability of those who prefer the myths to the realities of 1968 to see that this was a time not of 'world revolution' but of international, indeed 'tricontinental', counter-revolution.

The years from the mid-1950s to the mid-1960s had seen a spate of revolutions and less dramatic but real changes across what was becoming known as the 'Third World': in Indochina (Vietnam, Cambodia, Laos); in the Arab world (Egypt, Iraq, Algeria, Yemen); in Africa (the Congo, South Africa, Ghana, Kenya); and in Latin America (Bolivia, Brazil, Cuba). From the mid-1960s, however, a series of events indicated that the tide was beginning to turn. The coup in Brazil in 1964; the fall of the moderate Soviet leader Nikita Khrushchev in the same year; the coup in Indonesia; the invasion by the United States of the Dominican

Republic and South Vietnam in 1965; the coup that ousted Kwame Nkrumah in Ghana in 1966; the coup in Greece; the six-day Arab-Israeli war; and the death of Che Guevara in 1967: all heralded a global shift to the right, of which Richard Nixon's victory in the US presidential election of 1968 represented the culmination.

It took until the mid-1970s for a further sea-change to occur, with the end of fascism in Portugal and Spain in 1974–5 and a spate of revolutionary victories (Vietnam, Angola, Mozambique, Ethiopia, Iran, Nicaragua) in what was not yet known as the 'Global South'. The 'Second Cold War' of the 1980s closed one cycle and opened another. By then, many veterans of 1968 had long exchanged thinking through the present for romanticised celebration of the past.

The most dramatic events of 1968, and the ones with the greatest long-run consequences were not, however, in either Europe or North America, nor in the Third World, but in the Second (that is, communist) World. Two events in particular – the August 1968 Soviet invasion of Czechoslovakia, which crushed the liberalising 'Prague spring' under Alexander Dubcek, and the apogee of China's Cultural Revolution in 1967–8 – signalled the brutal imposition of authoritarian and coercive bureaucratic communism. In Prague, Moscow and Beijing – all a world away from the liberal and culturally experimental milieu of Paris or Berkeley – it was not the emancipatory imagination but the cold calculation of party and state that was 'seizing power'. Yet in the longer run the counter-cyclical reinforcement of hard-line communist rule in its two major centres proved less durable than appeared likely at the time.

Indeed, the repression of 1968 contained the seeds of the demise of the regimes that deployed it. In Europe, the decision by Leonid Brezhnev and his associates to invade Czechoslovakia in effect killed the last threadbare hopes that a progressive evolution of communist societies was still possible. The casualties included the next generation of intra-party reformers, who thus had few reserves of loyalty or enthusiasm to call on beyond the party nomenklatura and who were challenged by dissidents now hardened by experience to contemplate only the demise of communism rather than its reform. The brief flowering of optimism under Mikhail Gorbachev proved as evanescent as that under Nikita Khrushchev, but this time with far more serious results for the communist edifice. In Western Europe, the collapse of faith that the Soviet system deserved even a modicum of trust was even more damaged by the Red Army's invasion of Czechoslovakia than by that of Hungary in 1956. At least the wholesale evacuation of members from Moscow's 'brother parties' in 1956 did not damage their core; but Prague led the communist leaderships (in Italy especially) onto the road of coalition-seeking 'Euro-communism' and thence to effective oblivion.

In China, the violence, fear and societal damage inflicted by the Cultural Revolution were on such a vast scale that the generation which came to power after Mao Zedong's death in September 1976 sought to pursue a moderate and reforming path. The system survived, but it lost its inner doctrinal conviction. What is left is nationalism and fear of the people: whom it can appease only as long as 'market socialism' delivers the goods. For all their zealotry, the years following 1968 spelt the end of revolutionary commitment.

Much of the Left in Western Europe and the United States feted China's Cultural Revolution in displays that mixed political misjudgement, exoticist fascination and infantile irresponsibility in equal measure. The warnings of older and wiser observers such as Isaac Deutscher and Herbert Marcuse against the dangers of collectivist frenzies were heard, but also ignored.

It is clear in retrospect that 1968 did not bury European capitalist democracy or American imperialism. It did, however, set in train the death and burial of the Russian and Chinese revolutions and of communism in Western Europe: a fine example indeed of the cunning of history.

3.   WHAT WAS COMMUNISM?
16 October 2009

Few occasions are more propitious for forgetting the past than moments of historical commemoration. Amidst fond recollections of the fall of the Berlin wall, and in a time of at least temporary improvement in relations between Russia and the West, few may spare a thought for what it was that ended two decades ago. On two issues History has given its ultimate verdict: the Cold War, the third and longest of the three chapters that made up the great global civil war of 1914–91, will not return; the USSR, both as a multinational state and as a global ideological and strategic challenge to the West, is indeed dead. However, on a third component of this story, the worldwide communist movement, the verdict is, as yet, less clear.

Communism, embodying the ideology and the social aspirations underlying the Soviet challenge, and the worldwide echo evoked by that challenge remain to be interred. To bury communism can only be done on the basis of a recognition of what it represented; why millions of people struggled for and believed in this ideal; and what it was they were struggling against. It can also only be done when the legacy of this ideology and movement is assessed, and not simply forgotten or conveniently – and in violation of all historical evidence – dismissed as an 'illusion'.

Judging by the politics and intellectual debates of today, neither those who celebrate the end of communism nor those who are now articulating a radical alternative have carried out such an assessment: between the still resilient complacency of market capitalism and an increasingly uncertain world of liberal democracy, on one side, and the vacuous radicalisms that pose as a global alternative on the other, the lessons of the communist past remain largely ignored. And so, as they say, they will be repeated.

The question of what kind of political and social system communism was has occasioned several candidate explanations. These explanations include: a dictatorial tendency whereby revolutionary elites seized control of societies; a flawed movement for the self-emancipation of the working class; an expression of messianism; a product of oriental despotism; and a failed developmentalist project.

Communism embodied features of modern politics that should not be abandoned: a belief in mass participation in politics; a radical separation of religion and state; a promotion of public, political and economic roles for women; hostility to inter-ethnic conflict; and an insistence on the need for the state to intervene in the economic and social affairs of its people. Joseph Stalin and Gosplan may have discredited a particular form of 'planning', but the general application of rational scientific, managerial and political thinking to human affairs, the better to manage the future, is an entirely legitimate and necessary aspiration, not least in an age of resource depletion and looming ecological crisis. Communism had no monopoly on these ideas – any tough-minded liberal could have supported them – and the interpretation given to these values was authoritarian, bloody, in some cases criminal. This does not mean, however, that these goals, democratically and humanely conceived, are not necessary parts of a contemporary politics.

On the other hand, we have to look unambiguously at the failure of communism, rather than avoiding the issue which too many retrospective analyses have dodged: the fact that its failure was necessary, not contingent. This system, denying political democracy and based on the command economy, did not just fail because of a false policy here or there, let alone because classical Marxist theory was abandoned. As even sympathisers like Rosa Luxemburg realised in 1917 itself, it was bound to fail from the beginning.

It is common, and somewhat too easy, for defenders of Marxism in the contemporary world to argue that Marxist theory and communist practice were divergent, hence the theory bears no responsibility for the communist record. This raises the question whether another Marxism, a more liberal, 'genuine' or 'democratic' version – or, if you incline in the other direction, a more resolute, militant and disciplined one – could have prevented the collapse of the communist states. The answer is no.

There were certainly choices for the Soviet system throughout its seventy-year history: the New Economic Policy (NEP) could have been continued after 1928; there could have been a different trajectory in the mid-1930s if Stalin and not Sergey Kirov had been assassinated, or Nikolai Bukharin had become party leader; if Nikita Khrushchev had not been ousted in 1964, economic reform of the kind Mikhail Gorbachev would attempt after 1985 might have begun twenty years earlier. And so on. As for the final period, the Soviet system could certainly have continued for another generation if another Soviet leader, a conservative like Grigory Romanov or Viktor Grishin, had come to power in March 1985 instead of Gorbachev. But, in the longer run, neither the prevailing CPSU ideology, nor, in my view, any variant of the Marxist tradition remotely related to 1917 could have saved, let alone developed that regime. It had reached a dead end, but that aporia, although contingent in timing and form, was inevitable sooner or later.

The revolutionary socialist movement was not, however, some mistake, some aberrant illusion: it was at once a global movement of collective purposive action across all continents and a product of the structural tensions within the development of capitalism over the past two centuries. It is therefore pointless to begin a critique of it by seeing it in those terms. It had its illusions, but so do the capitalist ideology which posits that everyone can become a millionaire, the newly fashionable 'wellbeing' fantasy that the process of ageing can be halted or reversed, and the irrational belief in divine beings and afterlives that much of humanity still espouses and in many societies, East and West, tries to impose on others. Like these fantasies, socialism was an inevitability, as much as the other features of the development of capitalist modernity – be they democratisation and scientific change, authoritarian capitalism, war between states or colonialism.

For that reason, the revolutionary socialist movement was, in its very illusions and delusions, itself a creature of its times and of some of the chimeras that beset those times, not least a belief in a 'science' of human evaluation and action. That there were and to some extent remain elements in the Marxist tradition that contributed not just to the revolutions, but to the particular bloody and criminal records of these regimes is due especially to four central elements of the communist programme: the authoritarian concept of the State; the mechanistic idea of Progress; the myth of Revolution; and the instrumental character of Ethics.

First, and as central to revolutionary Marxism as it is to the radical politics of the Islamic world, is the anti-democratic Jacobin theory of politics and of the 'state': this, rather than the self-emancipation of the masses, or workers, or oppressed Muslims, is the core concept, indeed the core goal, of all modern revolutionary politics, secular or religious, from Lenin to Osama bin Laden. Secondly, and equally central to modern revolutionary thought, is the supra-historical concept of 'progress'. Of course, it can, in certain ways, be defended: there has been progress in, for example, medical knowledge, or human wealth, or the development of capitalist democracy. This does not mean, however, that history has a destination, an 'end' in the sense of a goal or telos, and of the kind implicit in most nineteenth-century thought. Even less does it imply that the pursuit of such a telos guides or legitimates political action or, in more than a few cases, the killing of 'reactionary' people.

Closely related to the myth of 'progress' was the third dangerous myth, that of 'revolution', not just 'revolution' as a historical moment of transition and a means of making the transition from one historical epoch to the other, but 'Revolution', indeed 'The Revolution', as a historical myth, a cataclysm that was both inevitable and necessarily emancipatory. Part of the rethinking of the socialist tradition has to be a re-evaluation of this myth, one that is almost as powerful and surely as destructive in modern times as that of 'nation'. As with nations, it is possible to make a distinction between what one may term 'actually existing revolutions' (such as Russia, 1917; China, 1949; Cuba, 1959; Iran, 1979) and the broader ideological, myth; this latter myth, included within which was the idea of the 'irreversibility' of socialist revolutions, was shattered between 1989 and 1991.

The related myth that somehow 'Revolution' in the mythic sense remained possible within developed capitalism was disproved long ago, arguably by the failure of the German revolution in the early 1920s but in my view much earlier, in the failure of the revolutions of 1848. What Marx termed 'the sixth great power', in contrast to the five powers that dominated nineteenth-century Europe, became more and more confined to the semi-peripheral world. On the other hand, the reality of revolutions as historical moments – inevitable and voluntaristic, emancipatory and coercive – is central to the history of the modern world. Not only did these revolutions transform the countries in which they occurred; by forcing the dominant classes in the counter-revolutionary states to reform, they transformed capitalism in considerable measure as well.

Underpinning these three ideas – 'State', 'Progress' and 'Revolution' – was the fourth component of this legacy, the lack of any independently articulated ethical dimension. Of course it did supposedly exist – whatever made for progress, crudely defined as winning power for a party leadership and gaining power for a mythical working class, was defended. However, the greatest failure of socialism over its two hundred years, especially in its Bolshevik form, was the lack of an ethical dimension in regard to the rights of individuals and citizens in general, indeed in regard to all who were not part of the revolutionary elite, and the lack of any articulated and justifiable criteria applicable to the uses, legitimate and illegitimate, of violence and state coercion. That many of those who continue to uphold revolutionary socialist ideals and the potential of Marxist theory appear not to have noticed this, that they indeed reject, if not scorn, the concept of 'rights', is an index of how little they have learnt, or have noticed the sufferings of others. Unless and until they do, they have no right to claim that they are advancing the cause of human emancipation.

Communism failed and was bound to do so, given its internal weaknesses as well as the vitality of its opponents. However, we should not forget that this attempt to escape the conventional path of capitalist development was for a time remarkably successful, not least in the ideological and military challenge it posed to the West. But it was in the end forced to capitulate, and to do so almost without any semblance of resistance. If nothing else, the communist collapse deserves careful study from the perspective of those who believe in elite-led or state-dictated social and economic development: this is certainly one 'lesson' of communism.

There is, however, another equally important aspect of communism, which is too easily overlooked in post-1989 triumphalist Western accounts. As much as liberalism, communism was itself a product of modernity, of the intellectual and social changes following on from the Industrial Revolution, and of the injustices and brutalities associated with it: in the Industrial Revolution itself, whose early impact on the city of Manchester Friedrich Engels described so vividly in 1844; in the cycles of boom and slump that culminated in the 1930s; and in the violence of colonial occupation, exploitation and war. If Engels were to return today to the shanty towns of most Asian, African and Latin American cities, and not a few cities in the developed world, he would not be that surprised.

The greatest achievement of communism may well turn out to have been not the creation of an alternative and more desirable system to capitalism, but its contribution to the modernisation of capitalism itself: no account of the spread of the suffrage, the rise of the welfare state, the end of colonialism, or the economic booms of Europe and East Asia after 1945 could omit the catalytic role which, combined with pressure from within, the communist challenge played from without.

This was not just a utopian project but a dramatic response to the inequalities and conflicts generated by capitalist modernity. The continuation of many of these same inequalities and conflicts today suggests that further challenges of an as yet indeterminate nature will result.

4. A LUNCH WITH MARIO SOARES
29 April 2005

Lisbon. Mario Soares, or 'Dom Mario' as he is universally known, is at once relaxed, inquiring and perceptive over lunch in an Italian restaurant near the research foundation that bears his name in central Lisbon. Now eighty, the former foreign minister, prime minister and president from

1986 to 1996 is the most respected politician in this land of 11 million people and is busy in national and international politics. Portugal has been a republic since the 1910 revolution, one of the string of upheavals in semi-peripheral states, from China, Turkey and Persia to Russia and Mexico, that presaged and in some degree provoked the First World War. Yet today, over three decades since the Carnation Revolution that toppled the fascist state in 1974, there is one man who is regarded by many as the uncrowned monarch of this country.

Soares now articulates four great themes, tirelessly emphasised in speeches, interviews and newspaper articles at home and abroad: the critique of American power, in particular of US policy in Palestine and Iraq, and of the American abandonment of commitment to international law and institutions; the need for a strong federal Europe to play an independent role in the world; alarm at the spread of uncontrolled global problems; and defence of the social and political gains of the European socialist movement over the past decades. But he has remained loyal to some of the less fashionable ideas of his radical Portuguese past, not least anti-clericalism, as well as to his first love, poetry. The day we met, he was to spend the evening with three other Portuguese politicians to discuss their favourite poets, in his case all Portuguese.

Denounced in the 1970s by the Portuguese Left as an agent of US imperialism, Soares is today one of the most prominent radical critics of contemporary world politics, the most senior presence at the Porto Alegre summits and a tireless critic of the US role in the Middle East, of neo-liberal globalisation, of the short-sightedness of contemporary European Union rulers and indeed of the banal, visionless and timid mentality that prevails across the Western world. Since leaving the presidency in 1996 he has, if anything, become more radical, more pessimistic about the range of global problems, from human trafficking and the drugs trade to the spread of disease, than he previously was. Yet he retains a resolute optimism: he is, he takes care to point out, not a social-democrat but a socialist; an opponent of violence on the one hand and a committed opponent of contemporary capitalism on the other.

Under the Salazar dictatorship, Soares, like his father before him, who had been a minister in the democratic years before 1926, was imprisoned and for a time exiled. As a young man in 1944 he joined the Communist Party, both in anger at the indulgence shown by Western democracies to Franco and Salazar and on the grounds that it was the only organisation actively opposing the dictatorship, but six years later he broke with it because of its lies. He began to read Arthur Koestler, Hannah Arendt and George Orwell, and later to travel to Western Europe and the USA to denounce the fascist state. As the wars in Africa began to wear down the regime, he took the opportunity to voice greater criticism. In 1972 he re-founded the Socialist Party, originally established in the nineteenth century but eliminated after 1926.

Soares was in Germany when the 25 April revolution took place. There were no air links, so he went by train through Spain: arriving at the first railway station, Vilar Formoso, he found a crowd waiting with banners to greet him. To his amazement, he was asked by the commanding officer of the troops for instructions. There followed a year and a half of drama in Lisbon: an attempted coup by General Spínola, the conservative who had become president in April 1974; attempts by the Communist Party and elements of the far Left, entrenched in the military, to take power; culminating in the events of November 1975 when a far Left coup, ambivalently supported by the CP, failed.

Soares is scathing about CP leader Alvaro Cunhal's violent romance with the prospect of an armed seizure of power on the Bolshevik model, and only once shared a platform with him. It was Cunhal who, returning from exile, climbed on top of a tank; he also gave the game away in an interview with Oriana Fallaci by saying that parliamentary democracy would never establish itself in Portugal. But when it came to the April 1975 elections, the Socialists won 37 per cent of the vote and the Communists only 12 per cent. Soares is equally scathing about another person he met at that time, the US Secretary of State Henry Kissinger. Kissinger told him that Portugal was lost to the communists; that he was, in effect, 'the Portuguese Kerensky'. However, the American opined, this would be a good thing, since it would inoculate France and Italy from the danger of communism. Unlike Kissinger, who appears to have learnt nothing from his years in power, Soares is insistent on how much the events of those years altered his thinking.

As foreign minister in the post-revolutionary government, Soares was responsible for establishing relations with the Soviet bloc and for overseeing negotiations on a rapid departure from the African colonies where war had been raging – Angola, Mozambique and Guinea. One person about whom he tells an unexpectedly favourable story is the Soviet Foreign Minister Andrei Gromyko: Soares recounts how, on his first visit to Moscow in January 1975, he spent the evening dining with Gromyko and his wife and discussing the Russian poet Pushkin. He also has warm words for the European socialist leaders of that time, James Callaghan, Willy Brandt and François Mitterrand, who supported him politically and financially in the stabilisation of democracy in Portugal.

In retrospect, and through his words, the Portuguese revolution of 1974–5 was not, as it seemed to many at the time, an insurrectionary moment of workers, landless peasants and radical soldiers that promised the first socialist revolution in Western Europe since the Second World War, but a late and confused move by Portuguese society to catch up with the rest of Western Europe. For all the drama and uncertainty, the military posturing and the land seizures, less than twenty people died in Portugal in those months. Democratisation, abandonment of African empire and entry into the European Union were to follow. For all the drama of the months after April 1974 and the theatrical politics of the communists, radical military and Maoists (who counted among their youth leaders one José Manuel Barroso, now President of the European Commission), Portugal was like Spain and Greece undergoing that 'Catching-Up Revolution' which was to be experienced a decade and a half later by the countries of Eastern Europe.

The key to understanding Dom Mario is historical context. Soares is one of the last survivors of a generation of European socialists who fought and in the end overcame the fascist epoch that has dominated so much of the continent in the last century. The anger he felt at American and European acceptance of Franco and Salazar after the Second World War has never entirely left him. While most of those who made their name opposing communism have lapsed into silence or eccentricity, it is noteworthy that it is those who lived through and fought fascism, be it in Central Europe and Italy up to the 1940s or in the Iberian Peninsula up to the 1970s, who retained the most resolute commitment to democratic and secular values, and to a critique of capitalist globalisation. Politicians such as Willy Brandt and Soares and philosophers such as the late Norberto Bobbio and Jürgen Habermas share an intellectual and moral steel that is rarely matched by opponents of the former Soviet Union: there is rather a gap between these figures and the inanities of Lech Walesa and Natan Sharansky.

After years of right-wing rule, Portugal has now acquired a socialist government under José Sócrates, forty-eight years old and elected leader of his party only four months before the elections of 20 February. In a coincidence that Soares has hailed with excitement, for almost the first time in modern history Spain and Portugal both have socialist governments. It remains to be seen if, in a manner less colourful but perhaps more effective than in the dramatic chapters of the last century (Spain 1936–9, Portugal 1974–5), these two countries, isolated for decades from mainstream European politics, can revive and sustain some of the democratic and steady values that Dom Mario has so long embodied.

5.   THE FORWARD MARCH OF WOMEN HALTED?
4 May 2006

In 1981, before the dissolution of democratic socialism in Western Europe and the collapse of communism in the East, the Marxist historian Eric Hobsbawm published *The Forward March of Labour Halted?*, a short study on the state of the socialist movement. This perceptive and timely text, originally delivered as a lecture in 1978, pointed to a major reversal of left-wing and more generally emancipatory optimism across the world. Hobsbawm, a chronicler of working-class struggles, identified factors pointing to the stalling of a trend that had been in evidence since the early nineteenth century. Events have confirmed Hobsbawm's judgement and forced a revision of history and perspective regarding the socialist cause.

A similar rethink may now be in order regarding another great modern goal: the emancipation of women. While important differences exist, there are similarities between the workers' and the women's movements: in the ways in which a commitment to women's equality and fulfilment has eroded, strong opposition to this commitment has emerged, and the movement has lost the unity of purpose and vision and the clarity of ambition that sustained it in earlier times.

If fewer people today, in politics or everyday life, call themselves socialist, it would appear that even fewer proclaim a commitment to feminism. While never aspiring to the organisational unity associated with socialism, feminism has suffered from a lack of formal national or international cohesion. At the same time the earlier association of feminism with a broader programme of social emancipation and rationality has been eroded by the collapse of the broader trend and through a diversion of much 'third-wave' feminist theorising and debate into epistemological and political blind alleys

Still, there are many factors today which militate against such a conclusion. In politics, women have become more prominent in several countries, evidenced by the recent elections of presidents Michelle Bachelet in Chile and Ellen Johnson-Sirleaf in Liberia. Bachelet, a former political prisoner under the regime of General Augusto Pinochet, was herself tortured, and her father died in prison. When she took power, crowds took to the streets of Santiago shouting: '*Ya van a ver, ya van a ver! Cuando las mujeres tengan el poder!*' ('They will see, they will see! When women have the power!')

In a range of countries across Europe it has become widely accepted that there need to be quotas for election candidates and ministerial appointments. In Spain, half of all ministers are women. In Germany and the Scandinavian countries, quotas are generally respected; in France (where they are not), the major parties have been fined for not meeting the stipulations of the law. In Italy, even outgoing Prime Minister Silvio Berlusconi has conceded the principle of 30 per cent women in the cabinet. Germany has its own first woman prime minister, Angela Merkel. And in Finland, where a woman, Tarja Halonen, was re-elected president in January 2006, schoolchildren reportedly ask if, in their country, a man is allowed to run for head of state.

The impact of three decades of feminist engagement with politics and the law is also evident in a number of changes in public policy across the world. To give a few examples: as a result of work by feminist international lawyers, rape has been classified for the first time as a war crime, categorised by the international tribunals on former Yugoslavia and Rwanda as a form of torture; sexual discrimination and maltreatment have been accepted by some countries, among them Canada and Spain, as grounds for political asylum; while, according to Amnesty International, thirty-six countries in the world maintain laws that discriminate against women, gender discrimination in employment has been outlawed in many countries and major overt discrimination within the same employment and pay scale has markedly declined in some countries; and organisations involved with aid to the Third World and development policy in general have put gender concerns at the centre of their donation policies. In a related policy shift, the issue of world poverty – and associated questions such as mortality, education and HIV/AIDS – have come to be formulated in gender terms, with a clear realisation that it is women who bear a disproportionate share of the costs.

To have achieved all this in the space of one generation is a major achievement of the feminist movement, which, emerging in the 1960s and 1970s, sought to develop an overall critique of the ways in which gender and sex continued to structure all areas of social, economic and political life. In the area of social science that I specialise in, international relations, a rich literature on issues of war and peace, international law and development, peace and security, rights and social movements has brought the question of gender into even this most recalcitrant of academic disciplines.

Yet on the horizon, other trends can be observed. There is a marked turning away by many states from the formal commitments on women's emancipation made in the 1960s (covenants on social and economic rights), 1970s (the United Nations Convention on Discrimination Against Women of 1979) and 1990s (the Beijing International Women's Conference of 1995). The most dramatic non event of 2005 was an illustration of this: while the states and diplomats of the world rushed to hold review conferences for such issues as nuclear proliferation and the Barcelona Euro-Mediterranean process, no such meeting was held to mark the tenth anniversary of the Beijing conference, or of earlier such decennial events at Copenhagen (1975) and Nairobi (1985).

This retreat from past commitments is most evident in the former communist countries, and in now marketised post-communist dictatorships such as China and Cuba, where the earlier, albeit authoritarian interventions of the state in favour of women have been abandoned. Inequality in terms of employment and social provision is growing, and in a gesture to the Catholic Church and the new anti-feminist mood, the new Polish government abolished the position of minister for women altogether. The British government has done almost as well, having allocated the job to a little-known MP who receives no additional compensation for the responsibility.

State defection is matched by a shift in public mood. In a range of countries and a variety of rhetorical registers, respect for women and for the goals of decency and equality proposed by feminism has declined. Arnold Schwarzenegger's rise to the governorship in California was marked by grotesque and vulgar strutting, as well as by his sneering at opponents as 'girlie-men'. Italy's Prime Minister Silvio Berlusconi makes much of his macho activities, while President Pervez Musharraf of Pakistan dismisses rape victims' protests by asserting that for many women, a claim of rape is a way to get financial compensation and perhaps a visa to live abroad. President Hugo Chávez of Venezuela, meanwhile, entertains his audiences with sexist jibes at Condoleezza Rice, the US Secretary of State.

More serious and sustained, reflecting a definite and organised commitment, is the spread of anti-feminist social movements and religious groups across many countries. In the United States, the Supreme Court ruling that legalised abortion, Roe vs Wade (1973), is now under serious attack, and the abortion issue has become a major dividing line in US politics. In Europe, the Catholic Church – now led by the conservative Pope Benedict XVI – is openly calling for more church intervention in social and political life and a return to 'traditional' values on marriage, sex, women and homosexuality. The argument that the church's policies – such as its prohibition against the use of condoms – are responsible for endangering the lives of millions of people through AIDS has received relatively little attention. Instead, we see the emergence in Italian political life, and potentially elsewhere, of a 'theo-conservative' political trend, bent on rolling back the clock on advances in social and gender equality.

The situation in the Islamic world is even more catastrophic. Here the spread of Islamism as a social and political force is universally accompanied by an erosion of respect for women and their rights, and greater use of the law and state power to impose a new authoritarian set of norms. Just as in the Cold War, both communist and capitalist states combined their rivalry with each other with the imposition of social and political controls at home, so now in the 'long war' between the West and politicised Islam, a similar, mutually reinforcing reconsolidation of conservative values is taking place.

At the same time, the conservatives states of East and West – Iran, Saudi Arabia and Qatar on one side; the US, Vatican City and almost certainly a newly assertive Poland on the other – ally in UN conferences on the family and other issues to impose their agenda.

These shifts in political and social attitudes are compounded, however, by the endurance and, in the context of globalisation, reinforced inequalities of the workplace and life. Studies produced on the most recent International Women's Day (8 March 2006) showed that across developed countries, overall discrimination in work remained resilient although discrimination within specific professions may have declined. Poorer-paid jobs are still allocated to women, who suffer enduring discrimination across their working lives because of the interruptions of child care. In Spain, the overall pay gap is 40 per cent. In Britain, many women are confined to the sectors known as the 'five C's': caring, cashiering, catering, cleaning and clerical work. In the United States, under the pressures of combining parenthood and work, the percentage of women in the labour force has declined in recent years.

In a tone that is both encouraging and profoundly misleading, much is made of the ability of women to 'juggle' work and home; but as anyone who has tried it for long knows, this 'juggling' is often stressful and suffocating. It may be too early to draw up a balance sheet, but there are strong indications that globalisation, with its increased strains and demands (not least concerning hours worked and the erosion of social services) is enhancing gender differences across both the developed and developing worlds.

There are other, far worse, trends; the terrible incidence of violence against women in many contemporary wars, such as the estimated 40,000 rapes in the Democratic Republic of the Congo in the past six years; the high levels of violence against women in developed as well as developing countries (in the US, an estimated 700,000 women are raped per year); the spread of female infanticide in India and China; and the impunity of men engaged in 'feminicide', or the systematic killing of women. In Ciudad Juárez, Mexico, 4,500 women have disappeared and hundreds have been found dead (and often tortured) in recent years, with almost no police or state response.

Above and beyond all of this, there are the gendered consequences of the dramatic times we live in, notably the 'War on Terror'. The response in many Western societies, particularly the US, to Islamic extremist violence has been to reassert conservative and male so-called 'family' values in the face of an alien culture and its associated threat. In the Muslim world, the sense of hostility towards the West is associated with a cultural nationalism that denies modern or liberal Western concepts of women's equality and rights. The terror groups themselves play a role in this, vaunting a male form of violence and protest that allows no place for women. In their rhetoric and political objectives, as well as in the fear and violence they spread, these groups also defy any culture of tolerance, democratic debate and openness – all preconditions for the advancement of feminism.

This contempt for and rejection of all that women's emancipation and its associate democratic norms entail was brought home to me in one dramatic incident during the summer of 2004. On a visit to Madrid to see where the Islamist terrorist groups responsible for the 11 March bombings had been active, I went to the suburb of Leganés, a district of modern four- and five-storey apartment buildings much favoured by young families. There, on a leafy street, was the mangled wreckage of the block where seven Islamists had blown themselves up. Looking around, I noticed that the streets all had feminist names: the Avenida Petra Kelly and Calle Flora Tristan – named, respectively, for a German peace activist and founder of the Greens, and for a nine-teenth-century French writer active in workers' struggles for social justice. Other streets carried the names of Spanish and Latin American women writers.

Evidently, the local authorities in Leganés were committed to feminism and to the heroines and writers of that movement. But for the terrorists this had meant nothing; had they known what these names represented, they probably would have hated it all the more, just as their accursed associates in Bali and Egypt attacked night clubs and hotels where people relaxed. In this, and in all the fear and masculinist violence they have spread, they are representative of a much wider, more ominous global trend. The forward march of women may not have halted, but it is certainly having to engage a much broader range of fronts, with varied success.

6.   FEMINISM IN THE MIDDLE EAST: TWO PIONEERS
20 April 2008

The intellectual, moral and historic confusions that mark the contemporary age – the Middle East as much as any other region – make the loss of thoughtful and humane voices all the more bitter. When these voices have illuminated the central issues of women's rights and human progress, the gap they leave is indeed impossible to fill.

This is certainly true of two outstanding public intellectuals, the Iranian scholar and activist Parvin Paidar and the Lebanese artist and publisher Mai Ghoussoub, the cruelty of whose deaths is accentuated by how much they had still to give (Parvin died in October 2005 at the age of fifty-six, Mai in February 2007 at fifty-three). But if they deserve commemoration, it is for what they did and embodied as much as for their premature end, for in these too lie their legacy.

What is striking about each of these figures was their resolute clarity of commitment on perhaps the single most burning question of our times: the full emancipation of women. In light of the experience of the different countries that had formed them, they resisted oppressions both international and domestic; refused to accept the silence and subjugation demanded of them (by nationalist and religious leaders, but also by authoritarian parties of the Left); and engaged confidently and enthusiastically in the global debates about gender and politics in the 1970s and 1980s through which their generation of women transformed themselves – and their menfolk. They were the finest and most principled exemplars of that proud and unheralded tradition, that of modern Middle Eastern feminism.

For many of us who originated outside the Middle East yet whose professional work demanded that we understood it, the writings, criticisms and examples of Parvin Paidar and Mai Ghoussoub were a sure guide – as much as their encouragement and humour were life-affirming. Both Mai, who came to London in 1979 and (with André Gaspard) founded the unique publishing house Saqi Books in 1983, and Parvin, who after studying in London made a distinguished career with the United Nations where she promoted women's rights in Afghanistan and Central Asia, made generosity into an art-form.

Their writings leave a complementary legacy. Mai fused literature and political analysis to dissect the mix of political dogmatism, violence and nationalism that tore apart her Lebanese homeland in civil war and also disfigured much of the Arab Left. Her poignant short stories (*Leaving Beirut: Women and the Wars Within*, Saqi Books, 1998, reprinted 2007) and her reflections on art and memory (*Selected Writings*, Saqi Books, 2008) interweave the domesticity and fantasies of Lebanese women with the political upheavals that afflicted her country and speculations on the place of women in contemporary art. In retrospect, her excoriating earlier critiques of Arab nationalist violence and sexism – published both in the *New Left Review* and in the independent journal *Khamsin* (which she co-edited with comrades from Palestine, Iran, Israel, Syria and Iraq) – are distressingly prophetic in regard to 'Islamo-nationalist' groups such as Hamas and Hizbullah.

Parvin's experience grew out of the debates and struggles of the independent Marxist left that emerged in Iran in the last years of the Shah's rule, and the confrontations with the new authoritarianism of the Islamic Republic that emerged from the 1979 revolution. Indeed Parvin and the Iranian feminist current she helped to develop quickly took the measure of the zealous patriarchy of the Ayatollah Khomeini regime – a vivid lesson that women's equality, and the freedom not to wear oppressive clothing, were (as the orthodox left believed) primary not secondary issues. Parvin was one of the founding editors of the Persian feminist journal *Nimeh-ye Digar* (The Other Half). Her PhD at London's Birkbeck College (of which I had the honour of being one of the two examiners) set the experience of women in the Iran of her time within the broader sweep of modern Iranian political and social history; published as *Women and the Political Process in Twentieth-Century Iran* (Cambridge University Press, 1995), it won deserved acclaim as one of the finest books written on modern Iran. Indeed, in tracing the intertwining of gender and politics through Iran's tumultuous decades from the Constitutional Revolution of 1906 through monarchism and nationalism to the Islamic revolution, it is an outstanding work in the entire field of scholarship on women and public life.

Their personal and political experience made these two women profoundly internationalist. Each came from countries with a variety of religious and linguistic groups; each was consciously part of the broader international embracing of women's rights that (in the Middle East as much as in Europe or Latin America) broke through in the 1970s; each, in exile, sought to join with feminists and independent socialists from other nations and ethnic groups.

At *Khamsin* and later Saqi Books, Mai worked with a variety of colleagues from Israel, other Arab countries and Iran, as well as with some of us from Europe and the Americas who were fortunate enough to know and collaborate with her. Parvin, after finishing her doctorate, lived in Uzbekistan and Afghanistan, working on behalf of Save the Children and UNIFEM, promoting women's rights and economic participation in the face of the religious, tribal and often violent groups that had emerged from the wreckage of communism.

This quality is even more vital in light of the political, social and intellectual trends in the broader region in recent years: increasing marginalisation of and violence against women, and the emergence of a slippery, relativising discourse on women's rights (on such issues as the imposition of the veil). The whole cast of Mai's and Parvin's work stood against the grotesque and pervasive re-masculinisation of public space that has swept across the Middle East, symbolised by barking and bearded clerical leaders; and against such confections as 'Islamic feminism', 'cultural difference', 'tradition', 're-veiling' and 'identity politics'. Faced with misogyny and mystification, they insisted, without concessions to particularity or nationalist sentiment, on the right of women to speak, dress, work, organise and love freely.

There are many in the Middle East, women and men alike, who have, despite all obstacles, threats and depredations, remained true to the egalitarian, feminist and universalist commitment exemplified by Mai Ghoussoub and Parvin Paidar. Yet it is notable that – as in other regions of the world – it is those of a liberal (and often individualist) orientation who do more to defend the collective rights of women, gays, ethnic minorities or workers than the supposedly more principled and combative groups of the socialist or Marxist Left.

In regard to women in the Middle East, the Arab women intellectuals who have produced the *Arab Human Development Reports* – documents that hold Middle Eastern societies to account in terms of universal performance indicators – are liberals of a progressive, United Nations-centred persuasion. They, as well as lawyers like the heroic Shirin Ebadi and other women in Iran and across the Arab world, carry the torch of progress with little support from what remains of the political left. The work of this new generation of feminists – whether or not they would so describe themselves – is also a testimony to the pioneering trail Mai Ghoussoub and Parvin Paidar lit a generation ago.

Two

Shadows of Cold War

1. THE AGE OF THE THREE DUSTBINS
30 January 2005

The onset of the New Year winter sports season also signals the time of high rhetoric and visionary posturing about the contemporary world. This week the thinkers and managers of world hegemony assemble amidst the snow in Davos, Swizerland, while the anti-globalisation forces convene in the tropical summer of Porto Alegre, Brazil. On 20 January 2005, the inauguration of the third George W. Bush presidency occasioned an orgy of recidivism in Washington. The political classes in Europe are in their own way also shaping up for the contests of the year ahead: Spanish debate is starting to focus on the referendum on the European Constitution in February; a battered but seemingly resolute Tony Blair faces the polls in the spring; while Gerhard Schröder, exploiting his high-profile response to the tsunami disaster in which so many Germans were involved, seems to have found a second breath amidst the disarray of his Christian Democrat opponents.

In some ways, the international system in early 2005 presents a much clearer, more resolved picture than that through which the world has moved in the fourteen years since the collapse of the USSR and the end of the Cold War in 1991. In the first place, after some years of mixed signals, since 2 November 2004 the landscape of American politics, domestic and international, is now clear. The confused idealism of the Clinton 1990s and the discredited outcome of the 2000 presidential election delayed recognition of how the most powerful country in the world has evolved since the collapse of its global rival. Like it or not, this is the America we all have to live with.

Now we can see a president confident of his support, resolute in international bellicosity as much as in domestic dissolution of the welfare state, and a Washington elite and national consensus that are arrogantly indifferent to external concerns. Secondly, over three years after the event, we can see the impact of 9/11, within the US and internationally. The battle lines of a confrontation that is militarised in Iraq and Afghanistan but whose ideological and political ramifications are global are now drawn. Al-Qa'ida, inheritor of a transnational Islamist insurrection that began in the 1990s and which was defeated in several key states (Egypt, Algeria and Afghanistan), does not have the capacity to destroy the West. It does have, however, the power to mobilise, directly and indirectly, for years if not decades to come. Abetted by great sympathy amongst many young Muslims, it and its loosely coordinated allies have, in Ariel Sharon and George Bush, found two stalwart recruiting sergeants. More important than either of these clarifications, however, has been the consolidated rise of China in both economic and strategic domains. After five centuries when the Atlantic was the strategic and economic centre of the world, the focus has now shifted to East Asia and the Pacific. This, not Iraq, is the dominant story of 2004.

In all these respects, the world is now a more comprehensible and firmly defined place. 2004 marked the end of the interregnum following the end of the Cold War, itself the third chapter in the great European civil war that began in 1914 and within which the world wars comprised the initial two chapters. Yet in another respect this apparent distance between the contemporary world and the Cold War is delusory – and dangerously so. The intellectual challenge is how to characterise this condition. Here it would seem, if public debates and headlines over the past decade are anything to go by, that the only way to grab attention is to come up with some grand, if preposterous, theory: thus we have had the New World Order, the New Middle Ages, the End of History, the Clash of Civilisations, and now the War on Terror. In a no doubt vain attempt to match these tall stories of our time, and as a way of comprehending the contemporary international system, this article proposes another narrative, the Three Dustbins Theory.

The Three Dustbins Theory rests on the claim that despite the receding of the Cold War we are still prisoners of its legacy in key respects and will, unless we face up to these questions, remain so. As with all unacknowledged influences from the past, these repositories of conflict and myth are the more powerful because unacknowledged. Dustbin Number One contains the legacies of the Soviet and communist periods. Among its contents are: an array of uncontrolled and unmonitored nuclear materials, the maintenance and regulation of which has in large measure been discarded; a set of unresolved and, it would seem, irresolvable sanguinary inter-ethnic problems inherited from the Soviet period and its international extensions – Bosnia, Kosovo, Trans-Dniestr, Nagorno-Karabagh, Chechnya and Eritrea–Ethiopia – in all of which the costs of ethnic expulsion and fragmented government have provided a context for the entrenchment of mafioso power; and the consolidation, in nearly all of the former Soviet Union and much of formerly pro-Soviet Africa (as in the Horn of Africa and the recent Mozambique elections), of corrupt dynastic elites – a transition not to democracy but to post-Marxist kleptocracy.

Most significant of all of these   and now more clearly recognisable than ever – is the political character of the two most important states to have undergone the communist experiment: the neo-authoritarian dictatorship of Putin in Russia, and the consolidated and politically immobile dictatorship of the communist leaders in China. No transition to democracy here and none likely, not least because these two groups of rulers have made sure that they play the coquette to Washington in the matter of their 'wars' against, respectively, Chechen and Uyghur opponents.

The Second Dustbin is that of the West, the USA in particular. One of the costs of winning the Cold War is that the West has failed to rethink its assumptions about the conduct of international relations. Instead, and above all with the Bush administration, we have seen the recycling of policies that were as wrong then as they are now: the fabrication of threats by hostile states, accompanied by dire warnings about how time 'is running out'; the repetition ad nauseam of platitudes about the role of force in international affairs that no first-year student of the subject could get away with repeating; a suspicion, if not terrier-like disdain, for international institutions, notably the UN and international law; and a facile, historically short-sighted and grossly exaggerated set of claims about how many of the states of the world conform to an acceptable model (the 'Free World' of the 1950s and 1960s now recycled as claims about the number of states in the world that meet the criteria for democracy). Of the cruel and intellectually bankrupt certainties of neo-liberalism, which has undermined the social provision and regulation roles of the state across the world, there is no need to say more.

The greatest and least acknowledged legacies of the Cold War on the Western side lie, however, in two other domains. Here pervasive denial compounded by self-righteous declamation reigns supreme. One such legacy concerns the origins of the terrorist threat itself: al-Qa'ida and its ilk did not arise suddenly in 2001, or from the subconscious of the Islamic or Arab minds, but from the Cold War, in particular the financing, training and arming of tens of thousands of jihadi militants by the USA, Saudi Arabia and Pakistan for the war in Afghanistan in the 1980s. That war was to the early twenty-first century what the Spanish civil war of 1936–9 was to the mid-twentieth: the devil's kitchen in which the ailments and criminal practices that would later be unleashed on the world were first brewed. It is the greatest, if far from being the only, solecism of Bush's anti-terrorist campaign that he is incapable of recognising how far the USA helped to prepare this movement, just as it did the bands of UNITA murderers in Angola, the Contras in Nicaragua and, at one remove, RENAMO in Mozambique.

The other legacy of the Cold War on the Western side is both simple and all-pervasive: the mental attitude accompanying the exercise of power over other peoples, and the discussion of it by Washington; one predominantly of arrogance, ignorance and instinctive resort to force. This mindset, often bedecked with frothy claims about 'Imperial Burdens' and 'Grand Strategy', was evident in the Cold War itself, not least in the grotesque continuation of a nuclear arms race over four decades; it also draws in the USA, as it does much of post-imperial Europe, on the unacknowledged cultural legacy of colonialism. The West has still not learnt to treat the rest of the world on an equal footing, a point most graphically illustrated by the photographs from Abu Ghraib and the British army prison in Basra: it was not because the victims were Muslim, Arab or even non-white but above all because they were from a subordinate people that they were tortured with such levity and sadism.

It might be thought prudent to stop the argument there, with a generic denunciation of the powerful in East and West. But the unacknowledged legacy of the Cold War does not stop there and is equally to be found amongst those protesting against globalisation and convening this week in Porto Alegre. The Third Dustbin is that of the contemporary global protest movement, to a considerable degree a children's crusade of intellectual demagogues, dreamers and unreconstructed political manipulators of the old and new Left, whose claim to moral and analytic superiority too often masks a set of unexamined, often recycled platitudes from the Cold War period and, indeed, from the ideology of the Communist world. It is as if, having appeared to die in 1991, the anti-capitalist world movement leapt from the coffin in 1999 like Joyce's Finnegan at his Wake, having learnt nothing at all.

The contents of this Third Dustbin are familiar enough: a narcotic incantation of 'No War' that avoids any substantive engagement with problems of international peace and security; a set of vague but un-thought-out, un-costed and often dangerous utopian ideas about an alternative world; a pleasing but vapid invocation of global human values and internationalism that blithely ignores the misuses to which that term was put in the twentieth century; an innocent when not indulgent attitude towards political violence (witness the cult of Che Guevara, a cruel and dangerous man, and the delegates from Northern Ireland, Palestine and Iran to name but three at London's European Social Forum in October); a capitulation that would have shocked their earlier socialist forbears to nationalist and religious bigots (witness the reception by the supposedly left-wing mayor of London, Ken Livingstone, of Sheikh Yusuf al-Qaradawi, the Muslim Brotherhood ideologue, which is on a par with his earlier dealings with the knee-cappers and murderers of West Belfast); a vapid and politically ineffective attitude to nature, forgetting, as the tsunami should have reminded all of us, that nature can also kill; a rhetorical affecting of concern for the fate of women that wallows in irrationalism and is a million miles from the resolute, egalitarian and rational critique of male power pioneered in earlier times by writers such as Simone de Beauvoir. All of this is mixed up with a shallow, repetitive critique of globalisation and a naive and resolutely uninformed analysis of the USA.

Here in essence is the Three Dustbins Theory. That unchallenged ideas and political legacies take their toll was familiar to the wise of earlier times. Marx remarked that the legacy of past generations weighs like a nightmare on the brain of the living. Keynes said that behind the ideas of every politician lay the thought of some dead economist. Freud warned us of the toll taken by the repressed. All would find much that is familiar in the world today. We can await the outcome of discussions in Davos and Porto Alegre to see if thinking on the current crises of the world has moved on. Here they must meet what I term the 'Vilanova Test', named after the distinguished Spanish academic Pere Vilanova, who on the basis of years of engagement and debate in Spain, Catalonia, Europe and the Arab world has argued consistently for *pensamiento duro* ('tough thinking') in the contemporary world. We certainly have and may again be treated to plenty of the other.

2. LOOKING BACK ON SADDAM HUSSEIN
9 January 2004

The images of Saddam Hussein in custody brought back a mixture of memories. Throughout my life as a scholar, activist and someone with close friends from across the Middle East, the issue of Iraq has been in the forefront of discussions, meetings and campaigns. Saddam's influence has shaped, distorted and poisoned thinking and passions across forty years, in a way that defies straightforward narrative. The 1958 revolution in Iraq unleashed a powerful and often uncontrollable set of political conflicts. These continued even after the first Ba'ath Party (anti-communist) coup of 1963, in which thousands of Iraqis were killed, and were only partly settled by the second, definitive, Ba'ath seizure of power led by Saddam in 1968.

Around that time, the Iraqi Communist Party, one of the largest in the Arab world, split into two groups: a cautious pro-Soviet party and a more critical and independent one. The latter group had representatives in the United Kingdom who worked with the Bertrand Russell Peace Foundation; it later despatched key members to start a guerrilla war in the southern marshes of Iraq, a venture which ended in defeat in 1969.

Many Iraqi leftists regarded Saddam Hussein as an obvious *'amil bri-tani* (British agent) and a 'fascist'. I and those who thought like me could not persuade our Iraqi comrades that this was perhaps not the case. We did not like Saddam, and unlike some on the British left never took his dinar, nor his theatrical forms of solidarity; but we felt that given his control of a state with vast oil revenues, he was, in the language of the time, 'relatively autonomous' of Washington. Right from the start, the projection of Saddam as a stooge or agent disempowered those critics from dealing with their own realities.

For those in thrall to it, 'agent' talk was confirmed when the civil war broke out in Jordan in 1970 between King Hussein and the Palestinians. Iraq remained neutral, even though it had 12,000 troops in Jordan, posted there in the aftermath of the Arab–Israeli war of 1967. The Palestinians later claimed that Saddam had encouraged them to act against the king. Saddam's complicity with Western imperialism was equally evident in 1975 when he signed an agreement with the Shah of Iran ending the two countries' six-year border war and closing down the exile operations and radios of their respective clients. When he invaded Iran in 1980 and was supported by Western allies like Saudi Arabia and Jordan, as well as receiving financial and intelligence backing from the United States, it was beyond doubt. For some, Saddam's invasion of Kuwait in 1990 was the final proof of his subservience to the CIA, since it provided the US with the cast-iron excuse to deploy its forces in the region and impose even stricter control on the local satraps, emirs and sultans.

A striking quality of the post-1958 period was the vitality and the highly influential role of the Iraqi left intelligentsia and of the artistic, theatrical, literary, musical and architectural groups associated with it. Indeed, even in a predominantly anglophone political and academic context in the West, it was Iraqis themselves, other Arabs influenced by them, or people involved in the politics of the country who wrote much of the literature of modern Iraq. Majid Khadduri, Abbas Kelidar, Sami Zubaida, Faleh Abd al-Jabar and Isam al-Khafaji are just some of the best known.

The most monumental social science book on any Arab country is that of the Lebanese academic, the late Hanna Batatu: *The Old Social Classes and the Revolutionary Movements of Iraq* (Princeton, 1978; reprinted in 2004 by Saqi Books). As lecturer at the American University of Beirut, Batatu influenced a generation of Arab political scientists and intellectuals. A vivid memory from a 1981 Exeter University conference is of

Hanna Batatu faced by a squad of menacing Ba'athist 'academics' from Iraq, refusing to be silenced by their complaints and intimidating gestures as he detailed the vicious nature of the Ba'athist state. As one Iraqi in the front row slowly and demonstratively drew his finger across his throat, Batatu declared: 'I am a free man.' This was a principle he held to throughout his productive and formative intellectual life.

Hanna Batatu's dignity is not the only memorable thing about that conference. Equally so is the participation of some United Kingdom citizens who had (perhaps) taken money from Iraq for public relations and translation work, and of others who were, to judge by their fulsome praise of Iraq's leaders, the core members of what one can only call the English branch of the Ba'ath Party. They were mainly Conservatives, old 'friends of the Arabs'; though in more recent times Saddam may have sought to recruit and reimburse at the opposite end of the political spectrum.

In its way that conference was a microcosm of the political and intellectual currents of the time flowing around the issue of Iraq. Its organisers even wanted to open the proceedings by having its participants send a collective telegram supporting Saddam in his recently-launched war with Iran   something the rest of us only just managed to prevent. It had also been preceded by a revealing incident involving the (dis-) invitation of a prominent American expert on Iraq, Joe Stork, then co-editor (with Jim Paul) of the influential journal Middle East Research & Information Project (MERIP), later director of the Middle East and North Africa division of Human Rights Watch. After Joe had, as instructed, sent his conference paper to Exeter in advance, the professor in charge cancelled his airline ticket.

This called for some gentle but persuasive solidarity. As it happened, King Khaled of Saudi Arabia was in London at the time. In keeping with the replication of tribal mores in the jet-set age associated with his regime, he had invited all his UK-based clients and friends to stay with him for a week at the luxurious Claridge's Hotel.

For the first time in my life, I entered Claridge's to meet the responsible Exeter professor – a curious, swashbuckling character – for breakfast. He began with predictable indignation against Joe, but as the meal wore on I was able to warn him that the scurrilous magazine *Private Eye* had already been alerted to a possible scandal and were calling me about it. Of course, I had not told them anything but these things had a way of getting out ... 'You understand the English, and their ways.' Joe was duly re-invited.

The crimes of Saddam Hussein against his people, becoming well-known even in 1981, were chillingly documented in Kanan Makiya's books *Republic of Fear: The Politics of Modern Iraq* (Pantheon Books, 1989) and *Cruelty and Silence* (Jonathan Cape, 1993). Both were widely denounced by Arab intellectuals, and some expatriate ones, for feeding Western prejudice against the Arabs. In the 1970s I had already made the acquaintance of an Iraqi diplomat, then quite active in London, who (it emerged) was given this job in recompense for his wife having been kidnapped and raped by some of Saddam's guards. But it was a visit to Iraq in 1980 to give some lectures at Baghdad University that offers me the opportunity to add a modest charge to whatever bill of indictment may now be presented to the captured dictator.

Saddam was at that time trying to portray Iraq as *qala'at al-thawra al-'arabiya* (the citadel of the Arab revolution). A big summit in Baghdad to that end coincided with the anniversary of the founding of the Ba'ath Party, an event surrounded by elaborate ritual blended from European fascist and Soviet communist festivals. During an interview with an unctuous party 'theoretician', a group of schoolchildren arrived with much fanfare and photographers to garland him (and by extension his visitors) with bouquets of flowers. This man had defected to Iraq from the rival Ba'ath regime in Syria. Saddam had won a major coup in intra-Ba'ath rivalry by inducing one of the two historic founders of the party, Michel Aflaq, to live in Baghdad. Aflaq, a Syrian Christian, argued – as many Arab nationalists still do – that the Arabs have a special link to God through Islam. Michel Aflaq was never seen in public, but as he lay dying in 1989 a rumour was diffused that, as the culmination of his life as a Ba'ath leader, he had converted to Islam. Even the slogan of the party he co-founded, 'One Ba'ath Party with One Eternal Message' (... *risala khalida*) exploits the dual political and religious resonances of the word 'message' (the Prophet Mohammed is the *rasul*).

The Syrian Ba'athist brought another element to Iraq, one that reinforced an existing prejudice which was inculcated through the nationalist school textbooks of the monarchical period: hostility to Persians. These neighbours ('Zionists of the East') were presented as the greatest long-term enemies of the Arabs – far worse than their more recent and less populous counterparts in the West. The mass expulsion from Iraq in the 1980s of people with Persian names or antecedents, no less than the making of an epic film celebrating the Arab victory over the Persians at Qadisiya in 637 CE, rested on this deep ideological morass. This is further exemplified in the title of a book written by one of Saddam's uncles, Khairallah Tulfah, and made compulsory reading in schools, *Three Things Which God Should Never Have Created: Persians, Jews and Flies* (note the order).

The Ba'ath Party had borrowed more than ritual from Europe's totalitarian regimes; it used their techniques of violence, fear and the corruption of language. In April 1980 a filmed party meeting showed Saddam singling out inner-party rivals who were dragged from the room, then executed after show trials. He had learnt the most basic lesson of all dictatorships: that it is one thing to kill the guilty, but what really works is to kill the innocent. Saddam and his cronies attended these executions; members of the Ba'ath Party, including students in Britain, were summoned to the embassy in London's South Kensington to view a video of the occasion.

I have visited some unsavoury regimes – from Ayatollah Khomeini's Iran (where I saw 100,000 people march past shouting 'Death to Liberalism' and realised that, among others, they meant me) to Ethiopia's Red Terror – but never have I sensed such fear as in Iraq. One could cut it with a knife. A professor said to me, resignedly; 'When I open the paper in the morning I do not know if I have been appointed ambassador to the United Nations or condemned to death. In either case I would not know why.'

In that spring of 1980, the rising tension with Iran led to the expulsions of tens of thousands of people across the Iranian border. In the bazaar, people were concerned about the impact of the Iranian revolution next door and its calls to Iraqis to rise up against the *Yazid* (that is, Saddam – a reference to one of the early Sunni rulers who oppressed the Shi'a). I asked one man why Iraq could not have a friendlier attitude to Iran and he replied: 'Look, I am happy they had a revolution. But why do they have to shout so much? We were Shi'a before they were. We had a revolution before they did. They should quieten down.'

On the day we were supposed to meet Tariq Aziz, the perennial front man for Saddam's regime, an alleged Iranian agent had tried to assassinate him while he visited Baghdad's Mustansariya University. Saddam appeared on television the next night to promise revenge: 'Blood will be answered with blood.' He denounced his enemies as 'cowards and dwarfs' and in typical style proclaimed that 'the Iraqis will dance merrily on the wings of death.'

Saddam's rhetoric put the eclecticism of any other modern leader to shame. It mixed twentieth-century demagogy with invocations of knights on horseback, the interpretation of dreams and evocations of the battles of early Islam. (In the 1991 and 2003 wars, he denounced George Bush, Senior and Junior, as 'Hulagu' – this was the name of the Mongol leader who captured Baghdad in 1258.) An image he used a lot, which English translators usually got wrong, was to call his enemies bats. This did not mean he thought they were mad (as in the English idiom) but that they were indeed like bats – beasts of the night who would be scattered to the four corners of the earth once the light, in this case the Ba'ath Party, had broken over them.

In September 1980, Saddam launched the Iran–Iraq war by invading Iran. It lasted for eight years and cost an estimated one million lives. This was by far the most destructive war in the modern Middle East (in the five Arab–Israeli wars, plus Israeli incursions into Lebanon and two Palestinian intifadas, the total deaths are estimated at 70–80,000); it was also the second longest inter-state war of the twentieth century, only two months short of the 1937–45 Sino-Japanese conflict.

Leaving Baghdad at the end of that 1980 visit presented a problem. At every meeting I attended, the Iraqi host would give me a two-volume set of Saddam's speeches. It was too risky to do what one normally does and chuck them into the waste-paper basket. So I carried six pairs, twelve books, in my suitcase – intending to find them a suitable home in London university libraries. (Much later, I met a linguistics student in Oman, Abdullah al-Harrasi, who had written a fascinating and, in a macabre way, funny doctoral thesis on the speeches of Saddam – Metaphor in Arabic-into-English Translation, with Special Reference to the Metaphorical Concepts and Expressions in Political Discourse – great read, which puts all the irony, metonymies and deconstruction of the postmodernists to shame). Arriving in the early morning at Heathrow airport, somewhat befuddled by the flight, I foolishly lent far over the luggage carousel to grab my bag. The disc slipped, the pain of this encounter with Ba'athism ran up my spine, and for a month I was flat on my back. This, too, may be counted among Saddam's crimes.

It is worth recalling, as he languishes in jail, some of what those who met Saddam reported. An Australian journalist in Baghdad was once woken in the middle of the night for an interview with the president. After stumbling unprepared via a translator through a number of banal questions, he resorted to asking Saddam what his favourite film was. The answer came in English: *The Godfather*. It was said without irony, and may be corroborated by the ways in which Saddam, born in Tikrit in northern Iraq, modelled himself on another moustachioed mass murderer, born only 720 kilometres away in Gori, Georgia: Joseph Stalin. Said Aburish's perceptive biography of Saddam contains a revealing anecdote about a visitor to Saddam's home, who witnessed the dictator in an austere spare room lined with fourteen books about the Soviet leader. (I suspect that Stalin's sinisterly measured way of shifting from one foot to the other while delivering a speech was copied by his Iraqi admirer.)

A Palestinian economist, Yusuf Sayigh, was attending a conference on economic development in Baghdad in 1974 when his party was marshalled late one night into a bus and driven to an unknown destination. A youngish man, with a moustache and a pistol, joined them around a table, professing a desire to learn about economic development. But his only question was how to use economic power to strengthen his state. Saddam had no education; talking to him, Sayigh soon realised, was a waste of time.

A leading Iraqi economist, Mohammad Salman Hassan, once told me never to forget that in the economic relations and agreements of the Arab world, there were never state-to-state relations, only person-to-person. Yet even here there are strange counter-currents. An Iraqi friend in London in the 1960s – an Arab nationalist of the Nasserist rather than Ba'athist persuasion, a *wahdawi* (unionist) – had been studying in Cairo a decade earlier, and was asked to help a man who was on the run from Iraq. My friend let the man sleep on his sofa for a few weeks. A few years on, he discovered it had been Saddam. When the latter came to power he called my friend to give thanks for the refuge. Saddam also said that while he expected other academics to join the Ba'ath Party and follow its line, my friend should feel free not to do so and even occasionally to publish limited criticisms of the government – something he did indeed do. I have a sense that when the war with Iran came, my friend's two sons, by then of military age, were not sent to the front. I have also recently heard that my friend, resorting to the unexpurgated nationalist myths of his youth, has explained the United States occupation of Iraq as 'the revenge for Nebuchadnezzar' (that is, for the captivity of the Jews in 586 BCE). I hope this report is untrue.

It is a curious fact that the last surviving original signatory of the United Nations charter in 1945 was an Iraqi, Fadhel al-Jamali, who would become prime minister and later the star of a theatrical show trial after the revolution in 1958. He denounced all the judges and his accusers in ringing tones – and was spared the firing squad. I once met him walking in North London's Highgate woods with his two sons. He was on a visit from Tunis, where he worked as an adviser to the then president, Habib Bourguiba. His interesting autobiography, still unpublished, contains a long section on the Palestine issue at the UN and Iraq's role. The distance from his diplomatic (and sartorial) era to the current one is reflected in reports from Iraq that observe the rise in tribalism, with people adopting flowing robes in preference to Western clothes. (One man, asked where he was from, said Ealing, the West London suburb and iconic home of British cinematic comedy.)

Indeed, for all the horrors and conflicts of the Middle East, it is a rich ground for political jokes – a fact I have tried over the years to instil into my students. Among my recommendations was the book *Arab Political Humour* (Quartet Books, 1985) by Iraqi author Khalid Kishtainy (a worthy companion to the volume by Steven Lukes and Itzhak Galnoor, *No Laughing Matter* [Routledge & Kegan Paul, 1985]). Khalid, a noted translator and novelist, writes a daily column in one of the main Arab newspapers, published as they nearly all are outside the region, in London. My Arab, Turkish and Iranian students all liked Khalid's book; so did the Israelis. But for the Europeans and Americans it was impenetrable, and in a certain way far too serious.

One Iraqi story Khalid told me involved a conversation between God and the Archangel Gabriel. Gabriel wanted to please God; what could he do? God replied that, following George W. Bush's 'axis of evil' speech, he wanted Gabriel to go down to earth, find Saddam and assassinate him. Gabriel duly set off, but at the first armed checkpoint near Saddam's palace, he was seized, taken to prison and badly tortured by Saddam and his guards. When Gabriel finally returned to heaven, he told God what had happened, and God replied: 'I am glad you made it back here, but I hope you didn't tell Saddam who sent you.'

Khalid has just returned from Baghdad with a new stock of Saddam Hussein jokes; they are, like many such stories in the region, unprintable. But with exact timing, he has produced a children's book on the Ba'athist terror, *Tomorrow is Another Day: a Tale of Saddam's Baghdad*.

It is about a man released from jail who, failing to find employment, discovers that if he marries a woman widowed by the war with Iran he will be awarded a grant of money and a Chevrolet. In the end, he marries four widows at the same time ... and this is only the beginning of his troubles.

One last thought from an Iraqi recently returned from Baghdad. Asked about the security situation in Iraq, he replied: 'Well, the overall security situation is terrible. You know, even the president got himself arrested!'

3.   COLD WAR ASSASSINATIONS: SOLVED AND UNSOLVED
11 August 2005

The rioting in Khartoum over the death in a helicopter crash of John Garang, veteran leader of the Sudan People's Liberation Army (SPLA) and very recently installed as Sudan's vice-president following the January 2005 peace agreement, highlights one of the recurrent problems of modern global politics: the belief that whatever the evidence, no death of a political figure, whether in a plane, a car or as a result of 'natural causes', can be accidental.

The Sudanese government, newly committed to a coalition with Garang's former guerrilla opposition in the South, has promised an independent inquiry, but given the political passions and suspicions involved, few can believe this will resolve the issue. In all of this, the Sudanese are not alone: the death in November 2004 of Yasser Arafat, for reasons that are still unclear, has led many in the Arab world to believe he was poisoned by the Israelis. When King Faisal of Saudi Arabia was stabbed to death by a deranged young male relative in 1975, the Arab world was full of conspiracy theories: the Russians, the Americans; it seemed everyone was involved.

In perhaps the most prominent assassination of the twentieth century, that of President John F. Kennedy in Dallas in November 1963, a vast industry of myth, plot and insinuation grew up, from the work of the lawyer Mark Lane (a tireless proponent of alternative theories revolving around the Book Depository and the Grassy Knoll) to Oliver Stone's film *JFK*. A free phone service called 'Dial-a-Conspiracy' even produced a different version each day of a seamless web involving JFK, his brother Bobby, Marilyn Monroe and a cast of thousands. Such addictive conspiratorialism serves as background and caution to evaluating an issue on which some recent research has cast new light: the role of political murder in the Cold War.

The Cold War lasted more than forty years, from the late 1940s to the collapse of East and Central European communism in 1989–91. During this period, Europe was (the Greek civil war and intermittent terrorist campaigns excepted) largely at peace; elsewhere, more than 20 million people died in multiple conflicts in what was for most of the period known as the 'Third World'. From Korea to Vietnam, Afghanistan to Guatemala, Angola to Nicaragua, Cambodia to Iran, the Cold War reaped a devastating harvest.

But between comfort zone and killing field, the Cold War generated another form of violence – assassination, covert killing, state and judicial execution. (The subject of attempted assassination – the CIA is reputed to have initiated around twenty separate operations against Fidel Castro in the early 1960s – would require another article.) The revelations of the last decade raise fresh questions about the extent and nature of this violence, and the legacy it leaves to a world now steeped in a new global conflict.

Modern history is replete with assassinations that have a dramatic impact on national and international politics: the killing of Alexander II by anarchists in 1881 unleashed repression and anti-Semitism in the Russian empire; the shooting of Archduke Franz Ferdinand of Austria in June 1914 in Sarajevo sparked the Great War that drowned Europe in blood and inaugurated what Eric Hobsbawm calls 'the short twentieth century'; the assassination of the liberal Colombian politician Jorge Gaitán in 1948 (a day after he had met a Latin American youth delegation that included the twenty-one-year-old Fidel Castro) helped spark *la violencia* – a civil war that continues to this day; the shooting down on 6 April 1994 of the plane carrying the Rwandan and Burundian presidents, Juvenal Habyarimana and Cyprien Ntaryamira, precipitated the Rwandan genocide.

Such examples could be multiplied. The inception and the end of the Cold War era in Europe were marked by political deaths that had a direct relevance to the wider global stand-off between the two superpower blocs: the demise of the Czech liberal politician Jan Masaryk in

March 1948 when he fell from the window of Prague palace – a defenestration with many precedents in Czech history, and one that has never definitively been solved – marked a crucial step in the consolidation of communist rule; the judicial execution of Romanian dictator Nicolae Ceauşescu and his wife Elena on 25 December 1989, after they had tried to flee from a popular uprising, symbolised the end of communist rule in much of Europe.

During the Cold War period, there were other examples of political killings that had a profound impact on domestic and international politics: the murder of the Congolese nationalist leader Patrice Lumumba by soldiers with the connivance of the CIA in 1961; the killing of the captive guerrilla leader Ernesto Che Guevara in Bolivia on the orders of the CIA in 1967; the assassination of two anti-Portuguese guerrilla leaders, Eduardo Mondlane in 1969 and Amilcar Cabral in 1973; and the death – apparently by suicide with a gun gifted by Fidel Castro – of Chile's president, Salvador Allende, in the Pinochet coup of 11 September 1973. None of these incidents had consequences as momentous as those of 1881, 1914 or 1994, but they revealed the violence that the confrontation of superpowers sanctioned outside their core domains.

Today, almost sixteen years after the Cold War's end, can new information resolve, or at least broaden understanding, of some of these killings? In relation to some of the more spectacular incidents – the Kennedy assassination in 1963 or the plane crash that killed President Zia ul-Haq of Pakistan in 1988 – these years have added little to the sum of knowledge. The death of Cape Verde and Guinea liberation hero Amilcar Cabral in Conakry in 1973 was attributed at the time to Portuguese forces, but some now suspect it was the work of elements within the regime of his Guinean hosts. However, new information has come to light about other murders and deaths during the forty-year global freeze : Dag Hammarskjold, the United Nations secretary-general killed on 18 September 1961 in the Congo was in a plane that crashed, rather than being shot down, as a result of attempts by Belgian agents – working to split Katanga from the Congo – to force the plane to land against its consent; the death of Mehdi Ben Barka, the Moroccan socialist leader kidnapped and killed in Paris in October 1965 – when he was working with the Vietnamese and Cubans to launch the Tricontinental Organisation in Havana – has often been attributed to the CIA and Mossad, but he seems to have been the victim of Morocco's security chief Mohamed Oufkir (himself to die in a failed coup against King Hassan II); Georgi Markov – the Bulgarian dissident with privileged insight into the circle of long-term dictator Todor Zhivkov, who became a BBC journalist in London and was stabbed with a poisoned umbrella on Waterloo Bridge in 1978 – was killed by an Italian contracted by the Bulgarian intelligence services; Haile Selassie, the veteran Ethiopian emperor, was last seen being bundled into a Volkswagen by revolutionary army officers in 1974: it is now known that his successor as head of state, Mengistu Haile Mariam, had him killed in captivity and his body buried underneath the palace lavatory the military dictator used.

The biography of Mao Zedong by Jung Chang and my brother Jon Halliday contains fascinating, macabre revelations about the death of three of Mao's most important opponents within the Chinese Communist Party leadership: Lin Piao, Liu Shao-chi and Peng Te-huai. Lin and Peng, opponents of Mao's more grandiose political and economic schemes, were imprisoned, tortured and left to die in misery and obscurity; their deaths were concealed from the Chinese people as long as Mao lived. Lin, at one point Mao's chosen successor, sought to flee to Russia after a failed coup attempt; his hurried commandeering of a Trident jet without sufficient fuel led to a crash in Mongolia.

Meanwhile, United States National Security Agency intercepts of Chinese radio traffic during the Tiananmen massacre of June 1989 indicate that the situation was even more confused than appeared at the time, and that the Chinese army did not have a clear plan deliberately to kill students protesting in Beijing's central square.

The mid-1970s inaugurated a period of superpower negotiation known as 'détente'. But it was also a moment when the collateral damage of violent (and, for a time at least, unexplained) deaths intensely impacted on those of us active and engaged in the political arguments of the period: Orlando Letelier, Chile's ex-foreign minister, exiled by Pinochet's coup and director of Washington's Institute for Policy Studies (for whom I then worked), who was blown up with a colleague, Ronni Moffitt, on the way to work in September 1976 – the result of collaboration between the Chilean secret police (DINA) and Cuban and American right-wing extremists; David Holden, Middle East correspondent of the *Sunday Times*, who was shot in still unexplained circumstances in Cairo in September 1977 – his paper's year-long investigation concluded that 'for every possible explanation, there was a good reason why it could not be the case'; Malcolm Caldwell, a lecturer in South-East Asian studies at SOAS, London, who was killed in Phnom Penh in December 1978 on the eve of the Vietnamese invasion of Cambodia; and Ruth First, South African Marxist scholar and writer, who was killed in Maputo by a parcel bomb sent by Pretoria's security services in 1982.

How far any of the Cold War's individual deaths, assassinations and killings altered its course is debatable. The full facts about some of these murders may never be known. It may also be that the incidents with longer-term effects are not always the most spectacular: Akbar Khyber, an Afghan communist, died in April 1978 during a demonstration in Kabul; few people may have noted, or now recall, this incident, but it sparked the communist seizure of power a few days later. Nur Muhammad Taraki, the Afghan communist leader, was smothered by his sinister rival, Hafizullah Amin, in October 1979; this act persuaded a doddering Leonid Brezhnev to order the Soviet invasion of Afghanistan in which Amin himself was killed, and which provoked the militant jihadi campaign of the 1980s. Abdullah Azzam, a Palestinian Islamist leader, was killed with his two sons by a car bomb in Pakistan in 1989; again, few noticed at the time, but Azzam (rather than his then-protégé Osama bin Laden) both controlled the jihadi forces who had fought in Afghanistan and opposed the extension of the Islamist war to targets in the non-Islamic world. Whether or not his subordinate organised the killing, it was the death of Abdullah Azzam that delivered leadership to Osama bin Laden, and thus opened the door to 11 September 2001 and all that has followed.

4. A CONVERSATION IN HAVANA
   19 February 2008

The announcement of Fidel Castro's serious intestinal illness at the end of July 2006, and the occasion of the Cuban leader's eightieth birthday on 13 August, inevitably have raised a mountain of commentary about the imminence or otherwise of a transition of power in the Caribbean communist state. But if 'what comes after Fidel' is a well-worn topic of op-eds and broadcast interviews, the focus of the answer is less often where it should be: on an assessment of the character – institutional, political and personal – of the Cuban revolutionary experience as a whole.

To approach the question in this way is also to recall the three informative encounters I have had with Cuban realities in visits to the island in 1968, 1981 and 2000. The third occasion offered most insight into where Cuba may go after Fidel, but the second also provided an illuminating sense of how elements of the Cuban political elite make sense of their place in the international environment – and of their leader.

The first time I visited Cuba was in 1968 with the Bertrand Russell Peace Foundation, when I helped organise a one-month, not very strenuous working visit by a few dozen British radicals to a coffee plantation in Pinar del Rio province. The project included a tour of the island and the experience of witnessing two characteristically marathon speeches by Fidel. The second visit was in 1981, when I was invited by the foreign ministry in Havana for discussions on the situation in the Middle East in the context of the then fairly new Israeli threat to Lebanon, which the Cubans saw through the prism of a possible attack on their close allies Syria and (closer to home) the Sandinistas in Nicaragua.

During the 1980s, I had further numerous discussions with Cuban diplomats in Europe on issues of concern to them: in the early part of the decade the threat of an American invasion of Nicaragua (and even Cuba itself) dictated their thoughts, but from the mid-1980s onwards the focus shifted to Mikhail Gorbachev's project in the Soviet Union and the gathering gulf between Havana and Moscow. In effect, therefore, the early 1980s were dominated by concern about the *yanquis*, the late 1980s by concern about what the Cubans always termed, with some irony and frustration, *los hermanos* (the brothers).

The Cubans spotted very early on that something was changing for the worse in the USSR and were not slow to express a view on it. As the years of Gorbachev's glasnost and perestroika gave way to the fall of the Berlin Wall and the wave of revolution in Eastern and Central Europe, Cubans were particularly interested in (and, it seemed, alarmed by) the uprising against Nicolae Ceauşescu in Romania in December 1989, which they saw as a KGB-inspired military coup that could be a dry run for Cuba.

This mistrust was evidently reciprocated. Soviet officials I met during those same years in Moscow seemed still to be anxious about the Cuban propensity for 'adventurism' in domestic and international matters. There was graphic evidence of this mutual suspicion in the huge tower of the purpose-built Soviet embassy building down the road from

Havana's Institute for International Relations (IRI) in the suburb of Miramar. Cubans joked that although the Soviets justified the building in terms of its function as a source of electronic surveillance of the United States, its real purpose was to invigilate them.

The IRI, the academic institute attached to Cuba's foreign ministry, was at the centre of my third visit to Cuba in 2000. There I lectured to diplomats and policy specialists on international relations, and had occasion to consult more closely with some senior staff. It was an impressive group: witnesses of four decades of revolutionary upheaval and international drama, familiar with the leaders and inner workings of the Cuban state, well read and well travelled, committed to the broad aims of the Cuban revolution, sceptical of much of what passed for Marxist or radical writing in the West, and devoid of the kind of rhetorical posturing that so often characterises officials of such regimes.

The conversation ranged over the fate of Third World revolutionary regimes, the possible evolution of United States domestic politics, and the impact on Cuba of the post-1991 period of economic hardship (caused by the ending of Soviet economic support) known as the 'special period'. There was by then already a sense of the end of a phase in Cuban history; the revolutionary advances of the previous two decades abroad had disappeared (Angola, Nicaragua) and Cubans domestically were more and more preoccupied with making ends meet, working in multiple jobs or relying on dollar remittances from relatives in the US.

The occasional roaring of passing *camellos* ('camels', the improvised mass-transport system based on converted lorries) underlined this crisis. Tourism was doing OK, but there was much corruption in the system associated with it, and it involved regulations – such as the denial of access to Cubans themselves to certain beaches and hotels – that my interlocutors found especially insulting. Much was blamed on the continued US blockade, though not all – hence the joke about a mid-air collision in which a plane carrying Fidel Castro hits one carrying the president of the United States. 'Who escapes? Eleven million Cubans.'

Despite this background of a certain familiarity and a degree of realism about the Cuban revolution, I was surprised during the course of the evening – as the discussion inevitably turned to the issue of what would happen after the death of *el comandante* – when my companions expressed considerable respect for the figure of Francisco Franco, the victor of the Spanish civil war and dictatorial ruler until his death in November 1975. The reason for this admiration was not any hankering after fascism, right-wing authoritarianism or the supremacy of the Catholic Church in national life; it was based on the belief that General Franco had prepared the foundations for a democratic transition after his death. Franco's famously enigmatic saying, '*todo está atado y bien atado*' ('everything has been tied up, well tied up'), was seen by my Cuban colleagues as an indication that Franco had – through the opening of Spain to European capitalism and the installation of Juan Carlos as the leading figure in overseeing the post-Franco era – foreseen and made provision for the transition of Spain to democracy in the late 1970s.

The point was not just a fascinating contrast with the hard-right Spanish political figure for whom Fidel Castro himself has long expressed affection, namely Franco's long-standing ministerial colleague (and Fidel's fellow *Gallego*), Manuel Fraga. It was, rather, not about Franco at all, but about Castro. They all knew Fidel, admired him and sympathised with his defence of radical and Cuban nationalist goals. But they were deeply concerned at how, over the years, he had retreated more and more into isolation, surrounding himself with young acolytes from the *Juventud Comunista* (the communist youth organisation) who told him what he wanted to hear: that Cuba was the most admirable country in the world; that the anti-globalisation movement was gaining ground across the world; that imperialism was in crisis.

In the early years of the revolution, some of its ablest leaders and thinkers left its embrace (among them the guerrilla commander Huber Matos and the writer Carlos Franqui); others once close to Fidel who had been able to speak the truth to him had passed away (including Carlos Rafael Rodríguez, the ablest of the Communist Party leaders; Osvaldo Dorticós, the long-time president; and, not least, Celia Sánchez Manduley, Fidel's companion of many years, at whose graveside he exhibited profound distress). The advent of a new generation of admirers and sycophants from Latin America, with Hugo Chávez in the lead, had done little to instil a belated sense of realism into Castro's worldview.

On only one issue were my interlocutors uneasy, even as they upbraided me for what I had written in a recent comparative study of Third World revolutions. This concerned one of the most contemptible episodes in the history of the Cuban revolution, the Ochoa affair of 1987 which involved a group of senior military officials associated with the Cuban war in Angola. It appeared that Fidel and his associates had staged a show trial of popular radical figures that might have challenged his authority. In the worst tradition of communist trials of this kind, the defendants had been tricked into making professions of loyalty and self-implication with the hope of leniency, only to find themselves either shot or sentenced to thirty years' imprisonment.

This introversion and protracted entropy of the Cuban revolution in the 1990s is not, however, some sudden break with an earlier utopian phase. It points, rather, to problems throughout the history of the revolution itself – problems which astute sympathetic observers noted in the early 1960s but which supporters of the Cuban state (quick to suspend judgement) seek to avoid. The most evident is the personality of the leader himself: a man of vision, courage, honesty and charisma; but also of demagogy, inconsistency, episodic vindictiveness and cruelty, grotesque verbal self-indulgence, intolerance, contempt for intellectuals and homosexuals, and plain administrative ineptitude.

Cubans have long known that in Cuba the solution is also the problem, and that it lies at the top. What the besotted visitors Jean-Paul Sartre and Simone de Beauvoir saw in 1960 'the dialectical unity of Fidel and the masses', a crazed rush of statements, changes of course and interventions – soon became a mixture of inefficiency, arbitrariness and whim. Such personal failings – ones that history, far from 'absolving', in Castro's famous phrase at his 1953 trial, only made worse – have been compounded by the choices he and his associates have made in regard to the administration of the Cuban economy.

Many observers rightly point out that Cuba has had an exceptional record in the field of social services – health, education and poverty reduction. But its overall macroeconomic record has been dismal, and this is a result not just of the US blockade (as the regime's friends and apologists so easily claim) but of a series of disastrous policies. These range from the utopian experiments with 'non-monetary accounting' (a fantasy of Che Guevara's) and 'voluntary labour' (a form of highly inefficient forced mobilisation) to the reimposition of state controls and the crushing of small markets and farmers in the ill-conceived 'rectification' campaign of the 1980s. The latest catastrophic switch came in 2003, when the regime drastically reduced the circulation of US dollars in the economy and antagonised foreign investors with a new set of controls. Today, even after some recovery from the special period, per capita annual income in Cuba is estimated at $3,000. Pensioners receive $7 a month, and can often afford meat only twice a month.

These defects of personality and policy have been accompanied by something else that visitors to the island, bemused by its superficially easy-going 'tropical' atmosphere, too easily miss: namely, a climate of fear. Cuba's record is not the most bloody among modern revolutions – though it is important not to forget the revolutionary show trials of the early 1960s, over which Che Guevara presided and which so disgusted his father that the latter left the country; or the mass imprisonment of dissidents, gays and others in the re-education camps of the 1970s and 1980s. In any case, these are only the most visible evidence of the tight restrictions on free expression, let alone free organisation, in Cuba.

The political system, for all its vaunting of 'people's power', is tightly controlled from the top. Those writers and other intellectuals who have over the years offered even friendly critiques have too often become the object of official persecution and slanderous denunciation: the group of Cubans associated with the Institute of the Americas, whose permission to travel and publish was abruptly withdrawn when they began to write about democracy, is but one example. Scorn has also been poured on external observers such as the French agronomist René Dumont, the Polish-French Marxist writer K. S. Karol and the American historian Oscar Lewis.

Such persecutions, and the attitudes that go with them, are not just a result of the inevitable growth of dictatorship after revolutions, or of imperialist pressure from outside. They also stem from Castro himself. His great hero is the Jacobin leader Robespierre, a biography of whom was published some years ago in Cuba: austere, cruel, at times fickle, and ultimately a victim of the very revolution he sought to lead.

This character trait is evident most of all in the inability of the Cuban leader to follow the model that Cuban officialdom professes to admire: China. Since 1978 the Chinese leadership has understood that its people want to make money and have a better life. Recently, Castro has made some moves in this direction, aided by the financial support of Hugo Chávez. But he remains the prisoner of a moralistic hostility to material wealth and improvement, and resorts time and again to appeals for greater moral purity and the ridding of Cuba of corrupt consumerist values. For all that Castro proclaims himself to be in the tradition of the nineteenth-century nationalist leader José Martí, he ignores Martí's view that a country of small property owners is a rich one.

Hence, perhaps, the mid-1990s Cuban anecdote about Fidel Castro finding himself in a cage with Bill Clinton and Boris Yeltsin, where they are all being threatened by a ravenous lion. Clinton and Yeltsin bravely tussle with the beast, but retire seriously mauled. Fidel tells them to leave it to him. He approaches the lion and whispers something in its ear: the animal pauses, frowns and rolls over dead. Bill and Boris take a break from licking their wounds to question the *comandante* about the magic words. Fidel replies: 'Well, I said what I always say – *socialismo o muerte*' ('socialism or death'). Every joke, *pace* George Orwell, tells a tiny truth as well as being a tiny revolution. Most Cubans are respectful of Castro as a leader and proud of their national independence, but they are fed up with their economic, social and political system and want a change – the sooner the better.

True, there is also widespread anxiety in the island about the possibility of violence after Castro's death, either between factions on the island itself, or between exiles returning from Miami and the forces of the Cuban state. The ideal – notwithstanding scenarios long nurtured in Miami and Washington about the regime's imminent fall – is of a peaceful transition to democracy which preserves both the independence of the island and the social gains of its revolution. As in East Germany and Eastern and Central Europe in the 1990s, this may be an illusion. If things do go badly and get out of hand, part of the blame will lie with venomous and ill-informed exiled politicians in Miami and New Jersey; and with the crass and ignorant complicity of successive US presidents with them. But some too will lie with Fidel Castro and those around him for having so long prevented political change in the island, mismanaged its economy and driven so many of its citizens into exile. Much of what is wrong with Cuba is the result not of imperialist mischief, but of post-revolutionary dogmatism, stupidity and arrogance.

Francisco Franco's true intentions for Spain after his death are a matter that may never be resolved. The one person who might give an authoritative answer, King Juan Carlos, will probably never do so. A few months ago, after giving a public lecture on Cuba at Barcelona University in which I mentioned the story of my Havana encounter with Franco's fan-club, I was approached by a student in his twenties who said that his father had been the CIA station chief in Madrid in the Franco regime's twilight years and knew the old dictator well. Franco, the young man assured me with the authority of his father, had no wish to see democracy being introduced into Spain; the general's '*todo está atado y bien atado*' meant only to indicate that the authoritarian regime he founded would continue.

My Cuban interlocutors were, it seemed, mistaken in their view of the Spanish dictator. But democracy did, after all, come to Spain; so the Barcelona version, if true, may nonetheless contain a grain of hope for Cubans after their authoritarian leader of (currently) forty-six years finally departs the scene.

5. BOADICEA IN THE SOUTH ATLANTIC: THE LEGACIES OF MARGARET THATCHER
3 May 2007

A few years ago, in my office at the London School of Economics, I was visited by the shrewd former foreign minister of Argentina, Guido di Tella, then a visiting scholar at the University of Oxford. Di Tella, who belonged to a family of prominent liberal intellectuals, had been speaking to a seminar at LSE on the theme of Argentina's relations with the rest of the world.

His interpretation of his country's predicament has stayed with me. After all Argentina's modern dramas – the two regimes presided over by the populist military leader Juan Domingo Perón and his wives, Evita and Isabel (1945–55, 1974–6); proletarian insurrection; ferocious military repression; flamboyant but fatally deluded guerrilla struggle; a rollercoaster economy which in the 1920s was amongst the most prosperous in the world; and, not least, the Malvinas war of 1982 itself – di Tella made a heartfelt plea for Argentina to become a normal, serious, even boring country. 'For once let us be like Austria, or New Zealand,' he remarked. To many Argentinians in his audience, and even to some like myself who had been exposed over the years to the charms and rhetoric of its politics or the twisting passions of its football or its tango music, this seemed a vain hope. But liberal optimist and inveterate Anglophile that he was, di Tella persisted.

The reason Guido di Tella came to see me was more specific. The Malvinas war had ended over a decade earlier, and after a decade of cold peace Britain and Argentina had in 1995 reached an agreement to open up the fishing areas around the islands, to allow regular flights from southern Argentina to the islands' capital Port Stanley, and, in general, to a reduction in tension. Then President Carlos Menem had even put aside his Peronist, populist credentials to visit Britain and pay his respects to the British war dead.

But di Tella was worried: the British government and the Falkland Islanders were deluded if they thought this peace would last. Britain's long-term possession of the islands was an anomalous and outdated arrangement, against which Argentines across the political spectrum would continue to push. At least let discussions begin on joint sovereignty or other mechanisms to close the gap between the two sides. Di Tella had tried to get the attention of the British political elite and had even, in one of the more extraordinary peace initiatives of modern times, tried to woo the islands over Christmas by sending each family a letter containing a Winnie the Pooh bear. His initiative led to no change in British or Argentinian public positions. Instead, what he predicted has come to pass. The islanders, backed by the British government, are reaping the benefits of the 1995 fishing-rights deal. In a boom largely fuelled by Spanish firms, they now have the highest per capita income in Latin America (around $60,000) and foreign reserves of $360 million. The official British position remains unchanged: they will not move unless the islanders so wish, and there is little sign of that.

In Britain the twenty-fifth anniversary of the start of the war – which coincided with the overrated dispute with Iran over the detention of British naval personnel – occasioned much nostalgic and blimpish commentary, usually linked to militaristic banalities about the prime minister of the time, Margaret Thatcher. It was less often noted that the political climate in Argentina is changing in significant ways.

The current president, Néstor Kirchner, has challenged the 1995 agreement and repudiated some of its key terms. Direct flights from Argentina are now banned, and only one weekly plane, run by the Chilean firm LAN Chile, makes the journey from Punto Arenas to Port Stanley. The national claim to the Malvinas islands has again come to be a live issue in Argentina; on 2 April, the day when the start of the war was commemorated, a mass rally was held in Ushuaia, the southernmost town of Argentina and the one nearest the islands, to commemorate the war and restate the Argentinian aspiration.

This nationalistic and militaristic impasse will, as di Tella predicted, sooner or later explode; it is to the discredit of successive British governments that they have refused to face up to this. The British claim to these islands, 12,800 kilometres from the 'homeland', is on any basis – rational, geostrategic or plain common sense – unsustainable; as if Japan were to claim part of Suffolk. It is one of the relics of colonialism and should be dealt with and despatched in that spirit. The islanders should, like all such displaced persons, be entitled to compensation and resettlement. A population of less than 3,000 hardly presents a major problem; there are many locations – Scotland, Wales, New Zealand and Australia suggest themselves – where they could feel comfortable.

The argument that London must respect the wishes of the islanders also lacks logic, on two grounds. First, it implies granting a population of 3,000 people the right to determine matters of strategy, diplomacy and economic interest, which is a grotesque indulgence. Second, it carries a suspicion of racism, given that at the same time as the islands were being defended by the British armed forces, Thatcher's government was negotiating with Beijing to hand over 6 million citizens of Hong Kong without consulting them.

But the lessons of the Malvinas war go deeper than that, for they exemplify a major issue involved in assessing the legitimacy of any war: proportion. Much of the jingoistic British press coverage of the Argentinian occupation conveyed the sense that two fantasy worlds had collided: as if the Wehrmacht had invaded the rural idyll of the long-running BBC radio soap opera, *The Archers*. But the image of terrible cultural crimes being committed by the occupiers was far from the prosaic reality. The islanders were not threatened with the crimes concurrently visited on Argentinian citizens under General Leopoldo Galtieri's junta – torture, massacre, dispossession and exile. After all, their cousins of British origin in Argentina formed a substantial community of around 100,000 people, and faced little or no persecution even during the dark years of dictatorship.

The war was not therefore about saving or protecting lives, but about protecting a way of life. Yet in pursuit of this nebulous but emotional cause, hundreds of young men had to die: 649 Argentinians (and another 1,068 wounded) and 258 British (777 wounded, including some terribly burnt and scarred for life). By no stretch of logic, law or humanity was this legitimate: that in support of an illegitimate war as many people (leaving aside the thousands of bereaved) were casualties as the total population of the islands themselves. This war was a paradigmatic crime, for which both governments should have been held responsible. It set a terrible example of wasted lives, and of the indulgence of wildly disproportionate (imperialist and nationalist) claims, to the rest of the world.

Its outcome was paradoxical. Britain and Argentina slowly re-established relations, aided by the return of democracy to Argentina in 1983, an event which the defeat in the Malvinas certainly precipitated. By a mixture of after-the-event planning and good fortune, the islands discovered a route to prosperity. The singularity of these effects reflected the way that, in some respects, the war was outside the broader Cold War pattern of international politics at the time. While the Soviet Union condemned Britain's role, I discovered during a visit to Moscow in July 1982 that Margaret Thatcher was extremely popular amongst many ordinary people and military officials in Russia. This fact was confirmed by the then Moscow correspondent of *The Times*, Richard Owen, who told me that, as many in the USSR considered his paper to be the official organ of the British ruling class and state, he had received hundreds of messages congratulating him and Mrs Thatcher on 'a great technical military victory in the South Atlantic'.

The temptation to see the Malvinas war as an isolated event should, however, be resisted. In particular, the covert United States–British collaboration which was central to eventual British victory helped to consolidate the far more momentous (and far less publicised) military project that was then being implemented, one whose destructive impacts are still reverberating across the region and the world: the jihad against the Soviet occupation of Afghanistan. In this campaign, Britain under Margaret Thatcher's leadership joined the United States, Pakistan and Saudi Arabia in training, financing and arming the *mujahideen* guerrillas, and in encouraging young Arab militants to go and fight there. British Special Forces (SAS) units were sent to Pakistan and into Afghanistan to assist the Afghan guerrillas, and Afghan fighters were brought to Britain for training – including in shooting down Soviet helicopters.

This concentrated effort helped create the conditions for the Soviet retreat from Afghanistan in 1989. But by then, the sorcerer's apprentices armed and incited by Thatcher, Ronald Reagan and their friends were no longer under the control of their paymasters, and they set about planning attacks on their former patrons. In this, the Malvinas war

– marginal to the main currents of global conflict as it may have seemed at the time and in retrospect – in fact played a significant part in consolidating the forces that were seeding future conflict and explosion far from the immediate theatre.

The real legacy of the 1982 war is, then, one of profound strategic and ideological irresponsibility, whose consequences were visible in the local wars and pitiless massacres perpetrated in many poor countries in the 1980s – El Salvador, Nicaragua, East Timor and Angola – by the friends of Margaret Thatcher. Those who seek to create a balance-sheet of the grisly record of that decade must complement their assessment of the adventure in the South Atlantic by putting it in the context of wars in the Hindu Kush and beyond, then and now.

6. THE VAGARIES OF 'ANTI-IMPERALISM': THE LEFT AND JIHAD
7 September 2006

The approaching fifth anniversary of the 9/11 attacks on the United States highlights an issue much in evidence in the world today, one that receives too little historically-informed and critical analysis: the relationship between militant Islamic groups and the Left. It is evident that the attacks, and others before and since on US and allied forces around the world, have won the Islamist groups responsible considerable sympathy far beyond the Muslim world, including among those vehemently opposed from a variety of ideological perspectives to the principal manifestations of its power. It is striking, however, that beyond such often visceral reactions there are signs in many parts of the world of a far more developed and politically articulated accommodation between Islamism as a political force and many groups of the Left.

The latter show every indication of appearing to see some combination of al-Qa'ida, the Muslim Brotherhood, Hizbullah, Hamas and (not least) Iranian president Mahmoud Ahmadinejad as exemplifying a new form of international anti-imperialism that matches – even completes – their own historic project. This putative combined movement may be hampered by 'false consciousness', but this does not compromise the impulse to 'objectively' support or at least indulge them.

The trend is unmistakable. Thus the Venezuelan leader Hugo Chávez flies to Tehran to embrace the Iranian president, while London's Mayor Ken Livingstone and the vocal Respect Party MP George Galloway welcome the visit to the city of the Egyptian cleric and Muslim Brotherhood figurehead Yusuf al-Qaradawi. Many in the sectarian leftist factions (and beyond) who marched against the impending Iraq war showed no qualms about their alignment with radical Muslim organisations, one that has since spiralled from a tactical cooperation to something far more elaborated. It is fascinating to see in the publications of leftist groups and commentators, for example, how history is being rewritten and the language of political argument adjusted to accommodate this new accommodation.

The most recent manifestation of this trend arrived during the Lebanon war of July–August 2006. The Basque Country militant I witnessed who waved a yellow Hizbullah flag at the head of a protest march is only the tip of a much broader phenomenon. The London demonstrations against the war saw the flourishing of many banners announcing 'We are all Hizbullah now,' and the coverage of the movement in the left-wing press was notable for its uncritical tone.

All of this is – at least to those with historical awareness, sceptical political intelligence or merely a long memory – disturbing. This is because its effect is to reinforce one of the most pernicious and inaccurate of all political claims, one that is made not by the Left but by the imperialist Right. It is also one that underlies the US-declared 'War on Terror' and the policies that have resulted from 9/11: namely, that Islamism is a movement aimed against 'the West'. This claim is a classic example of how a half-truth can be more dangerous than an outright lie. For while it is true that Islamism in its diverse political and violent guises is indeed opposed to the US, to remain there omits a crucial deeper point: that, long before the Muslim Brotherhood, the jihadis and other Islamic militants were attacking 'imperialism', they were attacking and killing the Left – and acting across Asia and Africa as accomplices to the West.

The modern relationship of the Left to militant Islamism dates to the immediate aftermath of the Bolshevik revolution. At that time, the Soviet leadership was promoting an 'anti-imperialist' movement in Asia against the British, French and Dutch colonial empires, and did indeed see militant Muslims as at least tactical allies. For example, at the second congress of the Comintern in 1920, the Soviets showed great interest in the Islamist group led by Tan Malaka in Indonesia; following the meeting, many delegates decamped to the Azeri capital of Baku for a 'Congress of the Peoples of the East'. This event, held in an ornate opera house, became famous for its fiery appeals to the oppressed masses of Asia and included calls by Bolshevik leaders, many of them either Armenian or Jewish, for a jihad against the British.

A silent-film clip recently discovered by the Iranian historian Touraj Atabaki shows the speakers excitedly appealing to the audience, who then proceed to leap up and fire their guns into the air, forcing the speakers on the platform to run for cover. One of those who attended the Baku conference was the American writer John Reed, author of the classic account of the Bolshevik revolution *Ten Days That Shook the World* (Boni & Liveright, 1919). (He died on his return journey from Azerbaijan after catching typhoid from a melon he bought on the way.)

For decades afterwards, the Soviet position on Islam was that it was, if not inherently progressive, then at least capable of socialist interpretation. On visits in the 1980s to the then two communist Muslim states – the now equally-forgotten Democratic Republic of Afghanistan and the People's Democratic Republic of Yemen – I was able to study the way in which secondary school textbooks, taught by lay teachers rather than clerics, treated Islam as a form of early socialism. A verse in the Qur'an stating that 'water, grass and fire are common among the people' was interpreted as an early nomadic form of collective production; while Muslim concepts of *ijma'* (consensus), *zakat* (charitable donation) and *'adala* (justice) were interpreted in line with the dictates of the non-capitalist road. Jihad was obviously a form of anti-imperialist struggle. A similar alignment of Islamic tradition and modern state socialism operated in the six Muslim republics of the Soviet Union.

Such forms of affinity were succeeded in the latter part of the twentieth century by a far clearer alignment of Islamist groups: against communism, socialism, liberalism and all that they stood for, not least with regard to the rights of women. In essence, Islamism – the organised political trend owing its modern origin to the founding of the Muslim Brotherhood in Egypt in 1928 that seeks to solve modern political problems by reference to Muslim texts – saw socialism in all its forms as another head of the Western secular hydra; it had to be fought all the more bitterly because it had such a following in the Arab world, in Iran and in other Muslim countries.

In a similar way to other opponents of the Left (notably the European fascist movements), Islamists learnt and borrowed much from their secular rivals: styles of anti-imperialist rhetoric; systems of social reform; and the organisation of the centralised party, a striking example of which is Hizbullah in Lebanon, a Shi'a copy of the Vietnamese Communist Party in nationalist, organisational and military form. This process has continued in the modern critique of globalisation and 'cultural imperialism'.

The ferocious denunciations of liberalism by Ayatollah Khomeini and his followers are a straight crib from the Stalinist handbook. Osama bin Laden's messages, albeit clad in Qur'anic and Arabic poetic garb, contain straightforwardly radical contemporary political messages: our lands are occupied by imperialism, our rulers betray our interests, the West is robbing our resources, we are the victims of double standards.

The hostility of Islamism to left-wing movements and the use of Islamists in the Cold War to fight communism and the Left deserve careful study. A precedent was the Spanish civil war, when Francisco Franco recruited tens of thousands of Moroccan mercenaries to fight the Spanish republic on the grounds that Catholicism and Islam had a shared enemy in communism. After 1945 this tendency became more widespread. In Egypt, the communist and Islamist movements were in often violent conflict up until the revolution of 1952. In the 1960s, Saudi Arabia's desire to oppose Nasser's Egypt and Soviet influence in the Middle East led it to promote the World Islamic League as an anti-socialist alliance, funded by Riyadh and backed by Washington. King Faisal of Saudi Arabia was often quoted as seeing communism as part of a global Jewish conspiracy and calling on his followers to oppose it. In Morocco, the leader of the Socialist Party, Oman Benjelloun, was assassinated in 1975 by an Islamist militant.

There are further striking cases of this backing of Islamism against the Left: Turkey, Israel/Palestine, Egypt and Algeria among them. In Turkey in the 1970s, an unstable government beset by challenges from armed left-wing groups encouraged both the nationalist right (the 'Grey Wolves') and Islamists, and indulged the assassination of left-wing intellectuals. In Palestine, the Israeli authorities, anxious to counter the influence of Fatah in the West Bank in the late 1970s, granted permission for educational, charitable and other organisations (linked in large part to the Muslim Brotherhood) in ways that helped nurture the emergence of

Hamas in 1987; Israel thus did not create Hamas, but it did facilitate its early growth. In Algeria, too, factions within the ruling national liberation movement (FLN) were in league with the underground Islamist group, the National Salvation Front; its French initials, FIS, gave rise to the observation that the FIS are *le fils* (the son) of the FLN.

In Egypt, from the death of Nasser in 1970 onwards, the regimes of Anwar Sadat and Hosni Mubarak actively encouraged the Islamisation of society, in part against armed Islamist groups, but also to counter the influence of the socialist left. This was a project in which many formerly secular Egyptian intellectuals colluded, in an often theatrical embrace of Islam, tradition and cultural nationalism. The trend culminated in the 1990s with a campaign to silence left and independent liberal voices: the writer Farag Fouda, who had called for the modernisation of Islam, was assassinated in 1992; Naguib Mahfouz, the Nobel prize-winning author, was stabbed and nearly killed in 1994 (allegedly for his open and flexible attitude to religion in his Cairo novels); the writer and philosopher Nasser Abu Zeid, who had dared to apply to the Qur'an and other classical Islamic texts the techniques of historical and literary criticism practised elsewhere in the world, was sent death threats before being driven into exile in 1995.

There were even worse confrontations between Islamism and those of a socialist and secular liberal persuasion. The National Islamic Front in Sudan, a conspiratorial group that explicitly modelled itself on Leninist forms of organisation, took power in 1989 and proceeded to arrest, torture and kill members of the Communist Party, all this whilst playing host to Osama bin Laden in Khartoum.

In Yemen, after the partial unification of the military North and socialist South in May 1990, the regime allowed assassins of the Islamist movement to kill dozens of Socialist Party members and army officers. This process precipitated the 1994 civil war, in which armed Islamist factions linked by ideology and political ties to bin Laden (most prominently the Abyan army) fought side by side with the regular army of the North to crush the socialist South. This was an echo of the war in Dhofar province in the neighbouring Arabian state of Oman during the 1970s, when the anti-communist government published propaganda by the British-officered intelligence corps denouncing the left-wing rebels for allowing men to have only one wife, and promising them four if they came over to the government side.

The historical cycle of enmity reached an even greater pitch in two other countries where the anti-communist and right-wing orientation of the Islamists became clear. The first, little noticed in the context of Islamism, was the crushing of the Left in Indonesia in 1965. There the independent and 'anti-imperialist' regime of President Sukarno was supported by the Communist Party (PKI), the largest in non-communist Asia. After a conflict within the military itself, a right-wing coup backed by the United States seized power and proceeded to crush the Left. In rural Java especially, the new power was enthusiastically supported by Islamists, led by the Nahdat ul-Islam grouping. A convergence between the anti-communism of the military and the Islamists was one of the factors in the rampant orgy of killing which took the lives of up to a million people. The impact of this event was enormous, both for Indonesia itself and the balance of forces in South-East Asia at a time when the struggle in Vietnam was about to escalate.

The outcome in the second country, Afghanistan, was also of great significance to the Cold War as a whole. During the Soviet occupation of the 1980s, the most fanatical Islamist groups – funded by the CIA, Pakistan and the Saudis to overthrow the communist government in Kabul – were killing women teachers, bombing schools and forcing women back into the home in the areas they controlled. Such enemies led the first leader of communist Afghanistan, Nur Mohammad Taraki, to refer to the opposition as *ikhwan ash-shayatin* ('the satanic brotherhood', a play on 'Muslim Brotherhood'). Bin Laden himself, in both his 1980s and post-1996 periods in Afghanistan, played a particularly active role not just in fighting Afghan communists, but also in killing Shi'a, who were, in the sectarian worldview of Saudi fundamentalism, seen as akin to communists. The consequences of this policy for the Arab and Muslim worlds, and for the world as a whole, were evident from the early 1990s onwards. It took the events of the clear morning of 11 September 2001 for them to penetrate the global consciousness.

This melancholy history must be supplemented by attention to what is actually happening in countries or areas where Islamists are influential and gaining ground. The reactionary (the word is used advisedly) nature of much of their programme on women, free speech, the rights of gays and other minorities is evident. There is also a mindset of anti-Jewish prejudice that is riven with racism and religious obscurantism. Only a few in the West noted what many in the Islamic world will have at once understood, that one of the most destructive missiles fired by Hizbullah into Israel bore the name 'Khaibar' – not a benign reference to the pass between Afghanistan and Pakistan, but the name of a victorious battle fought against the Jews by the Prophet Mohammed in the seventh century. Here it is worth recalling the saying of the German socialist leader Bebel, that anti-semitism is 'the socialism of fools'. The question of how many on the Left are tolerant if not actively complicit in this foolery today is a painful one.

The habit of categorising radical Islamist groups and their ideology as 'fascist' is unnecessary as well as careless, since the many differences to that European model make the comparison redundant. Slogans are not necessary for us to understand that the Islamist programme, ideology and record are diametrically opposed to the Left – that is, the Left that has existed on the principles founded on and descended from classical socialism, the Enlightenment, the values of the revolutions of 1798 and 1848, and generations of experience. The modern embodiments of this Left have no need of the 'false consciousness' that drives so many so-called leftists into the arms of jihadis.

7. THE DOMINICAN REPUBLIC: IN SEARCH OF A 'NATIONAL HERO'
23 April 2009

Hispaniola may have the distinction of being the only island in the world shared between two entire states (Haiti and the Dominican Republic), even if their intimacy belies very different trajectories. But the spacious city of Santo Domingo on the island's southern coast appears to transcend narrowing distinctions and embrace the whole history of the Caribbean: five centuries of invasions, colonial (French, Spanish, British) and neo-colonial (American), and recurrent but intermittent nationalist and socialist revolts.

This indeed was the first city established by the Spanish in their conquest of the Americas, and traces of the 1490s are still visible in the elegant villas and churches of today's Zona Colonial. Many later predators came this way, among them Sir Francis Drake, the English marauder who in 1586 burnt much of the city and turned the cathedral (like the city's university, the oldest in the Americas) into a stable. Rafael Trujillo, installed by the United States in 1930, ruled as absolute dictator until his assassination in May 1961; a son of this land, he was also a grotesque epigone of the worst in European tyrants (though few went as far as Trujillo in naming a city after himself). The melancholy list must also include Lyndon B. Johnson, the US president who ordered the US marines to occupy the country in 1965.

It was Trujillo's death in 1961 – re-imagined in a novel by Mario Vargas Llosa, *La Fiesta del Chivo* (The Feast of the Goat, Farrar, Straus & Giroux, 2001) – that sparked the most dramatic and internationally resonant phase in modern Dominican history. The elections in 1962 brought the moderate left-wing leader Juan Bosch to power; the results were overturned by a coup in September 1963 but in April 1965 an unprecedented alliance, whereby radical and popular parties and movements were joined by nationalist army officers, took power, proclaiming a return to 'constitutional' government. It was only days later that LBJ, reflecting Washington's fear of another revolutionary upheaval in the Caribbean so soon after Cuba and anticipating the invasion of Vietnam that followed weeks later, sent over 40,000 troops in what was to be the largest-ever US invasion in its own 'backyard'.

The 'constitutionalists' were led by their new president, Colonel Francisco Caamaño Deñó; he and his supporters held out until January 1966 before accepting a form of reconciliation agreement under which Caamaño and his fellow officers went into exile. From there they worked in vain to rally the Dominican opposition to their cause. No other help was forthcoming: Cuba was unable to do anything directly (though it did help Caamaño in 1973 in ways it could not then reveal); Charles de Gaulle's strong protest against the invasion remained verbal only; while the Soviet Union implicitly accepted the US action and found in it a convenient analogous justification for its own 'backyard' interventions in Hungary (1956), Czechoslovakia (1968) and Afghanistan (1979). The US occupation was completed with the installation in rigged elections of the neo-Trujilloist leader Joaquín Balaguer for his second period as president in June 1966, a position he was to hold for twenty-two of the next thirty years. The nationalist and socialist forces were gradually worn down: in the years that followed, hundreds of opposition members were killed in the poorer districts of Santo Domingo.

In the early part of this period Caamaño served in London as an increasingly frustrated military attaché, at odds both with Bosch and with the fractious Dominican revolutionary Left; he turned gradually towards an alliance with Cuba. After twenty months in Britain – including a memorable speaking engagement on 4 March 1966 at the Oxford University Labour Club (invited by me as its president) – Caamaño disappeared in disguise via Holland to Prague and then by plane to Cuba.

The constitutionalist president arrived in Havana in November 1967: six years later in February 1973, despite the best efforts of the Cuban leaders to persuade him it was not opportune to return, he led a small group of revolutionary guerrillas back to his country. Within two weeks he was captured and shot. The talk he had given to our student grouping in Oxford turned out to be the last time he ever appeared in public. Since then, history has seemed to bypass the Dominican Republic. The massive protests throughout Latin America in the months following the 1965 invasion were soon eclipsed by the international attention devoted to the escalating war in Vietnam, in which another US marine landing – in June 1965 at Danang – was a symbolic landmark. The Johnson doctrine of massive US military intervention in Third World crises seemed for a time to be working. But in April 1975, exactly a decade after the US troops landed at Santo Domingo, Saigon fell to the North Vietnamese forces and local insurgents.

In the Dominican Republic, a gradual transition to democratic politics began in the late 1970s. Juan Bosch again became president; return to office is a recurring pattern of Santo Domingo history. (Buenaventura Báez had five spells as president between 1849 and 1878.) In 1996 Leonel Fernández, a lawyer raised in New York, won the election; his party, the Dominican Liberation Party (PLD), presents itself as the centre-left inheritor of the 'constitutionalist' movement of 1965.

Today, Francisco Caamaño Deñó has received official recognition in his own country. He is designated a national hero and lionised in statues; his life and struggles are memorialised; he has foundations and an avenue named after him. His widow, Maria Paula Acevedo, and cousin, Rafaela Caamaño, shared his London exile; they recall visits to Portobello Road, Hyde Park (where Caamaño liked to fly model airplanes) and the maze at Hampton Court. Their welcome in Santo Domingo across decades of political and personal history is enthusiastic and warm.

It has been a long national journey too: the Dominican Republic is now far from the country of the revolutionary 1960s. 'Dr Leonel' had to surrender power in 2000 on account of term-limit restrictions, but the lifting of these in 2002 allowed him to run again and win election in 2004 and re-election in 2008. This thoughtful and engaging fifty-five-year-old politician has more in common with the cautious Spanish-Brazilian-Chilean left model than with the bolder one of Hugo Chávez or Evo Morales, yet many of those who have served in his three administrations are former members of the radical 1960s movement. A prominent minister in the first Fernández administration was one of only two people to survive the 1973 guerrilla expedition; another, now a television host and chair of a historical foundation, who interviewed me about Caamaño for an hour on his TV programme, graduated in 1967 from a Chinese guerrilla training school. A number of other recent ministers were educated in the universities of the Soviet Union.

One of the president's trademark themes is the potential of the 9 million people of the Dominican Republic. The last two decades have seen substantial progress in two areas, tourism and export-oriented industry: together they play a vital role in offsetting the annual $5.8 billion trade deficit. In the pre-recession years, the economy was growing at an average annual rate of 7 per cent. The large Dominican diaspora – most living in the US and some in Spain – sends considerable sums in remittances. There is great cultural pride in the award of the Pulitzer Prize for Fiction to the Dominican-American writer Junot Díaz for his Joycean novel relocated to the Caribbean, *The Brief Wondrous Life of Oscar Wao* (Riverhead, 2007); a refreshing variant for a country whose international reputation had hitherto rested on the prowess of baseball players. But the strains of the global economic crisis are becoming evident alongside such indices of progress, with exports down and remittances less certain. Moreover, the prospect of normalisation between Cuba and the US poses a major threat to the Dominican tourist industry.

At the same time, the Fernández leadership, now in its third presidency, has run into trouble. The president is criticised for appointing too many ministers and advisers with unspecified responsibilities. More questions are being asked about the deals the president has made with businessmen in order to secure his re-election, questions he has been obliged to answer via unscheduled appearances on television. The main preoccupation of those participating in a national conference in January 2009 (the

Summit for National Unity in the Face of the World Crisis) was the level of corruption in the country. The next items were the high levels of public expenditure (up nearly 20 per cent in 2008), the global economic crisis, levels of crime and violence, and the lack of competitiveness of Dominican exports. Some of those who admired and supported the president in his first and second periods in office are now markedly less enthusiastic.

These uncertainties are reflected in a continuing debate about the Dominican Republic's place in the world. The president has repeatedly stressed that the DR is in the US's 'backyard' and needs to avoid unnecessary confrontations with its powerful northern enemy. This caution is perhaps reinforced by something many people in Santo Domingo allude to: the sense of their country's geographic isolation. Haiti is a neighbour, its capital Port-au-Prince seven hours overland from Santo Domingo, but relations between the two states and peoples are strained. Cuba is geographically nearby to the west – Guantanamo is an hour's flying time, nearer to Santo Domingo than Havana – but, for political reasons, remote. Almost equally so is the US-controlled island of Puerto Rico to the east.

Dominicans often express the feeling that, just as their country was forgotten by the world after the attention of the Rafael Trujillo years and the 1965 events, so it is treated as outside the regional political and economic systems today – accepted neither as part of Latin America, nor of Central America, nor even in many respects of the Caribbean. It is a paradox indeed that this country, the centrepiece of the original Spanish colonisation of the Americas, and scene of one of the most tumultuous confrontations of the Cold War, should have slipped so easily from international attention. Perhaps it is time for the Dominican Republic to write another page. The five-hundredth anniversary of the denunciation of Spanish colonialism by Friar Bartolomé de las Casas, pronounced in Santo Domingo in 1511, could provide a suitable occasion for such an historical correction.

Three

Challenges of the Middle East

I. CRISES OF THE MIDDLE EAST: 1914, 1967, 2003
    15 June 2007

In *Variations on Night and Day* (Pantheon, 1993), the first volume of his great historical trilogy of the modern Arab world, the late Saudi writer Abdelrahman Munif describes the impact on the region of the First World War and the collapse of the Ottoman empire:

> The world, the whole world, in that quaking era, so full of anticipation and possibilities, looked around, as slow as a tortoise, as swift as a bolt of lightning, to question, to listen carefully for distant thunder, watching with dread for the approaching morrow. Then, everything was open to reevaluation, to reapportionment. ideas, regions, countries, even kings, sultans and little princes. New states rose suddenly, and others vanished.

This is a good time to recall such words. Amid all the retrospective analysis forty years after the Arab-Israeli war of June 1967 it is necessary to set this event in some perspective and context. It was arguably one of the most important moments in the modern history of the Middle East, on a par with the Iranian revolution of 1978–9 and the American invasion of Iraq in 2003 – but it was not the most important. That honour belongs to the early part of the twentieth century, the moment in relation to which the region today and all Arab–Israeli wars past and future have to be seen.

The First World War, more than any other since the rise the Ottoman empire in the fifteenth century, defined the modern Middle East. It was this war that created the system of states – around twenty of which are Arab and three non-Arab – that characterise the region today. It was also this event that drew the boxes within which modernity created the modern nations of the region, like some great historical colouring scheme, out of a motley collection of pre-existing peoples, geographical terms and myths (even as, like people everywhere else in the world, they proceeded to claim ancient affiliation). In larger measure, the map of the region has remained the same since Winston Churchill and his associates drew it around 1920: this was the founding moment.

The Great War of 1914–8 finished a process that began long before its outbreak. In the nineteenth century, colonial Europe had implanted itself on the other peripheries of the Ottoman empire: the French and Italians in North Africa; the British in Egypt, Cyprus, Aden and the smaller Gulf states. The formerly Ottoman Balkans had already been carved up by Russia and Austria, with bit parts for the Greeks, Bulgars, Albanians and Romanians. But it was after the defeat of the Ottomans in the Great War, a war they unwisely and unnecessarily chose to enter, that the French and British delimited and indeed invented (by transforming hitherto loose names into specific territorial boxes) what became Iraq, Lebanon, Syria and – not to be forgotten, for it did not exist before – Palestine.

In the territories that remained outside colonial control, new authoritarian and nationalist military regimes arose – modernising, secular and nationalist in Iran and Turkey, conservative and tribal in Yemen and Saudi Arabia. In Palestine, Zionism – the movement that aimed to create a Jewish state in the territories inhabited for a few centuries by the modern Jews' remote ancestors – received a green light from the British in the form of the Balfour Declaration of November 1917. The losers were those peoples who, trusting in the promises of British diplomats and of American President Wilson, had sought recognition and support from the Western states: the Kurds, who, despite a vague promise of consultation in the Treaty of Sèvres (1920), got nothing; the Armenians, who emerged from genocide with a rump state around the hitherto provincial town of Yerevan that immediately fell under Soviet control; and the Arabs, who found themselves fragmented and dominated.

Thus did the global conflict shape the territorial map and state character of the Middle East. No subsequent conflict – not the Second World War, the decolonisation that followed it or the Cold War – had any comparable effect. In the eight decades since the 1920 settlement, all attempts at Arab unity have failed, with the exception of the fusion of the two Yemens in 1990: the consensual unity of Egypt and Syria broke apart in 1961; Saddam's 'unity of tanks' failed in 1990. With regard to the Turks, it was one of the great achievements of Kemal Atatürk that after he completed his 'liberation war' in 1923 he got his people to accept the much reduced boundaries that eventuated from the Great War (even if his successors have eroded this: episodically in regard to northern Iraq, more enduringly in northern Cyprus).

On their side, the Iranians have not used force to pose any serious territorial demands on anyone in the past century and half: in today's tense times, it is worth remembering that the last occasion Iran invaded a foreign country was when Shah Nader Shah occupied Delhi in 1736 – a three-century record of non-aggression that no other significant state in the world, even including Scandinavia, can claim.

The same is true, despite all the changes of frontier and speculations about settlement and withdrawal, of the Arab–Israeli conflict. In summary terms, a civil war has continued with sporadic intensity between the two communities, Israeli and Palestinian, who have been formed in Palestine (neither a Jewish 'Israeli' nor an Arab 'Palestinian' nation existed before); yet the actual borders within which this conflict has been fought out are those of 1920. The first Arab-Israeli war of 1948–9 did repartition the area of Palestine between Israel and the Arab states (Jordan on the West Bank, Egypt in Gaza), but this redrawing of the map proved to be temporary: 1967 brought it all into one box again. This is all the clearer since 2000, when the collapse of the Yasser Arafat–Ehud Barak talks at Camp David and the outbreak of the second intifada marked the end of any realistic prospect of a two-state solution. The point about Hamas, reinforced by its combative campaign against Fatah in Gaza in these days of internecine conflict, is that it is not interested in what may be termed 'the agenda of 1967', i.e. some kind of compromise or repartition. Nor, as is evident, is the majority of the Israeli population.

Analysis of 1920 also serves another, much needed, function in regard to discussion of the Middle East: namely to discount, if not entirely eliminate, all claims about legitimacy, national identity or cultural continuity that predate this event. In a world where so many analysts within the region and outside fall back on explanations in terms of ancient history, holy texts, deep structures, climatic determination or perverse national character (not to mention 'Islam', 'clash of civilisations' or 'oriental despotism'), my challenge to all those who do so is for them to show how anything that happened before 1920 is relevant to explaining the Middle East of today.

My one and virtually only instinct about the current civil and internationalised war in Iraq is that whenever it ends, and it could be some years away, the territorial entity, the box created in 1920, will endure. Equally, for all the rhetoric and hype now surrounding talk of a new pan-Islamic Sunni community or *umma*, one that transcends existing Western-imposed states, this is very much a minority current; even if, in the form of al-Qa'ida and the various militant Sunni militias which have arisen in the Palestinian camps in Lebanon, this minority is, as the British Foreign Office likes to say of itself, punching above its weight.

1967 served, therefore, to pull the region back into the box created in 1920, even if it took another three decades for the chimera of partition and of a two-state solution, undoubtedly the best way out, to be cast aside. It had, however, other important consequences, which echo Abdelrahman Munif's dramatic words about the First World War: kings did indeed fall. Just as after the Suez crisis of 1956 the Iraqi monarchy fell in 1958 with consequences that continue to be felt, the 1967 war led to a widespread change in the Arab world.

The first manifestation of this was in Aden, the longest-standing British colony, where the weakening of Egypt in the war with Israel had the paradoxical consequence of unleashing a far-left guerrilla movement that took power in the wake of the British withdrawal in November 1967 and established the People's Republic of South Yemen, later the only case of an Arab communist state. The second was in July 1968 in Iraq when the Ba'ath Party definitively took power, leading to the thirty-five-year rule of Saddam Hussein and his associates; the third was in Libya in September 1969, where the radical military around Colonel Muammar al-Gaddafi overthrew King Idris.

The reverberations of 1967 were also felt much nearer home: the Nasserist experiment in 'Arab socialism', already under criticism within Egypt for its corruption and inefficiency, and for the creation of a new class of military bureaucrats and entrepreneurs, began its move to the right: Gamal Abdel Nasser's successor Anwar Sadat would promote this when he took over in September 1970. In Jordan, the Palestinian guerrillas emerged as an independent force, breaking the controls which the Arab military regimes had imposed on them before June 1967: it would take King Hussein's military repression of September 1970 and the long agony of the first phase of the Lebanese civil war (1975–82) before the Arab states were able to bring the Palestinian armed movement under control again.

Three processes – the discrediting of Egypt and Syria in the war in 1967, the rise of the Palestinian *fedayeen* (freedom fighters) in Jordan (with calls for the conversion of Jordan into the North Vietnam of the Palestinian revolution), and the triumph of the radical National Liberation Front in South Yemen – led some leftist commentators within the Arab world to foresee a new, more radical phase in the region, what was at the time termed 'the crisis of the petty-bourgeois regimes'. The fall of Ahmed Ben Bella in Algeria in 1966 was, for a time, seen as part of the same process.

But in the long run, the crisis of the petty-bourgeois regimes led not to the rise of the workers, peasants, progressive fishermen, nomads and intellectuals, but to something very different: the rise of the conservative Arab oil states. These, especially after the Arab–Israeli war of October 1973 and the associated OPEC rise in oil prices, were able to use their oil revenues to turn the Middle East significantly to the right; towards Islamist conservatism and, in the context of Afghanistan in the 1980s, to active support for and incitement of the tribal and jihadi counter-revolution in Afghanistan. This brings the story to 2003. For all the dangers of speculating on the long-term significance of recent events, it is at least plausible to say that the United States invasion of Iraq in that year, with all its consequences for Iraq and the region, may prove to be as important an event as 1967 and in some respects on a par with the reordering of the region after 1918. It has already set in train six major processes, which will take years to work themselves through: the wholesale discrediting of the US, its allies – particularly Britain – and any campaign for the promotion of democracy in the Arab world; the unleashing across the Middle East, and more broadly within the Muslim world, of a revitalised militant Islamism, inspired if not organised by al-Qa'ida, which has used the Iraq war greatly to strengthen and internationalise its appeal; the shattering of the power and authority of the Iraqi state, built by the British and later hardened by the Ba'athists and the fragmentation of Iraq into separate, antagonistic ethnic and religious zones; the explosion for the first time in modern history of internecine war between Sunni and Shi'a in Iraq, a trend that reverberates in other states of mixed confessional composition; the alienation of all sectors of Turkish politics from the West and the stimulation of an authoritarian nationalism there of a kind not seen since the 1920s; and the fomenting, albeit in slow motion and with some constraints, of a new regional rivalry between two groupings: Iran and its allies (including Syria, Hizbullah and Hamas) versus Saudi Arabia, Egypt and Jordan – a rivalry made all the more ominous and contagious by Iran's pursuit of nuclear weapons.

This is, in Abdelrahman Munif's words, very much a quaking era. People within the region and without are alert to the distant thunder; they do most certainly await the morrow with dread. As should all of us. 'Mission Accomplished' indeed.

2. AMERICA AND THE ARAB WORLD AFTER SADDAM
12 May 2004

The images of insensate torture, humiliation and abuse from the prison of Abu Ghraib represent a moment of truth for the world. It is one that, in a sudden, unforgettable shaft of illumination, binds together the reality of what Iraq has become under the hands of its American masters with what it was during the thirty-five long years of dictatorship under Saddam Hussein's Ba'ath Party. Such a moment calls for both an immediate moral and political accounting of this Iraqi reality, and a larger perspective that attempts a direct understanding and appreciation of what Iraq also represents against the canvas of the larger geopolitical crisis of which it is now inextricably part. These are what I seek to provide.

The Iraqi people had Saddam, and then they had post-Saddam. Both have failed them. It is time to allow them to chart a new course, while indeed there is still time. But if it is to happen, and if the Iraqi people are to secure the justice, freedoms and stability they deserve, this can be guaranteed only by establishing a principle that neither Saddam's terrible rule nor the chaos, brutalism and indifference of the occupiers have conceived: listening to the experiences and voices of Iraqi people themselves. My central focus, then, is Iraq – its people, its recent history, its sufferings and its future. Too much Western discussion, in its concern with internal, domestic disputes and agendas, ignores this dimension, and pays scant attention to the 25 million people at the centre of Iraq's own experience. In the West, the tendency to a self-proclaimed anti-imperialism that fuels a relentlessly moralising posture is too often but the obverse of the arrogance and brutality of the occupying forces themselves. Yet whatever our analyses and views may be, there is now a vigorous debate taking place in the Arab world, in Iraq in particular, as well as in Iran, about their future. It is one which demands our attention far ahead of the fantasies, tergiversations and half-truths of London, Washington and Paris.

In Iraq, and more broadly in Western Asia – a term I use deliberately – a fire is burning and it is impossible to know how long it will rage, or who will emerge victorious. But Iraq is not simply at the centre of that fire. It is at the core – historically, politically, intellectually, culturally – of much of the modern Arab world. Of all the intelligentsias of the Arab world, Iraq's is the most sophisticated, historically conscious and rooted in the real concerns of its society. I can attest from recent conversations that it has survived even the ravages of Ba'athist rule with its pertinent and mordant sense of humour intact. It will, if permitted by foreign occupiers and domestic insurgents alike, play a decisive role in the future of its country.

In 1980, I travelled from London to lecture at Baghdad's College of Law and Politics (later renamed after the dictator). It was a time of great tension. The previous year Saddam had taken power openly for himself, and had staged a show trial and execution of his supposed opponents – including the popular leader Abd al-Khallaq al-Samarai, who had been imprisoned for several years. Party members had been dragged screaming from political meetings as Saddam stood, cigar in hand, at the microphone. The top party leadership had been instructed personally to attend and, some report, participate in the executions. All Ba'ath Party members had been ordered to watch a video of them.

This was all presented by spokesmen for the regime as quite normal, one of whom told me that in a country like Iraq you had to apply *al-qiswa* (harshness), and that the reports of Amnesty International and other bodies about torture and executions were quite true. This was not, in my experience, the standard response in Third World repressive states.

The Iraqi regime was then at the height of its economic power, after the oil rises of the 1970s, and its social programmes were well advanced. But it was also feeling vulnerable: to the machinations of its Syrian Ba'athist rivals to the west, to the then vocal and insurrectionary Iranian revolutionary mullahs to the east, and even to a possible attack from the Soviet Union.

In its thirty-five years in power, the Ba'athist regime wrecked the best-endowed of all Arab countries. It killed hundreds of thousands of its own people – Arab and Kurd; deported millions from their homes in forced resettlement programmes; gassed the Kurdish population in the north during the 1980s; destroyed the society of the marsh Arabs in the south; forced millions into exile; and, attacking Iran in 1980 and Kuwait in 1990, plunged the country into two catastrophic wars. This was in addition to its murdering of opponents and moderate Palestinian leaders abroad; its attempts to undermine rival radical states such as Syria and South Yemen; and the systematic programmes of bribing foreign diplomats, journalists and intellectuals that stretched well into Europe and Latin America, as well as across the Middle East.

What exactly was this regime? It was clearly rabidly nationalistic and (through conscious borrowing) fascistic in its rhetoric. Yet its leader also modelled himself explicitly on a communist leader, Joseph Stalin – whose deliberate menace and nuance he copied in his speeches, whose biographies he had studied and whose birthplace in Georgia he secretly visited in the 1970s. Moreover, the unified state–party system he established derived from a communist model, replete with hierarchies, secretiveness, party privileges; and its political economy was comparable to other oil-producing states (republics as much as monarchies), whose rulers appropriated substantial sums from their peoples yet also used this money for broad welfare policies – hence the now preferred term 'distributive state' rather than the older 'rentier state'.

All this is brilliantly portrayed in *The Republic of Fear*, the classic book by Kanan Makiya. This book, written during the height of Saddam's influence in the 1980s, found it hard to get a publisher in the

West or the Middle East alike. When it did so, and like his later *Cruelty and Silence*, the majority of the Arab intelligentsia and their Western, supposedly anti-imperialist, collaborators, excoriated it.

At the summit of the Iraqi system of power stood an omnipotent individual, who drove the accumulation of military potential and strategic ambition, but who by that very fact destroyed his country through the fantasies and ignorance that lay at the centre of his thinking. In addition to the intellectual influences of East and West, there was something more direct: foreign political and military support. The Ba'athist regime in Iraq benefited over many years from the support and indulgence of the West – including Britain, France and the United States. During his time as a student in Cairo in the late 1950s, Saddam was a visitor to the US embassy and received money from them. In the original Ba'athist coup of 1963, when several thousand communists and nationalists were killed in a few days, there was active, close, cooperation between the murderers of the Ba'ath and the US intelligence services.

After the second, decisive, coup of 1968, the Ba'ath depended on the support of the Soviet Union. But following the Iranian revolution of 1979, when the Iranians foolishly and cruelly detained 53 American diplomats as hostages in the Tehran embassy (*jasuskhane* or 'spy-house' in their terminology), Iraq re-established closer relations with Washington. The state was, during the eight-year war with Iran that followed its illegal invasion in September 1980, supported and encouraged by the West.

Saddam was not in any simple sense an 'agent' or ally of the West, as he had his own nationalist and militaristic agenda, but he benefited in many ways from its support: when he invaded Iran in a clear violation of the UN charter, Western powers helped block action at the UN Security Council and, even when a resolution was adopted, made sure it called for a ceasefire in place, not a return to the original frontiers.

During the Iran–Iraq war, and especially after the Iraqi setbacks of July 1982, many states – Britain, France, the US, as well as the Soviet Union and India – armed, financed and provided intelligence on Iranian forces to the Iraqis. The list of those responsible for keeping Saddam and his regime in power, killing a million Iranians in the process, is long: it includes British politicians (Margaret Thatcher, Michael Heseltine, Kenneth Clarke), French (François Mittérrand, Jacques Chirac, Jean-Pierre Chevènement and Claude Cheysson) and American (Ronald Reagan, Robert Dole and Donald Rumsfeld).

Amidst all the debate on the self-righteous Spanish withdrawal from Iraq, the record of Spanish companies and political parties in relation to Saddam in the 1980s and 1990s is worth examining. The same is true, evidently, for many Arab rulers, including the rulers of Saudi Arabia and Kuwait: they were all upset when Saddam invaded Kuwait in 1990 but – as with Osama bin Laden and al-Qaʻida – they had helped to create and sustain the monster who now leapt at them.

If, then, we ask why we should be concerned about Iraq, and involved in its present and future, here is one answer: we in the West helped sustain that dictatorship, and we compounded the failure in withholding support from the nationwide popular uprising of Arabs and Kurds, Sunni and Shiʻa, in 1991, in the aftermath of the Kuwait war, as well as several serious coup attempts during the 1990s. In short, we in the West, and in the Arab world and Russia, owe a debt to the people and society of Iraq. The crisis in Iraq, and the broader post-9/11 crisis that surrounds it, will clearly last for many a year yet. It will affect many areas of life: security (inter-state, internal and personal), the economy (its effects on the world oil market, business confidence and broader macroeconomic change), domestic politics, and inter-ethnic and inter-religious relations in Europe and the Middle East. This combination of impacts across a wide arc of nation-states – the Arab world, Israel, Turkey, Iran, Afghanistan and Pakistan – amounts to what I called three years ago the 'Greater West Asian Crisis'.

In short, in the spring of 2004 we are in the midst of one of the greatest, most intractable and global crises of modern times. It is not a world war, a strategic military conflict between major states – the form of conflict that, with two world wars and the Cold War, dominated the twentieth century; nor is it a major international economic crisis, as was 1929 and (less seriously) 1973. But at every level of social and political life, we confront a situation that is likely to affect everyone on earth and have serious global consequences.

At the outer rim of involvement, there is the situation in the developed West. Events of the past two years, more than any since 1945, have divided the countries of the Western alliance, their governments and, more importantly, their public opinions. Washington stands alone, with Britain on its side, while on the European continent, governments and public opinions are overwhelmingly hostile. In Western Europe, and including large sections of the British public, there is a groundswell of antagonism to the US. At the level of political leadership, it is an open question whether the American president or the British prime minister will survive the pressures on them – let alone salvage for posterity any reasonable political legacy.

In this light, it should be remembered that the Middle East has been the graveyard of many political reputations in the post-1945 period. The Suez adventure in 1956 destroyed the career of Anthony Eden, Winston Churchill's successor as British prime minister; the war in Algeria (1954–62) destroyed both the reputation of many French politicians, and eventually the Fourth Republic itself; and Iranian (1979, 1985–6) humiliations defined the limits of American presidential power.

The role of Iran and the Persian Gulf region should not be under-estimated: the revolution of 1978–9 and the subsequent hostage crisis helped destroy Jimmy Carter in the 1980 election; the Contragate scandal of 1985–6 dented the reputation of Ronald Reagan and broke several of his subordinates; and the mismatch between his preoccupation with the Kuwait crisis of 1990–1 and his domestic economic failures sealed the fate of the first President George Bush. These major strategic and psychological setbacks for the United States demonstrated, in ways that should be relevant to present thinking in Washington but appear not to be, that the capacity of American military, political and ideological power to bend others to its will was not absolute.

The geopolitical climate appears very different now. Washington, shorn of the responsibilities of Cold War, is not just blissfully ignorant of the fact that both national and global security requires alliances and coop-eration with other states: it affects not even to care. 'You are either with us, or against us', is the refrain. The clearest exposition of this line of thinking is the Bush administration's National Security Strategy of September 2002. It argues, in line with what is generally termed 'neo-conservative' thinking, explicitly for a doctrine of US superiority and unilateral capa-bility that dispenses with consultation with allies. This is not confined to official statements: a senior European foreign minister who recently met Dick Cheney reported that, in defiance of even minimal diplomatic norms, the vice-president showed absolutely no interest in talking to him.

For Europe, the consequences are very serious. The long-term costs of political division in the European Union – at a moment when ten now querulous new members have joined, with a still undeveloped defence and intelligence policy, and a constitution not yet agreed or applied – could be considerable. All these difficulties are magnified by the bombings in Madrid. 11 March 2004 has now become the second chapter of 11 September 2001 – an event horrendous in itself, with serious political consequences in Spain, and one that opens the prospect of great uncertainty in Europe in the coming years: in electoral politics, economic confidence, inter-ethnic relations and (because so many people across Europe, as in Spain, blame Europe's vulnerability on the United States) in transatlantic relations as well. 9/11 was such a terrible event, even beyond its human cost, because it unsettled so many areas of life. It was an earthquake of the collective psyche, an abrupt end to the period of liberal optimism which for some, and with a certain good reason, had followed the end of the Cold War in 1991. Madrid's 11 March reproduces all of this; but, coming at a time of great crisis in the Middle East, the area of the Third World nearest to Europe, it acquires an added strategic and cultural dimension.

A key to understanding this broader dimension is to pose the question in blunt terms: one year after the fall of Saddam Hussein, who has 'won' and who has 'lost'? There is no doubt as to which country heads the list of those who think they have won in the current climate. This is the country which has had for 3,000 years a hegemonic political and cultural relationship with Iraq; which commands some cultural if not political respect from 60 per cent of the Iraqi population; and which has fought two inter-state wars with Iraq in recent decades – both the devastating 1980–8 conflict in which it lost a million people, and the less recognised but still decisive border and subversion war of 1969–75. That country is Iran, whose political and media establishment is highly encouraged by what has happened. The United States has destroyed Iran's arch enemy, while itself doing great damage to its own credibility in the region; Iran's own political allies in Iraq, among Kurds and Shi'a, are integrated into the new government structure and have never been stronger; and the country is now poised to play a major, if not decisive, role in the formation of any new Iraqi political and social system.

Iran does not want to see the break-up of Iraq, but it is not unhappy to see the Americans bogged down there for a lengthy period, at considerable cost. It is delighted that, for the first time in the politics of any Arab country, the Shi'a community – 10 per cent of all Muslims, but a majority in Iraq (60 per cent) and Iran (80 per cent) – has now acquired public, legitimate, internationally recognised status. But this Iranian optimism is not entirely wise, for three reasons. First, although the Iranians like to compare themselves to the Chinese – that other great, 3,000-year, post-revolutionary state – there is one major difference between them. The Chinese have, since 1978, embarked on a dynamic economic path, whereas the Iranian economy is mired in inefficiency and corruption, run by an elite of trading mullah and *bazaari* elements who exploit oil income for their own purposes, and shackled by substantial un- and under-employment. (Ayatollah Khomeini notoriously said that 'economics are for donkeys', an unwise statement in a country with a population expanding towards 70 million, predominantly young, people.)

Second, the Iranians repeat as a mantra that the US can deal only with one crisis at a time: embroiled in Iraq, they will not invade Iran. Indeed they will not – not even Richard Perle or John Bolton advocate that option, despite ritual mutterings about 'regime change' in Tehran too. But the issue of Iran's nuclear programme will not go away. Bolton recently highlighted Iran's failure to satisfy International Atomic Energy Agency (IAEA) rules and warned of the likelihood of this going to the UN Security Council; this process would trigger serious, protracted sanctions on Iran, much more severe than those currently in place for US firms under the 1996 Iran–Libya Sanctions Act (ILSA).

More seriously, however, no one should reasonably doubt that, if they wanted to, the US and Israel could launch air strikes against Iran if they identified nuclear targets to hit, on the model of Israel's destruction of Iraq's Osirak plant in 1981. Washington ought to be constrained, in dealing with Iran, by the need to keep talking to Tehran over the political futures of Afghanistan and Iraq – for in both countries Iran has a decisive say. But it is unlikely that this prudence will prevail, especially as Israel is now increasingly citing Iran as the source of support – ideological, financial and military – for Hamas.

A third area of concern should equally be a worry to Iran: the relationship between Sunni and Shi'a Muslims, both in the Arab world and elsewhere, especially Afghanistan and Pakistan. The current Iranian line, emanating from the dominant faction around the *rahbar* (spiritual leader) Ayatollah Khamenei, is that Iraq marks the decisive arrival of the Shi'a world onto the broader international stage, after more than two decades of isolation of the one officially Shi'a state, Iran itself.

Any such outcome has, however, been preceded by two decades of internecine Sunni–Shi'a violence – exemplified in attacks on Shi'a and their places of worship in Pakistan; in recurrent, virulent anti-Shi'a propaganda by Saudi *ulema*; and, in Afghanistan, the mass killing of Shi'a in the 1990s by the Taliban, evidently assisted by their fundamentalist Sunni allies in al-Qa'ida. A sharp sense of this sectarian antagonism, and of the deployment of ancient myths for modern murderous purposes, can be gleaned in the Taliban's use of a great Afghan (and Pashtun) hero, Sultan Mahmud Ghaznawi (971–1030) – a tenth-century commander who was patron of the great scholar al-Biruni, and a scientist and linguist who learnt Sanskrit and translated Indian classics into Arabic. But while cultivating literature and science at his court, Sultan Mahmud also conducted brutal extermination campaigns against Shi'a, whom he considered apostates, and against the Hindu population on the plains to the south.

It was the Taliban's custom, the night before sending fighters into battle against the Shi'a, to take them to the tomb of Sultan Mahmud. According to Kate Clark, a BBC correspondent who visited his tomb during the Taliban period, the young *mujahideen* were told that Sultan Mahmud had been killing 'communists' – a loose translation of the Qur'unic term *moshrikin* (polytheists or 'sharers'). My local Pashtun grocer told me the other day that Sultan Mahmud had invaded India a hundred times. 'Why only a hundred?', I asked him.

Both Iran and Iraq fuelled this sectarian conflict after the Iranian revolution of 1979 and the Iran–Iraq war that followed. Khomeini denounced Saddam as 'Yazid', the Sunni tyrant who killed the founder of the Shi'a belief-system, Hussein; while Saddam called his war Qadisiya, after the battle in which the Arab armies of Islam defeated Zoroastrian Iran – the implication being that Khomeini was not really a Muslim. Each side denounced the other for being Israeli agents.

If the Iranian revolution and the wars in Afghanistan in turn heightened the communal tension, the American occupation of Iraq has opened a third chapter. The two modern precedents show that when sectarian and political aspects of the Sunni–Shi'a divide come into alignment, the result can be not simply distorting of truth – involving the conventional misuse of text, symbol and tradition – but destructively violent. At present, in the context of Fallujah and the equalisation of Iraqi experience under occupation, there is much talk of Sunni–Shi'a alliances in Iraq. This may not last, and for their part the Iranians should not be too confident that in this domain things will continue to go their way.

The second country that can, if more quietly, claim to be a benefi- ciary of the crisis is Turkey. Turkey matters to Europe, and the world, for several reasons. First, it occupies a position of unique political, cultural and strategic importance between Europe and Asia; more particularly, it links the Balkans, the Black Sea, Transcaucasia and Central Asia to Western concerns.

Second, almost a century after the Turkish revolution of 1908, the challenges, goals and hopes of the modernisation project in Turkey continue to shape the aspirations and destiny of West Asia as a whole – even though they are as yet unfulfilled in their country of origin. The convulsive events that followed – the revolutions in Egypt (1952), Iraq (1958), Iran (1979) and, crucially significant for the Cold War and the subsequent rise of reactionary Islamism, Afghanistan (1978) – have striven to fulfil the agenda of the 1908 revolution: modernisa- tion of the state; emancipation from foreign domination; seculari- sation of society and the robust separation of Islam from politics; the forging of a new national consciousness; reform of the position of women; and modernisation of education and language. Thus, the Turkish revolution of 1908 remains the benchmark – at once aspira- tion, model to be rejected and constant implicit critique – for all the radicalisations that followed in Western Asia, and those that are yet to come.

Turkey's suspicions of the West are reinforced by memories of what its diplomats refer to as the 'Sèvres syndrome', in relation to the 1920 treaty that imposed severe and unworkable conditions on the Ottoman empire. But Turkey had no love for Saddam Hussein. This was mani- fest in the crisis over Kuwait in 1990–1, when Turkey supported the US operation in several ways short of direct involvement: allowing the use of its military bases, moving 100,000 Turkish troops to the Iraqi fron- tier, and cutting the oil export pipeline from Iraq.

There is indeed very little sympathy for the Arab world in Turkey. The disdain can be traced back to perceived Arab betrayal in the First World War, and finds its contemporary manifestation in the consolidation (since 1996) of an active military relationship with Israel. But Turkey is at least a semi-democracy, and its public opinion – while mainly con- cerned in recent months with Cyprus and the European Union – is also overwhelmingly against the US intervention in Iraq, not least because it is seen as furthering the agenda of the Kurdish nationalist movement in the northern regions of the country, setting a bad example for the continuously restive Kurds of Turkey itself.

This time, in 2003, Turkey did not allow its bases to be used. But the ostensibly Islamist Justice and Development Party (AKP) government, in power since November 2002, responded actively and creatively to the crisis. It took advantage of disarray between the US and its putative European allies by pressing the need for strengthened Turkish relations with these countries, including closer links to the EU; and by deploying inside Iraq at least 5,000 troops of its own. The latter were used to support the Turcoman community of northern Iraq (variously estimated as between 0.5 million and 3 million) and strengthen its position in the disputed city of Kirkuk, and quietly build a Turkish-Turcoman security belt between the Kurdish region and the Arab heartland to the south.

Turkey can take heart from the consequences of its decisions over Iraq – even more since the rejection by the Greek population of Cyprus of the UN peace proposal makes the country appear on the international stage as a reasonable, stable regional actor.

There remains considerable concern, in Turkey and Western Europe alike, about the long term intentions of the Ankara government, how 'moderate' its Islamic social programme really is, and which shadowy groups are in reality supporting it. So far, things have gone well; but those of us concerned with the interplay of religion and politics might note that the US ambassador to Ankara recently commented that Washington supports the Turkish government's rejection of secularism. The continuing power of the Turkish army, which is the institutional bastion of precisely this secularism, makes it difficult to read this statement without a slightly ominous frisson.

The third country with a strong claim to be a winner in this crisis is Israel. Israel has been a strong supporter of a hard line against what it generically calls 'terrorism' and against states, such as Iraq and Iran, that appear to support it. After the Oslo Accords of 1993, there was some optimism that a substantive, just and lasting Arab–Israeli peace could be achieved, and on the basis of what had for decades appeared to any reasonable observer (and to a considerable number of Palestinians and Israelis) as the only basis for a settlement: namely, a two-state solution that involved Israel's retreat to its pre-1967 boundaries, still 70 per cent of historic Palestine, along with compromises over settlements and the 'right of return'.

In the late 1990s these hopes were dashed, all the more cruelly since, on several occasions, it seemed clear that a political settlement was possible. It was the failure of political leaders and their intellectual and security advisers on both sides that destroyed these possibilities. But the failure was shared by the broader diaspora and inter-state structures into which both Israelis and Palestinians were inserted: Arab nationalist and Muslim leaders, and members of the Jewish community abroad, were equally intransigent and stubborn, while neo-conservatives in Washington were determined to consign the Oslo process to the rubbish bin – along with the ABM treaty, the Kyoto agreement on climate change and the International Criminal Court.

This was made vividly clear in the tantalising but ultimately abortive non-encounters of mid-2000. Then, Israeli and Palestinian leaders misjudged their opponents, and the broader communities of both sides combined to override reason and the prospect of peace – by urging intransigence in the name of religious and/or national rectitude, and by failing to support, fund and endorse a compromise solution. The blame should be spread widely, and without equivocation, for the disaster is shared.

Since 2000, the Palestinian-Israeli conflict has escalated to a new level of violence, bitterness and irretrievability. Yasser Arafat and his people have acted with callous disregard for the interests of the Palestinians or their commitments to Israel; while Ariel Sharon, in his blinkered and militaristic initiatives, has acted as the recruiting agent for Hamas and al-Qa'ida.

If there was a realistic chance for peace in 1967, 1973 and 1993, where is the chance of it now? Whatever ceasefires, truces, peace processes or negotiations take place in the future, are we really condemned to witness a fight to the finish? If so, the human suffering will be great, the international ramifications enormous, the ultimate outcome catastrophic.

The deterioration no longer extends to the Israeli–Palestinian equation alone; rather, after decades of rhetoric and posturing, the Arab and Muslim world – 1.5 billion people – is now truly, and for the first time, mobilised against Israel and in favour of the destruction of a Jewish state in the Middle East. A hatred that was in the past verbal or formal has started to become real. Far too many young people in the Muslim world now see the destruction of Israel as a desirable goal in a way that was previously not the case.

Israel has military security, but its society is long shorn of its initial Zionist idealism and egalitarianism, and is now a semi-peripheral consumerist community of mid-Atlantic calibre. From all we know and see, the psychological toll on the nerves of Israelis has risen sharply. This is evident in two major processes of considerable import: the flight of tens of billions of Israeli funds from the country to safer markets abroad, and the departure (in Zionist terms, *yorda* [descent] as opposed to *aliya* [ascent]) of a significant proportion of the Israeli population to Western countries. Sharon and his allies may be able to hold power behind their fence, but Israel will be a society increasingly living on its nerves and on medication, losing funds and many of its most talented and independent-minded people. If the current conflict continues, this will become a land without a future, except one that is too menacing to contemplate.

A further important point relates to the policy of targeted assassination, part of what is in effect a continuing war. What is often missed in discussion of this matter is the particular significance, and legitimacy, of those Hamas leaders whom the Israelis have recently killed (with no doubt others to come): Sheikh Ahmed Yassin and Abdul-Aziz Rantisi. My personal observation from contemporary encounters in Iran and the Arab world is that the leaders who command particular respect are those – like these – who lead simple lives, are palpably honest in their daily dealings, and who speak in a clear, non-ideological, and often spare voice.

Within the Middle East as a whole, there is a crisis of political legitimacy, after decades of hot air and rhetoric – from nationalists and Marxists, Maoists and Islamists, and now World Bankists and globalists. On a visit to the tomb of Ayatollah Khomeini in South Tehran in 2000, I was struck by the way people there praised him for being *sade* (pure) and *dorost* (straight) – not like the others. And in the Arabian peninsula, I repeatedly heard praise of political leaders expressed in words like *tamam* (all right) and *mutawadi* (simple) – whether the revolutionary first president of Yemen, Abdullah al-Sallal (whom I interviewed for my PhD), or conservative leaders like King Faisal of Saudi Arabia; in either case the sense was that they were shorn of corruption, verbiage and vanity. These were the very qualities of Sheikh Yassin and Abdul-Aziz Rantisi. It is for this, more than their nationalist, let alone their religious, militancy that they are respected and will – with as yet unforeseen consequences – be avenged.

If Iran, Turkey and Israel are the winners in the present crisis, the losers in all this are if anything even clearer to identify: the Arabs and the Americans. The Arab world is now divided, between reluctant allies of the US and an enraged population, in a way that was never the case before. A growing sense of militancy has been evident since the late 1990s, one in which the composite issues of Palestine, Iraq, Afghanistan and Western support for corrupt dictatorships have fused, and in turn been linked to issues beyond the region proper like Afghanistan, to create the 'Greater West Asian Crisis'.

A combination of three elements – popular feeling from below, inter-state manoeuvring and rivalry from above, and the mobilisation by networks like al-Qa'ida and a genuinely transnational army of jihadis – has transformed the regional political and security situation. 9/11 in Manhattan and 11-M in Madrid reveal that this struggle knows no conventional national or state limits. Here, the United States has found itself, through the decisions of its leaders, in a monumental trap – and the emphasis felt in Washington on global 'credibility' makes it very difficult to imagine an easy exit. Even were fighting in Iraq to cease tomorrow, and the US to withdraw its military forces in the next few months, the combined damage to its reputation from its actions in Iraq and its folly in endorsing Ariel Sharon would continue to cost it and its allies dear.

As things stand, there may be little that George W. Bush or (in the event) John Kerry can do. The United States' predicament is compounded by the apparent lack of any coherent political control over its Iraq policy: the leadership in Washington is in seclusion or disarray; the political authorities in Baghdad, notably Paul Bremer, are in a bunker; and the initiative lies with military commanders – Generals Myers, Abizaid, Kimmitt and in Fallujah (it seems) local marine officers – who have no sense of political or diplomatic requirements. Moreover, throughout this crisis the US – true to the unilateralist instincts and policy of the White House – has shown scant regard for the views of any of its allies. The situation is, quite literally, out of control.

Those analysing the Middle East – as much as its residents – love to invoke history, but this is in effect often a disguise for a current interest rather than an innocent exploration of how the past determines the present. In the engagement with this region, I am ever reminded of James Joyce's observation that 'history is a nightmare from which I am trying to escape'.

But beyond the modern history of colonial state formation and later inter-state nationalist rivalry in the Middle East, history does indeed continue to exert its hold on the present, for both its inhabitants and its Western interlocutors. In the case of Iraq, no one can understand the mentality, and appeal, of Saddam Hussein without looking at the society in which he grew up. It is not necessary to concede much ground to generalisations about the 'severe' or 'harsh' character of Iraqi society and culture as an explanation for the brutality of the Ba'ath – among the defects of such explanations is their exculpation of the perpetrators of such actions from responsibility for them.

But an essential part of the context of the Ba'ath regime is indeed the history that formed it: the aftermath of the suppression by British forces of the nationalist uprising of 1941 led by Rashid Ali; the mass anti-state mobilisations over Britain's proposed Portsmouth Treaty in 1948 and again in 1952 (possibly the first time the word 'intifada' [uprising] was used in modern Arab politics); growing hostility to the pro-Western monarchy in the 1950s; the salience of the Palestine question; and, then, the 1958 revolution in Iraq itself.

In this trajectory, nationalist anger at Western control, direct and indirect, of their country has been a central feature of Iraqi politics for decades, and for good reason. This is apart from the confected, state-directed use of national heritage by the regime in which all precedents – whether the Kurdish anti-Crusader Saladin, or the tyrants of ancient Mesopotamia, Hammurabi (author of a famously severe penal code) and Nebuchadnezzar (conqueror of Jerusalem in 586 BCE) – are recruited to legitimate Saddam's rule.

On the Western side too, history also has its hold. The senior officials now running Washington are far from free of Cold War constraints, as they imagine: they are in fact prisoners of them. This is evident above all in two respects. First, the overall strategic vision of the Vulcans running policy in Washington, far from being some great response to the post-Cold War world, is a tired recycling of its themes. What no one has told them, or they have chosen not to see while ensconced in their Washington DC offices, is that the US official view was never an accurate account of how the world worked even during the Cold War (as many, including Mary Kaldor, Gabriel Kolko, Daniel Ellsberg and myself tried at the time to argue in our alternative accounts of post-1945 politics); and the world has indeed changed very substantially since 1991, presenting new opportunities and threats alike.

The great beneficiary of the Cold War itself, who has proved himself a good student of this change, with a range longer than any of the Vulcans, is Osama bin Laden. In his cave in the Hindu Kush he has a much more perceptive take on international politics than the supposedly visionary occupants of 1800 Pennsylvania Avenue. He also, as we have seen in Spain, understands a lot more about European domestic politics.

The Bush administration is a prisoner of the Cold War in one respect that goes to the heart of the deceptions over weapons of mass destruction (WMD): namely that, when unable to mobilise support for confrontational actions on more legitimate grounds (like international law or human rights) they resort to a well-worn and little-challenged ploy, 'threat inflation'.

During the latter phase of the Cold War (1973–83), and before coming to the LSE, I worked as a researcher on international issues for the Washington-based liberal think-tank, the Institute for Policy Studies, originally created by members of John F. Kennedy's White House staff who had become dissatisfied with his nuclear and Indochina policies. In a debate formed by the Washington consensus, our main job was to provide an alternative analysis of the 'Soviet threat'.

This broad challenge was subdivided into three parts: an alternative, critical, analysis of the arms races, nuclear and conventional; an alternative, less alarmist and more historically aware, account of the evolution of Soviet politics and society; and a critical rethinking of the alleged Soviet role in the Third World, not to exonerate Moscow from its support for dictatorships and its spurious arguments about a 'national democratic' path used to justify this, but to discover whether a closer analysis of what actually happened in countries such as Iran, Afghanistan, Palestine, Ethiopia, Angola and Nicaragua would reveal the Soviet factor to be much less important than the 'threat inflators' of Washington alleged.

My focus was on the last of these. I soon learnt that our work, informed and measured as it was, counted for nothing: the 'threat inflators' ploughed on, calling the alarm from Kabul to Beirut, Addis Ababa to Luanda, Managua to the tiny Caribbean island of Grenada. Now, thirty years after those days, the same arguments and the same stage army of inflators – Richard Perle, Frank Gaffney, Donald Rumsfeld himself – are back.

The identical mentality at work across these decades is evident in the arguments made about Iraq's WMD programmes. Saddam of course talked of a WMD programme, and he had bought (probably at great expense) bits and pieces of it; but he was no engineer, or manager, and his main items had been destroyed, either by Israel in 1981, or the UN in the mid-1990s – and the rest was junk. Washington's failure is a political one, not, as current investigations seem to think, an institutional or intelligence one – a failure that reproduces the mindset, and the mendacious practices, of the Cold War era.

In addition to these historical continuities, there is a further element in the present deep crisis that needs to be registered: the centrality of violence. All societies rest, as Max Weber and Antonio Gramsci insisted, on a core of violence. We who live in Britain have special reason to recall this: this country has over the centuries visited its armies on much of the world, and has been involved in violent conflict in every one of the fifty-four years that the current monarch has ruled.

Yet it is the violence of the rebel rather than of the state that invites particular attention here, in all its stages – the decision to take up arms (often an easier one than that to resist using weapons); the contagious impact of violence on society (particularly young men); the impact of retaliatory state violence; the casualties (physical and mental) of such violence; and the means by which a war once started becomes a way of life for many young people. Violence is a recruiting agent in itself.

In this perspective, it would be better to analyse al-Qa'ida not (for example) by looking for some elusive 'profile' or 'terrorist personality', but via a systematic study of the forms and consequences of violence in modern society. This would open the way to understand secondary, but not irrelevant questions: the relation of violence to culture and religion, the disposition of some social groups to violence, and how far violence represents either breakdown or continuation of politics.

Behind the questions of history and violence lies the issue, both ethical and political, that is now at the centre of public controversy: the right to intervene and the critique of Western action. Here, focus has been maintained on the question of WMD: as justification for intervention this was both empirically false and in any case highly selective, since if there was one rogue state that was spreading WMD around the region it was not Iraq but America's ally, Pakistan – a country very much part of my Greater West Asian Crisis but conveniently left off the edge of Bush's Greater Middle East Initiative.

The argument has been made that Bush and Blair could have made a much better case for intervention in Iraq on other, legal, grounds – namely Iraq's continued defiance of Security Council resolutions either on weapons inspections (in suspension since 1998) or on more 'humanitarian' grounds (regarding Saddam's refusal to implement the provisions over human rights and democracy contained in Resolution 688 of 1991).

The reasons why these leaders based their argument on WMD may never be entirely clear, but two suggest themselves: first, the advice of their domestic political advisers (Karen Hughes and Karl Rove in the case of Bush) that public opinion would not support a legal or human rights, only a crude security argument; second, from evidence in the media and from conversations I have recently had with serving British army personnel, the reluctance of the British armed forces at least to engage in a major 'do-gooding' operation, after so many inconclusive years in Bosnia, Kosovo, northern Iraq and Sierra Leone.

These arguments may be in part settled by later documentation, but in any case they seem to suffer from the absence of a concept that is both crucial and undervalued within the debate on intervention and the norms governing it: solidarity. It is this value which to my mind opens up a different way of looking at the problem of intervention. The question it entails is what are our obligations – as citizens of the world, and (where Western countries are concerned) as part of a democratic, internationalist and privileged society – towards people in other countries?

It was that governing ethic of solidarity that led several of us in Britain – politicians, intellectuals and trade unionists, from Jack Straw, Neil Kinnock, Stan Newens and Ann Clwyd to Eric Hobsbawm and Rodney Hilton – to work through the Committee Against Repression and Dictatorship in Iraq in the 1980s. This was a vehicle through which many in Britain first became interested in Iraq and in expressing solidarity with its people.

This emphasis on solidarity raises two further issues, both analytical and practical, with important consequences for policy. First, it is no secret that modern democracies – particularly those enjoying the comforts of globalisation and the post-Cold War world – find it hard to debate, let alone act on, their responsibilities in the field of international peace and security. The reasons for this are at once varied, inexorable and deeply disturbing. The Rwanda genocide of 1994 was a portent here: 'There were no takers for Rwanda' in the memorable words of one UN official.

In the midst of crisis, politicians are reluctant to act, the press is too easily swayed by short-term sensationalist irresponsibility, and professional armed forces are often doubtful about action, especially where it appears guided by humanitarian considerations. Yet if Western democracies, including the twenty-five members of the newly-enlarged European Union, do not wish to address the issue of solidarity with suffering elsewhere on the globe, others with fewer scruples will certainly take advantage. Osama bin Laden is certainly doing so.

A second point arising from a concern with solidarity is the issue of universal values. It is commonly argued in current debates of political and cultural theory that these are of limited salience – that even when people espouse them, their prime loyalty is actually to 'their own' specific (cultural, national, 'embedded' world). In Michael Walzer's terms, there is a contrast between the 'thin' international and the 'thick' internal system of value and meaning; similar assumptions underlie the work of Samuel Huntington, Richard Rorty, John Rawls and the 'communitarian' school of Amitai Etzioni.

This important debate allows for no easy resolution. But it has very little to do with what is happening, or being debated, in many non-Western countries – and it has virtually nothing to tell us about the current conflict in Iraq, and indeed makes very little reference to the extensive literature on the politics of modern Iraq – from Hanna Batatu's classic study of the 1958 revolution, *The Old Social Classes and the Revolutionary Movements of Iraq*, the greatest work of social science on the modern Middle East, to recent studies of Shi'a political thinking by Faleh Abd al-Jabar.

What is palpable in such works, as in the reality they depict, is that the supposedly internal and specific 'thick' is inextricably bound up with the categories and aspirations of the putatively 'thin'. Thus, the Iraqi convulsion is currently raising ideas of nationalism and independence, democracy and equality, federalism and women's rights, legal process and press freedom – quintessentially 'universal' concerns.

I would go further. Even when Islamic terms are used across the

Middle East to voice political concerns and aspirations (as in the 1978–9 Islamic revolution in Iran), the main stimulus to action tends to be eminently general, secular ideas like nationalism, democracy, justice, employment, honest government. The ideas may be articulated in language that may seem particular, but their reach and relevance are universal. Here, too, Iraq and its people belong to the same world as the rest of humanity, and solidarity with them is a recognition of this shared reality as well as a moral and political obligation.

Against the background of the 'Greater West Asian Crisis', and with the fires of war blazing in Iraq, it is both difficult and urgently necessary to recommend lines of policy engagement that have a chance of influencing those with power to ameliorate a desperate situation. In Iraq itself, it is obvious that the United States has, with spectacular mismanagement and blundering, destroyed the goodwill it initially enjoyed when it invaded Iraq in spring 2003. It is in danger of destroying the tolerance of Iraq's neighbours for its presence in the country. At the same time it has, through its reckless and illegal endorsement of Sharon's projects, alienated and undermined its allies across the region in a way no previous administration has ever achieved.

The responsibility for all this lies with the Bush administration itself, a coalition of retreads, zealots and incompetents whose errors in this region – as in the areas of environment, world trade and international law, perhaps also the management of the dollar deficit – will cost the planet dear for many years to come. Moreover, the United States will itself pay a heavy price for these blunders, and, in the eyes of many across the world, will deserve to do so. Its lack of clear strategy and the absence of any clear line of command in the everyday management of events in Iraq mean that it has forfeited any claim to tolerance or understanding there. At the same time, the militant armed groups that have arisen in Iraqi cities have no political strategy of their own, beyond the assertion of armed force; on the basis of all we know (including the balanced assessment of Yahia Said in his openDemocracy interview), they do not enjoy the support of the majority of the Iraqi people.

In brief, the only possible way out of this crisis lies through a decisive international intervention to secure the foundations of stable and just governance in Iraq, sponsored by the United Nations, backed by Iraq's neighbours (Arab, Turkish and Iranian), and in cooperation with those

Iraqi politicians and technocrats who have the ability and commitment to pursue such a transitional strategy.

At present, Washington shows a vestigial willingness to follow this course, but the signals underlying it are not good – from the militaristic bluster of Generals Kimmitt, Abizaid and Myers to the stalling rhetoric from Colin Powell and George W. Bush himself. Perhaps worst of all, however, is the proposed appointment as US ambassador to Baghdad of John Negroponte – a man without close knowledge of the Middle East despite forty years in the diplomatic service of the United States, who in Central America in the 1980s was notable for his championing of forces responsible for illegal and murderous actions, and who as US ambassador at the United Nations has proved a slavish apologist for Ariel Sharon's strategic project.

Indeed, it is the UN's views of the future of Iraq, embodied at present in the figure of Lakhdar Brahimi, a man I have known and admired for over thirty years, that should be heeded, not those of a John Negroponte. There are problems about the UN's role in the past – the corrupt handling of the oil-for-food programme has left many Iraqis sceptical, and both Kurds and Shi'a remember UN indifference to their plight. But Brahimi's understanding is vital, and is echoed among Western states and the Muslim world alike: this international intervention is the last chance to avoid a total conflagration in Iraq and the triumph of the extremists. On current form, it is improbable that Washington will listen.

Will Britain? In regard to Washington's closest collaborator, I would suggest that its leaders should specify the following five conditions for further collaboration with the Coalition Provisional Authority in Baghdad:

1. A clear, line-drawing restatement of the justifications for overthrowing Saddam and remaining in Iraq. Both WMD and the al-Qa'ida link are discredited, and the resort to international law is so contested as to be unusable. The only case now – and, I would argue, from the start – is one of humanitarian support to the Iraqi people; in a word, solidarity.
2. A clear, public and irrevocable guarantee from the Americans as to the integrity and authority of the UN position – what Kofi Annan has called the 'central role' of the UN in any political transition after 30 June 2004.

3. A clear, public and authorised statement from the White House as to the lines of command in regard to policy on Iraq, both military and political. The confusions, blundering and buck-passing of these months must end.

4. A clear, immediate break with the equivocation and bluff that have so far marked the British and American response to revelations about the torture of Iraqi prisoners, and the detention (in Afghanistan and elsewhere) of thousands of people in undisclosed detention centres. No purely American or British judicial procedure will command credibility: a tribunal must be set up, calmly and with due regard to international law, which will hear the charges and administer justice. Nothing less will do.

5. A clear resolution of these issues, and a substantive handover of authority to the UN, must take place before any more British troops are sent to Iraq. Moreover, active contingency plans should be prepared for the withdrawal of forces from an operation that had the potential to bring great benefit to the people of Iraq, but has been squandered by arrogance, incompetence and lethal bluster.

That is the challenge of this moment of truth in relation to Iraq. Meanwhile, we global citizens who are equally concerned with the issues and principles of public policy have a responsibility to provide what resources we can, however unwelcome or contested they may be:

1. A clarification of the analytic and normative, moral and legal issues involved.

2. A transparent account of how the past has really (as opposed to mythically) come to shape the present.

3. A critique of the illusions and propaganda of those involved, be they states or their opponents.

4. An attempt, provisional as it must ever be, to explain what has occurred.

5. Not least, the preservation of our own space for free exchange of ideas, without fear of government, threats or calls for boycotts or piety towards any of the parties involved.

Above all, and here I return to the beginning, we must focus our efforts on an interchange with Iraqi citizens, colleagues and friends. For many decades, and including recent months, their views have been ignored. But it is they who will in the end decide the outcome of their current troubles – and in doing so supply a solidarity of their own to those else-where who need it most.

3.   AL JAZEERA: A MATCHBOX THAT ROARED
      23 March 2007

Doha, capital of the small Gulf state of Qatar (adult citizen population around 80,000), was once the centre of the most retrograde of the region's British-ruled statelets. Things have changed a little since then. With around 15 per cent of the world's gas, Qatar now has the highest per-capita income on earth, at around $70,000; its capital is a fast-moving city of skyscrapers and seaside motorways; its emir, Sheikh Hamad bin Khalifa Al Thani (who came to power in June 1995 by following family tradition and deposing his father), a shrewd and ambitious ruler.

Yet for all the modernity, drivers here take their direction by ref-erence to roundabouts, most named after local landmarks or symbols – 'clocktower roundabout', 'oryx roundabout' and ... 'television rounda-bout'. Welcome to the studios of Al Jazeera, perhaps the most famous broadcasting station in the world. A few minutes from the centre of town, past a gatehouse with the proverbially sleepy guard, here it is: two extensive single-storey buildings containing respectively the studios of Al Jazeera's Arabic service (founded in 1996) and the newer English-language channel. At first sight the headquarters seem nondescript: Egypt's Hosni Mubarak, a regular target of criticism on Al Jazeera's pro-grammes, was heard to remark after a surprise midnight visit, 'All this trouble from a matchbox!'

In the 'English' building a relaxed and largely British staff of produ-cers and interviewers offer a set of programmes and view of the world that are not that different in feel from BBC World and Sky News. Famous interviewers such as David Frost (in London) and ex-CNN host Riz Khan (in Washington) have been hired. The Arabic service was originally staffed with journalists who had worked on the BBC's first attempt at an Arabic TV station; many lost their jobs in 1996 when the station's Saudi sponsors, Orbit TV, took against their coverage of Saudi Arabia. Qatar's new emir responded to the censorship with an inspired move: he hired the Arab journalists en masse. Al Jazeera was born.

After an interview on the Arabic service with the Lebanese and Tunisian hosts of a books programme about the dialogue of civilisations, I talked with one of Al Jazeera's senior editors, Aref Hijjawi (an ex-BBC man from Nablus), about the consequences for America of its impending defeat in Iraq. I suggested that, despite the regional effects, United States economic, technological and military power may not be any more affected at the global level than it was by the defeat in Vietnam. Hinjawi disagreed strongly, citing the Arabic saying: 'When the string snaps, the worry beads fly in all directions.' Meanwhile, a translator regaled me with stories of mistakes in Arabic rendering of English film scripts. Even now, we translate 'cool' as *barid* (cold) instead of his suggestion of *hilwa* (sweet), he lamented.

The English-language service took several years longer to set up than anticipated, thanks to personnel disputes and what were politely termed 'teething problems'. The hope that it would be entirely separate from the Arabic station was unfulfilled: Wadah Khanfar is managing director of both channels. But the difference in approach from that of the main Western channels is evident. On a routine news morning, while CNN led with the story of US troops fanning out across Baghdad to establish zones of security, Al Jazeera in English carried an account of the loss of US troops in a battle and the downing of an American helicopter by the Iraqi opposition – the latter event repeatedly illustrated by film of a helicopter falling out of the sky.

The flagship discussion programmes of the 1990s remain: *The Opposite Direction* (in Doha, hosted by Faisal Qasim) and *The Other View* (in London, hosted by Sami Haddad, a sparky Palestinian more at home in the Via Veneto than in Arabia). They have acquired a reputation for outspoken discussion, but a word of caution is necessary: they are not so much Arab, as very American chat shows whose purpose is provocation and whose 'moderator' acts as the chief agent of incitement.

I have occasionally appeared on Sami's discussion programme, which rather too often degenerates into a bun-fight of competing accusations. On one occasion he accused me of being a KGB agent who had helped run the Soviet occupation of Afghanistan; on another, I spoke alongside

Abu Qatada, a Jordanian clergyman who was reputedly al-Qa'ida's main ally in Europe (now detained in London), who justified the destruction of the Bamiyan statues in Afghanistan on the grounds that there was 'a world Buddhist conspiracy against Islam', aided by arms-carrying Japanese tourists to the (Shi'a populated) region. At one moment Abu Qatada rounded on me and, in front of millions of viewers, accused me of being a *kafir* (infidel). I also recall a shouting match, egged on by Sami, with the Arab newspaper editor Abdel Bari Atwan as to which nation was capable of the greatest evasion and verbal hypocrisy: the British or the Arabs. It was a sign of our friendship, and of Abdel Bari's graciousness, that after the programme had been broadcast he immediately asked me to write for his paper, *al-Quds al-Arabi*. I doubt if such an offer would have come after arguing with an American editor on Fox News.

These lively if not always responsible programmes continue, but many of the older, secular journalists and board members have been shoved sideways. Indeed, the Arabic service has also changed from its former iteration, in part to reflect a shift of mood in the Arab world towards a more Islamist and less traditionally Arab nationalist approach. A gradual increase in the influence of Islamist producers and journalists from Egypt and North Africa is notable in the past two to three years; there is regular observance of prayer time, and more bearded journalists. Much of this is attributed to the influence of Wadah Khanfar, a Palestinian Islamist. As a correspondent in 2003 he angered the Saddam Hussein government, which threatened to hang him for his critical reports from the Kurdish regions of northern Iraq. Today, he is aligning Al Jazeera more with the new militant nationalist and Islamist mood of the region.

No television station in modern times has created as much controversy as Al Jazeera. It made world news with its coverage of United States and British operations in Iraq in 1998; of the second Palestinian intifada from September 2000; of the invasion of Afghanistan in October 2001; then with the invasion of Iraq in March 2003. Above all, and beyond its insistent and critical denunciation of US and Israeli policy in the region, it has stimulated attention by broadcasting the video-communiqués of Osama bin Laden, Ayman al-Zawahiri and the al-Qa'ida leadership. But perhaps its greatest crime is the simple fact that for the first time in the history of the electronic media, a station outside the control of Western governments has reported in a live, independent voice from zones of combat.

This has made Al Jazeera the object of widespread denunciation and harassment. In both Kabul and Baghdad its studios were attacked by American aircraft; in the latter case one of its correspondents, Tareq Ayyoub, was killed (a memorial to him stands in the Doha studios). Al Jazeera was subject during the Afghan and Iraq conflicts to crude diplomatic pressure from the US and others, to isolation of its journalists and TV crews in the field, and to vilification in much of the American media. Saudi pressure on advertisers to boycott the station also has had an effect on the level of advertising on Al Jazeera. Yet this has become the most popular TV station in the Arab world: satellite discs in North Africa that were turned to Europe a decade ago now point towards the Gulf. Anyone who has seen the wooden, censored and completely dull fodder that is produced by conventional Arab TV stations will understand why this lively and informative channel has performed as well as it has. Just as the Kuwait war of 1991 'made' CNN (which was alone in broadcasting live from Baghdad – and denounced by US right-wingers as 'Chicken News Network' for its sins) – so Al Jazeera has made its name in moments of crisis and media opportunity in Afghanistan and Iraq especially; deservedly so, as the professionalism and courage of its correspondents and crews has shown.

Al Jazeera has also been the dubious beneficiary of an often indulgent mythology, especially from Western commentators who know no Arabic and ignore the station's political and regional context. It may be lively and something new for the Arab world, but Al Jazeera is not by any stretch of the imagination an independent broadcaster; nor is it an index of some new 'civil society' in the Arab world. Like every other satellite TV station in the Gulf (and very many elsewhere), it remains, in the last instance, the property of one very rich man. It is the arm of a state, and operates also as a function of Qatar's foreign and domestic policy.

The station's main function is very simple: to annoy Saudi Arabia, something it does very effectively. In February 2007 it obtained some video footage of a brawl in a Saudi university between students and security guards, which it broadcast over and over again. Its political connections mean that it is also heavily subsidised: its budget is not public, and all its claims of generating advertising revenue have been empty. This link to the Qatari state also explains what Al Jazeera can and cannot talk about. Qatar is engaged in a complex balancing act: providing base facilities to the US air force, army and intelligence services on its territory; maintaining diplomatic links with Israel; and seeking to assuage a nationalist and quite religiously conservative population. (A Doha joke is that when the US air force does decide to bomb the Al Jazeera studios there, it needs only to take off from one side of town and fly for a minute before descending on its target.) After the Iraq invasion, the emir was the first Arab head of state to visit Washington, where he was thanked by George W. Bush for 'his silent support' and for fulfilling his (unspecified) promises.

Qatar remains vulnerable. Kuwaitis, also criticised on Al Jazeera's programmes, like to say that when the Saudis invade Qatar (as Saddam did Kuwait) no one will now come to their aid. The emirate's solution is to offset realistic cooperation with Washington by broadcasting that meets domestic mood: acerbic towards the US and Israel and openly hostile to most other Middle Eastern regimes; leavened with a large dose of religious propaganda and conservatism, embodied in the figure of Sheikh Yusuf al-Qaradawi, a conservative and often demagogic Egyptian preacher and Muslim Brother who was given refuge in Doha in the 1960s. More recently, in what some in Qatar see as a risky move, both government and TV station have moved closer to Iran.

This context helps explain Al Jazeera's silences. Like all the rest of the media in the Gulf, including the universally craven English-language press, Al Jazeera is happy to report at length about developments far away but not so keen to report on those nearer home unless it suits state purposes. So there is little about the treatment of migrant workers in Qatar, or the facts of state finances, or the reasons for the dismissal of ministers (including the sacking of the crown prince, Sheikh Jasim, and his replacement by a younger brother). Nor does anyone probe corruption, inter-elite factionalism, or the feasibility of the many grand projects to which the government is committed.

The Qataris make much of their independent foreign policy and related initiatives, and in some cases rightly so: they have kept a door open to Israel, and to their great credit interview Israelis on Al Jazeera, while helping to keep the Palestinians afloat. There are darker realities too, from the assassination in February 2004 of the former Chechen leader Zelimkhan Yandarbiyev by Russian secret service agents to policies endorsed by Qatar within United Nations bodies and conferences on family and gender issues, which align with the most conservative global forces (such as the US, the Vatican and Iran).

Al Jazeera has occasioned a wider myth, to which both it and its opponents seem to subscribe: that alongside the real wars in the region there is another (in some ways equally important) 'media' or 'information' war. This leads Western governments, pressed after Iraq or over their support for Israel, to upgrade their own media and journalistic output in the service of 'public diplomacy'. True, the media matter in international affairs. Satellite TV has had an enormous impact on the Arab world, even if it is hard to quantify. But the general claim is flawed, and for a very simple reason: the problem with US policy is not that it has not been properly packaged or argued for in TV studies, but that it is in itself mistaken, and deeply offensive to most people in the Middle East. That is something that no amount of spinning, leaking, primetime interviews or public relations can solve.

Like any TV station, Al Jazeera faces the challenge of staying ahead. Its fundamental broadcasting challenge is that of keeping its edge in a relentless and increasingly internet-dominated media environment. As long as other stations in the region remain under tight censorship and transmit boring programmes, it should not find this too difficult. Al Jazeera Arabic also captures today's mood of anger in the Arab world following the Iraq debacle. The English-language station has a more difficult task: in seeking to put an alternative, combined 'North–South' view of international affairs, it risks falling into blandness: the kind of coverage of state conferences and development projects that was tried in the 1970s under the rubric of a 'new international information order'. Its current editorial inflexions suggest that its managers are seeking to give it a grittier, non-mid-Atlantic character. In this, they will be ably abetted by the blunders of the West and its allies in the Middle East itself. The matchbox may roar for some time to come.

4. YEMEN: MURDER IN ARABIA FELIX
13 July 2007

The killing of seven Spanish tourists in the Arabian state of Yemen on 2 July 2007 is a terrible and tragic event: for the victims and their families; for the people of Yemen, whose suffering and isolation it will only increase; and for all those who aspire to travel and explore beyond the confines of the enclosed hotels and beaches of the travel industry.

Yemen, with a population of 22 million, occupies the fertile south-west corner of the Arabian peninsula. It was known to the Romans as *Arabia Felix* ('Fortunate Arabia') to distinguish it from *Arabia Petrea* or *Infelix* ('Stony', i.e. desert, or 'Unfortunate Arabia'), and today this land of mountain vistas, spectacular roads, medieval cities and fierce national and religious traditions is among the poorest countries in Asia.

Yemenis regard themselves as *al 'arab al asliin* ('the original Arabs', a phrase they are fond of repeating), the most ancient of the Arab peoples. The tourists killed on 2 July died visiting an ancient sun temple at Marib, which Yemenis associate (without any historic evidence) with Queen Bilqis, the legendary Queen of Sheba who the Bible says visited Solomon in Jerusalem. Yemen is, indeed, one of the only four countries in the world – along with Egypt, Persia and China – that can legitimately claim three millennia of more or less continuous culture and statehood. Yemenis are proud of their ancient past, including the many languages (including Hebrew, ancient Himyaritic, Latin and Greek) that were once spoken there and which are visible on the inscriptions that lie in cheerful disorder in the museums. By the same token, Yemenis look down on the recently invented state of Saudi Arabia as a land of the uncivilised and uncultured.

Yemen has in some ways remained outside the flow of modern history and development. Yemenis' own variation on this theme is expressed in another favoured anecdote. Adam got bored in heaven and asked God to let him see the world once more; flying over London, Paris and Cairo he had to ask what the buildings he saw were called, but as he went down the Red Sea he turned to God and said: 'You don't need to tell me where this is, it is Yemen. It has not changed at all.'

In large parts of the country there is no state control; almost all men outside the cities and coastal regions carry arms; the main social unit is the tribe; educational and health standards, especially for women, are appalling; corruption is widespread and growing; and much of family income and time is devoted to the daily consumption of the mild, amphetamine-like narcotic, qat.

The reality of the economy is forever fixed in my mind by a conversation I had some years ago in the House of Commons. In a misguided gesture of promoting academic research, I introduced a French PhD student of mine, who knew Yemen and had good Arabic, to reputedly the richest man in Yemen, a hotel owner, trader and good friend of the president. A charming gentleman, he was keen to tell us that he had been minister of health in the first revolutionary government after the 1962 revolution, and was proud of his role in those years. (I had once acted as his translator at an official dinner with British government representatives in London.) On this occasion he was in town for a parliamentary reception for the leaders of the Yemeni community in Britain, which was born over a hundred years ago – the oldest Third World community in the country after the Chinese. My student explained in lively colloquial Yemeni dialect that she wanted to do a thesis on the Yemeni economy. The millionaire listened carefully and then said, with a sigh: 'Madam, I have to tell you: in Yemen there is no such thing as an "economy".'

Yet international history has not passed Yemen by. In a brutal but vivid inversion of the Trotskyist law of combined and uneven development, it is those few countries in Asia and Africa that escaped formal colonial rule, and were thus isolated for decades from economic and political development, which, in a violent spasm of accelerated change, are then the site of major, and sanguinary, upheavals, often marked by extremes of sectarianism and far-left authoritarianism: thus Ethiopia, Iran, Afghanistan and Nepal have all in recent years been the site of such belated and thereby more intense convulsions.

Yemen, which combines the non-colonial northern part with the former British colonial region beyond Aden, exhibits much of this pattern of revolution. In 1918 the North was the only independent Arab state, but it was cut off from the outside world by conservative imams until the 1962 revolution, when radical republicans inspired by Nasserist Egypt took power. An eight-year civil war followed, before the royalist counter-revolution was contained by the Yemeni and Egyptian republicans. It is conventional, not least in Egypt, to say that this was Egypt's Vietnam; that Nasser lost the war in Yemen: but this is not true. The republic that Gamal Abdel Nasser sent troops to protect survived, and even when the Egyptian troops left after the Israeli victory in June 1967 the royalists, aided at that time by British mercenaries, failed to capture the capital, Sana'a. In a dramatic seventy-day siege in the last weeks of 1967 a popular resistance movement, composed of an array of tribal and Marxist-Leninist militias vigorously and courageously backed by a continuous Soviet airlift of arms, pushed back the royalists, who were later (in 1970) forced to sign a compromise peace agreement with the republicans.

This siege had a curious witness. Many years later I met Vladimir Chubin, the main Soviet linkman with the African National Congress (ANC) in South Africa; a close comrade of Joe Slovo, Chris Hani and the rest of the ANC, and the South African Communist Party (SACP) leadership; and someone who was deeply involved both in the guerrilla war against apartheid and in the war in Angola. I asked him which of all the conflicts he had seen in southern Africa had left the deepest mark. His reply was 'none of them'. As a young Soviet special forces officer, he had flown into Sana'a at night and on a makeshift runway in the first military supply plane in December 1967. In all he had seen in Africa, he had never seen the equivalent of the fighting spirit and military skill displayed by the popular militias during the Sana'a siege.

The radicalism of the late 1960s was soon contained and crushed by the more conservative Yemeni army, and in 1982 the last elements of the socialist resistance movement in North Yemen negotiated a peace settlement with the government. Yemen was then ruled by President Ali Abdullah Saleh, a somewhat flamboyant and uncultivated artillery officer who had come to power in a coup in 1978 after the assassination (by hands never publicly identified) of his two predecessors. At the time few observers gave Ali Abdullah much chance of remaining in his position, but he held onto power with his own astute sense of politics and timely help from the Saudis, the CIA and, be it noted, the Soviet Union.

Today 'Abu Ahmad' as he is known, has been in power for twenty-nine years. (His son Ahmad is being groomed to succeed him; as part of this programme, he was sent for a time to the British military academy at Sandhurst.) Some political change has followed, but ultimately all major decisions, and much of the state revenue, are associated with the president. On one occasion, when a multi-party system or 'pluralism' was introduced into Yemen, I asked an official I knew why this had occurred. 'Why did we introduce pluralism? Because the president told us to do so!'

The smaller southern part of Yemen was, with its capital in Aden, a British colony from 1839 to independence in 1967. In the wake of the defeat of Egypt in the June 1967 war with Israel, and the withdrawal of Egyptian forces from the Yemeni civil war to the north, a radical Marxist-Leninist faction, the National Liberation Front (NLF), seized the reins. Two years later the People's Democratic Republic of Yemen (PDRY) was proclaimed, with the aspiration to form the core of a future united socialist Yemen. There followed the most thoroughgoing political experiment in modern Arab politics to date: in effect, the attempt to build an Arab Cuba.

At first the NLF leaders were attracted by Maoism, and in rhetorical denunciation of the 'petty-bourgeois' regimes of Egypt, Iraq, Libya and Algeria, they sought to export armed revolution to neighbouring Oman, to Yemen itself and to Saudi Arabia. If it were not to mix Arabian place names and ideological currents, it could be said that at that time Aden was the Mecca of Middle Eastern and what were then routinely known as Third World revolutionaries.

Researching my first book *Arabia without Sultans* (Penguin, 1974) in hotels and conferences in Aden in the early 1970s, I had occasion to meet a wide array of characters from across the world: revolutionaries from Eritrea and Ethiopia, Sudan and Somalia; volunteer doctors and teachers from Cuba; exiled MIR guerrillas from Chile; representatives of the far-left Palestinian groups; underground communists from Saudi Arabia and Bahrain; dogmatic Soviet political instructors and bibulous policemen from East Germany; French and West German Maoists; Lebanese Marxists purveying the ideas of Alexandre Kojève and Louis Althusser; and (on one memorable occasion) two feisty visitors from New York: *Monthly Review* editor Harry Magdoff and the American radical political scientist and inventor of the board game *Class Struggle* Bertell Ollman (who had at NYU taught the PDRY ambassador to the United Nations, the late Abdullah al-Ashtal, and who presented the Aden University library with a book by Wilhelm Reich).

One person not welcome in Aden at that time, and whose organisation was not permitted to open an office there for several years, was Yasser Arafat, leader of Fatah. Fatah was considered a bourgeois organisation by the PDRY, which gave priority to its Marxist Leninist conferences, the Popular Front and the Democratic Front, which had, like the PDRY itself, emerged from the radicalisation of the formerly pro-Egyptian Arab nationalist movement of the 1960s. What was not known at the time, and which later emerged in Germany, was that under the pretext of 'international solidarity' some of the radical Palestinians were bringing into Aden associates from West Germany and the Armenian diaspora who were involved in terrorist acts elsewhere.

In the first revolutionary years, foreign monopolies were nationalised (with disastrous economic consequences) and the 'popular alliance of workers, peasants, fishermen, Bedouin and nomads' was promoted. One party song, not content with conventional Leninist programmes on female emancipation, even had the refrain: 'We must arm the women!' But the NLF soon fell under Soviet influence and failed to overthrow the military-tribal republic in the North.

On two occasions after short wars between the two states, the leaders sought to promote unification of the Yemens. Yemeni unity, seen as a step on the road to a broader Arab unity, was a popular cause, even if in practice it amounted to little more than a pact of non-aggression. The PDRY leaders thought that, armed with the teachings of scientific socialism, they could outwit their Northern interlocutors, but it was not to be. On one occasion in 1972 the Southern president, Salem Robea Ali, said he would agree to unity with the North if the latter complied with two conditions: liquidation of the bureaucracy and of the bourgeoisie. To this the Northern president, Abd al-Rahman (Qadi) al-Iryani – a wise old man who had probably never heard of Karl Marx or Lenin – replied. 'I agree. But first you have to give me a bureaucracy and also give me a bourgeoisie. Once I have them, I can then discuss getting rid of them again.'

Socialism could not be built in half a Yemen. In the longer run the larger and more politically coherent North prevailed over the revolutionary South. In 1990, riven by factional differences and abandoned by the USSR, the South agreed to unity with the military regime of Ali Abdullah Saleh. Four years later, in May 1994, the president launched a pre-emptive civil war, dispersed his socialist enemies and took control of the whole country.

Little now remains of the socialist aspirations and sentiments of the first revolutionary years. All women in Aden are covered by black cloaks, and the only signals of those days are the Castro grocery store, some faded slogans and a caste of academics and officials who, by dint of their study in countries of the 'socialist camp', are fluent in Russian, Spanish, Hungarian and even Korean. The socialists retain some political liberty within the reunited Yemen, but they have little power and have not retained a hold on the younger generation.

The murder of the Spanish tourists (an eighth was declared brain-dead on 13 July 2007; two Yemeni men also died) has to be seen against this background – of a weak state, an often fractured and violent society, and the emergence in recent years of new armed opposition groups that seek, if not to overthrow, to discredit and weaken the government in Sana'a. There are at least three kinds of groups that may have been responsible for the killing of the tourists: tribal forces seeking to undermine the central government's authority in their area; al-Qa'ida operatives based in Yemen; and representatives of a radical Shi'a group that has been in violent conflict with the army for several years.

Al-Qa'ida certainly has support in Yemen: some of its local members, including the so-called 'Army of Abyan' based in a district of the former socialist South, allied with the president in crushing the Left during the 1994 civil war and in the assassination of socialist leaders that preceded and followed that conflict. As recently as 2001 the leader of the Yemeni Socialist Party (the successor to the NLF), Jarallah Omar, a former guerrilla leader who became one of the most respected politicians in the country (and whom I met several times in Sana'a), was assassinated while leaving a political meeting. In 2000, al-Qa'ida blew up and nearly sank the American warship USS *Cole* in Aden harbour, with the loss of seventeen lives. But al-Qa'ida has reason to be restrained in Yemen for the moment, since the country serves, in a covert way, as a rear base for the anti-American insurrection in Iraq.

The most likely culprits are the rebels formerly associated with the Shi'a rebel group linked with the tribal and religious leaders of the al-Huthi family. The al-Huthi, based in the Northern province of Sa'ada (relatively near the Marib site), rose up against the Sana'a government some years ago, reportedly calling for the establishment of an orthodox Shi'a state. The leader of this revolt, the clergyman Hussein al-Houthi, was killed in 2004. In a secret deal with the government, some of his followers agreed to go into exile in Qatar. But another faction refused to compromise and its members have continued to battle with government forces in the Sa'ada region. They have the greatest motive to carry out an operation of this kind, which was probably not focused specifically on tourists from Spain but on the broader credibility of the Sana'a government. Spain, Yemen and all who know and appreciate this extraordinary and beautiful country are the losers.

5. NAVIGATING MARE NOSTRUM:
THE BARCELONA PROCESS AFTER TEN YEARS
11 November 2005

Catalonia, the autonomous region in the north-east of Spain, is proud of commercial traditions and expertise that its people often trace to the early influence of Phoenician traders crossing from the other side of the Mediterranean Sea. Its capital, Barcelona, is about to host a conference marking ten years of a diplomatic initiative that seeks to cross cultural, political and human borders in not so different ways from those pioneers of 3,000 years ago.

The conference on 27–28 November 2005 takes place a decade after the launch of the Barcelona Process, designed in 1995 to foster dialogue between European Union member-states and countries on the southern and eastern shores of the Mediterranean – including the Arab states (among them the Palestinian National Authority, but not Libya), Israel, Cyprus and Turkey.

The key aim of this new 'Euro-Mediterranean Partnership' – as embodied in the wide-ranging Barcelona Declaration to which the participants in the first conference committed themselves – was to promote democratisation, security and economic growth in the countries to Europe's south and east. The challenge the partnership addressed was at least partly to demonstrate that the European Union could act in a united and effective manner around the sea – the Romans' Mare Nostrum ('Our Sea') – that nurtured the historic cultures that shaped modern Europe.

Today, there is considerable frustration in Spanish and European Union diplomatic circles at the apparently meagre results of this engagement, and uncertainty about what forward-looking proposals a review conference can elaborate. Yet an overall balance sheet of developments since 1995 reveals a mixed, even dynamic picture. The goals of the 1995 conference may not have been achieved, but four major positive developments are to the credit of the Barcelona Process.

First, Libya has become engaged. Three factors contributed: its decision to settle the Lockerbie affair by allowing two of its junior officials to go on trial before a Scottish court in the Netherlands, its subsequent renunciation of any nuclear programmes and the moderate turn in its foreign policy. True, Muammar al-Gaddafi's visit to Brussels in April

2004 was marked by a sharp difference of historical perspectives: from his tent outside European Union headquarters, Gaddafi rebuked Romano Prodi for the massacre of tens of thousands of Libyans by Italian colonial occupiers. But as United Nations sanctions have been lifted and even Washington is allowing some diplomatic and economic contact, Libya has again become part of the international community.

Second, there has been a marked change in the relationship between regional states and Islamist politics. In Egypt, an insurrection that was in full swing in 1995 has greatly receded, if not quite died. The mid-1990s alarm about the rise of Islamist forces in Turkey has given way to settled acceptance of the post-2002 government led by the reformist Islamic party, the AKP. The war in Algeria between the military regime and its various Islamist armed opponents – sparked by the regime's refusal to allow the Islamists to come to power through an electoral victory in 1991 – has ended. The regime's amnesty referendum on 29 September is part of its effort to contain discussion of its own forces' part in this brutal conflict, in which up to 150,000 people died.

Third, Lebanon has witnessed dramatic change in its relationship with Syria. The international revulsion following the assassination of former Prime Minister Rafiq Hariri in February 2005 forced Syria to withdraw the forces it had installed in Lebanon on the invitation of then President Suleiman Franjieh in 1976 – the first year of a civil war that was to last fifteen years and kill an estimated 150,000 people. The Syrians' departure has opened new uncertainties: both for a still riven Lebanon, and for a Syria whose regime under Bashar al-Assad is under pressure from all sides.

Fourth, the Balkans – an area central to Mediterranean and European security, though not formally included in the Barcelona Process – have returned to precarious stability after the devastating wars in ex-Yugoslavia from 1991 to 1995 and (in the case of Kosovo) 1998 to 1999. Even as the final constitutional status of Kosovo and Montenegro remains uncertain, it seems that 'Yugoslavia' has been reduced to its Serbian heartland, while the post-communist nationalist leader responsible a decade ago for Belgrade's rampaging military campaigns, Slobodan Milosevic, faces war crime and genocide charges in The Hague.

If these four areas of the Mediterranean show signs of progress, in three others there is a bleaker outlook. First, the Western Sahara question remains unresolved. Morocco continues to occupy the former Spanish colony – abandoned by its old colonists in 1975 – and to block calls by the United Nations for a meaningful referendum. A plan proposed by James Baker, UN envoy and former United States secretary of state, was rejected by Morocco, which is acutely sensitive to the inter-state dimension of its rivalry with Algeria on the issue as well as resistant to the claims of the native Sahrawis and their long-standing pro-independence Polisario movement.

Second, Cypus remains in effect divided into two states, as it has been since the right-wing Greek coup and the subsequent Turkish invasion of 1974. Here too, a UN peace plan was rejected – in this case by Greek Cypriots, swayed by nationalist and religious demagogues within their own community. The Turks in Northern Cyprus have made the most courageous moves in recent years, most noticeably in opening the border dividing the island, while the Greeks have held out against compromise and are now using the issue to complicate Turkey's accession negotiations with the European Union.

Third, the most prominent conflict bordering the Mediterranean – that between Israel and the Palestinians – remains paralysed. The first Barcelona conference in November 1995 coincided with the Tel Aviv assassination of Israeli Prime Minister Yitzhak Rabin. Perhaps, as many Israelis argue, the Oslo peace process was already in trouble by then, but Rabin's death marked the end of the dynamic in the process; the ten years since have seen if anything a degeneration in relations both between and within the two peoples involved. Its milestones are familiar: Binyamin Netanyahu's 1996 election victory, the collapse of Camp David and the outbreak of the second intifada in 2000, the building of the 'separation wall' and continued inter-ethnic violence.

An assessment of ten years of the Barcelona Process has also to take into account the broader patterns of international relations. Insofar as this European Union initiative was meant to displace the hegemony of the United States, it has clearly failed. Washington remains the key player in Palestine and in the Balkans, and indeed launched its own democratisation initiative on the Arab world in 2004 without any apparent reference to the existing Barcelona Process. Europeans themselves are as divided as ever in matters of security and foreign policy – as evident by the fissures over Iraq since 2003, inter-state competitiveness over the enlargement of the UN Security Council, the collapse of the constitution project after the French and Dutch referendums, and divisions over trade policy in the context of the Doha negotiations.

For all these difficulties, the Mediterranean region – whose richly overlapping worlds were anatomised by the great French historian Fernand Braudel – continues to pose a challenge that is collectively recognised by the states bordering on and associated with it. It has been the graveyard of many ambitions in the twentieth century: from Italian fascist dreams of a new Roman empire, through British and French imperial projects (Suez, Algérie française), to the radical social models embraced by newly independent countries (Yugoslavian and Algerian workers' self-management, Israeli agricultural communalism, Albanian communism under Enver Hoxha and Libyan 'anti-imperialism' under Gaddafi).

The fate of these earlier dreams is a warning to the admittedly more modest goals of today, but also a sign of the cycles of change within the Mediterranean region. If there has been only minimal progress towards democratisation in the Arab countries since 1995, the capacity for large-scale convulsion impelled by social division, population growth and technological revolution is clearly present. Meanwhile, there are some ominous developments in European lands – from corruption in Italy under Silvio Berlusconi to French anti-Turkish obsessions.

These cycles of change may even be said to include the geostrategic boundaries of the region itself. Iran, for the first time in 2,000 years, is beginning to play a military role in the eastern Mediterranean; while tens of thousands of migrants from sub-Saharan Africa are seeking to enter Europe at its first destination point, Spain. Many cities along its shoreline – Naples, Athens, Istanbul, Barcelona itself – are being transformed by immigration from Africa, Latin America and the former Soviet Union. There is not now, nor was there ever, one Mediterranean. Mare Nostrum, Our Sea, it may remain, but only to ask anew: who are we?

6.   IN AN UNHOLY PLACE: LETTER FROM JERUSALEM
   15 December 2006

Four months after the 'summer war' between Israel and Hizbullah, the longest the Jewish state has fought since that of 1948–9 and the only one in which it failed to emerge with a clear military advantage, there seems to be little optimism in this city. For sure, the cast of characters that make up Jerusalem remains as lively as ever: returning here after teaching the Arab–Israeli dispute in a seminar room thousands of miles away, you sometimes feel a bit overwhelmed, as if there is a PhD in every conversation.

An Israeli waitress insists to me that the old Sephardi–Ashkenazi division, which lasted into the 1960s, is for her generation no longer so important. Although her parents, with whom she now lives, are of Syrian origin, she and her generation feel a sense of common destiny with the Jews of European origin; a fact borne out by the school trip she made, as most young Israelis now do, to Auschwitz. 'I felt that they had killed my cousins,' was how she put it. She is studying law, goes every day to the gym and when I tell her I have lived in Yemen, recalls with a broad smile her time in a moshav (semi-collective farm) with her Yemeni boyfriend, where, as in Yemen, the men all chewed the narcotic qat, itself freely grown and commercially marketed in Israel. Her two years in the army, spent in Gaza, were the best of her life.

Meanwhile an Arab taxi-driver, whose family has lived in Jerusalem for generations, regales me with anecdotes about the arrogance of pro-Israeli visitors from the West, who usually get a shock finding their driver is an Arab. He begins by telling me he is not a Palestinian, but an 'Israeli Arab', from a part of Israel incorporated in 1967, distinct again from Arabs with Israeli citizenship, those dating back to 1948. This last group serve in the Israeli army, but his group do not have Israeli citizenship. But when I tell him that I met Arafat, once in Jordan in 1969 and again on his last visit to London in 1997, his eyes light up. When the PLO leader's body was brought back from Paris, he drove to Ramallah and stood with many thousands of people all night to see the helicopter return it to the Muqata, Arafat's half-destroyed headquarters.

The driver takes me to the Mount of Olives and the parapet overlooking the Old City from which so many TV interviews have been filmed, with Mount Zion and the Tomb of King Solomon rising to the left and the golden roof of the Haram al-Sharif shining on its esplanade below. An Israeli tourist guide is telling his visitors that it is untrue to claim that the area below them, now including a Jewish cemetery, was once inhabited by Arabs: when Mark Twain came to Jerusalem in 1863, he assures them, he reported that no Arabs lived outside the walls of the city. If the guide's charges are anything like the Evangelical Christians who inhabit my ersatz-oriental hotel – where, like the others it abuts, no newspapers, foreign or local, are for sale – he will not have too hard a time making his case. My fellow guests were obviously not interested in the Israel or Palestine in front of them: they had indeed come to see for themselves how the Jews had returned to 'their homeland' and were apparently satisfied, if a little confused, with what they had been shown.

On the Israeli side the mood is one of political recrimination and military reorganisation. In contrast to earlier decades of Israeli life, this is a time without strong leaders and personalities, military or civilian. In press and parliament, Israelis continue to dispute who got what wrong in the war itself, and to hold Prime Minister Olmert in low esteem: 'a lawyer, who was good at telling you how to avoid going to jail, but not a military leader' was how one friend put it to me. Numerous commissions of inquiry are looking into the technical side of the war, while military leaders are behaving like clan leaders, each with their own pliant journalists setting them in the best of lights. Netanyahu waits in the wings but he, too, lacks credibility.

One immediate consequence of the lack of victory in the summer has been a hardening of the government position. Before the summer war, Olmert, promoting a supposedly liberal version of Sharon's plan for partial withdrawals, talked of leaving parts of the West Bank on top of his predecessor's departure from Gaza. Now there is little talk of this, on the grounds that withdrawals, whether from Gaza in 2005 or Lebanon in 2000, only make Israel look weak in Arab eyes. In an ominous move, one that legitimates what had hitherto been regarded as generally unacceptable, or at least unspeakable, views, the Russian immigrant politician Avigdor Lieberman has been brought into the Olmert cabinet. Lieberman says that he wants to apply the tactics the Russians have used in Chechnya to the Palestinians, and forcibly remove Arabs from within Israel itself. Needless to say, he is all for bombing Tehran, a fact of some relevance since his ministerial position is that of long-term strategic planning.

All this Israeli argument and uncertainty masks, however, other realities that are of longer duration. The first, as an old friend from Haifa is quick to tell me, is that the war showed up Israeli weaknesses as never before: no missile defence system can protect every town in the north of the country. The showering of thousands of Katyusha and other rockets on Israeli towns and cities for a month left a deep scar. This was not because of the level of casualties, which were rather low, but because of the helplessness of government or populace to do anything about it. My friend told me that the shelters in which people had to spend hours were drab and ill-prepared (his family had one at the back of their flat but had long used it as a storage room and could not clear it out in time). The people under bombardment in the north felt that politicians in Jerusalem and the south had lost the ability to empathise with them. Driving less than an hour each day to work in Tel Aviv, bathed in normality, only accentuated his sense of two peoples.

The second and more serious reality is that most people now expect another war, if not in 2007 then in 2008. The phrase 'unfinished business' is on many lips, but what this involves is less clear. No doubt the Israelis can refit and protect their tanks and APCs and train their elite units in new kinds of counter-insurgency, but, as events in Lebanon show, they are not going to destroy Hizbullah as a political and military force. The main aim of the summer war, to force an international and Lebanese state intervention in the south of that country in order to control Hizbullah, has not been achieved. As the current political crisis in Beirut itself shows, this is all because of a long term problem that no one, not Syria, Israel nor before them France, has been able to fix, namely the weakness of the Lebanese state itself. Sooner or later, any attempt to 'finish the job' will bring a clash with Syria, maybe Iran. Israel's dilemma, like America's, is that if it presses Syria too hard it may undermine the Bashar al-Assad regime and bring the Muslim Brotherhood, the main opposition, to power. As for Iran, there is no excluding an Israeli air strike on Iranian nuclear facilities, if only temporarily to disrupt, rather than permanently prevent, development of that country's nuclear capability.

It must be assumed also, in the broader regional scale of things, that if Israel is drawing lessons from the war of last summer, others, particularly Iran and its allies, are doing so too. And here lies the third and most important outcome of the 'summer war': the strategic map of the Middle East, the one with which Israel, the Arab states, the Palestinians and the outside world have all lived since 1967, has now significantly, some would say fundamentally, altered. First, it is no longer just a matter of conflict between the Arabs and Israel, but of one between Israel and Iran, this latter power now developing a strategy designed to weaken the USA and its allies across the region from Iraq to Gaza. Secondly, the assumptions of that post-1967 epoch no longer hold: of territorial compromise, UN resolutions, the pursuit of mutual recognition, and international guarantees. In Iran, and in its allies Hizbullah and Hamas, Israel now has an enemy more resolute, organised and uncompromising than any it has faced since it was established.

Israeli public discussion is very concerned about Iran, almost to the exclusion of any recognition of the much nearer and more explosive situation developing in Iraq. This will, if nothing else, directly affect Israel's neighbours in Syria and Jordan and greatly enhance the regional power of Iran. But those in the Israeli armed forces who have come into contact with Hamas prisoners and militants see that they are up against a much more confident foe, and a look at the new strategic map shows that Israel has no easy options. This has implications for the internal dynamics of Israel itself. The agreements of the early 1990s gave hope to the more secular part of Israeli society, the coastal liberals and those in business who have made Israel a successful economic power. Now those hopes have gone and few seem willing to trust the Palestinians again. 'I guess we will have to wait, and go on fighting, for another thirty to forty years before the Middle East sorts itself out,' as one Israeli academic, who came within an inch of losing his life in Lebanon over the summer, put it to me. I could not bring myself to tell him I thought he was being a bit optimistic. Meanwhile, a significant section of Israelis, perhaps 20 per cent or more, have left the country, never quite saying they have emigrated, but somehow not coming back. These *yordim* ('descenders'), as Zionist terminology puts it, are, along with the much higher Palestinian birth rate, the two weakest points of Israeli society.

Opinion on the Arab side has if anything hardened even more. The electoral victory of Hamas and Hizbullah's showing in the summer war, 'the divine victory' as it is called by the latter, have given militant Palestinians a new sense of confidence, even as they have plunged others into despair. The voices of those who, in post-1967 mode, favoured recognition of an Israeli state and some sort of territorial compromise are less now: Hamas insists that all of pre-1948 Palestine is a *waqf* (Islamic trust). Arafat tried to finesse the question of the refugees' right of return in Oslo, but by the late 1990s this had become a major issue again.

This new mood was vividly put to me by an old acquaintance, formerly an intellectual representative of Fatah views, who came to see me one day. He was accompanied by a confident-looking younger man with a beard, who was introduced as a specialist on Islamic political thinking, in particular an expert on *hudna*, the classical Arabic and Qur'anic word for 'truce', much used by Hamas to suggest compromise with Israel. 'Why should Hamas cooperate with the remnants of the corrupt PLO?' my visitor asked me in reference to speculation about a coalition between Hamas and the old nationalist guard. President Abbas was just a puppet of the Americans and the Israelis. As for Hamas, it was, despite Israeli pressure, going from strength to strength. 'They have the people, they have the votes, they have the guns, they have the money,' he insisted, pointing out that Iran, some Arab states and the Organisation of the Islamic Conference had all promised to help the Hamas government financially. As if to confirm this perspective, Prime Minister Ismail Haniyeh left Gaza for a one-month tour of the Middle East, including Tehran, an index of how serious his fundraising tour would be and of how unhurried Hamas feels about finding a political solution within the Palestinian ranks. His bearded companion seemed happy to agree with all of this.

All of which suggests an unwelcome conclusion: that the room for external diplomatic mediation and impulsion is very small. Beyond ceasefires and some alleviation of economic pressure on the Palestinians, neither side seems at the moment – and probably for a long time to come – to be interested in a serious compromise. And so it would appear that, if you want good cheer and good news this Christmas, the Holy Land is not the place to start; not this year, not last year, and perhaps not for some years to come either.

7.   LEBANON, ISRAEL AND THE 'GREATER WEST ASIAN CRISIS'
18 August 2006

All wars are different, but the war between Israel and Hizbullah of 12 July–14 August 2006 proves indeed that some are more different than others. It may be that this war has resemblances to other conflicts in the recent history of the region, but it is in important respects both a departure from and more than its predecessors: it is more than an Arab–Israeli war of the kind seen on five previous occasions since 1948; it is more than another chapter in the Lebanese civil war, which began in 1975–6 and lasted until 1990; it is more than (even if linked to) the wars that have ensued from the Iranian revolution of 1979 in different parts of the region.

A first definition of its distinctiveness is that it is a war for supremacy and survival in the region as a whole: a newly emerged political and strategic space that encompasses India, Pakistan and Afghanistan as well as Iran, the Arab world and Israel. As with the United States-led regime changes in Afghanistan (2001) and Iraq (2003), so with the Lebanon war of 2006 – the causes also belong to, and the effects will be felt throughout, this region: from Beirut and Tel Aviv to Baghdad, Kabul and Mumbai.

This is the primary sense in which the war of summer 2006 is different: for this superficially quite localised war (in terms of its field of operations) is but one dimension of a complex of interlinked problems that connect Haifa to Herat and all points between. It is now possible to talk, without oversimplifying distortion, of a single, many-layered crisis that since the mid-1990s has both arisen from and given definition to a new world region: not just a 'Middle East' but a 'Greater West Asia'.

Each individual conflict in this region – Palestine, Iraq, Afghanistan, Iran and now Lebanon – may be interrelated, but it is the 'how' and the 'how far' that must be defined. It is a familiar part of political and intellectual discourse in the Middle East to seek to put events in individual countries or sub-regions into a broader regional or global context. This process can often be accompanied by a conspiratorial or secret agenda gloss (the Arab–Israeli conflicts, the Iran–Iraq war, revolution in Yemen, civil war in Sudan and Algeria, and sundry assassinations or oil price movements are just a few examples); it can also be impelled by reference to external agencies or institutional powers (the Cold War matrix, the global 'Zionist' movement, the machinations of old imperial powers such as Britain and France, and in recent years 'globalisation' and United States 'democracy promotion' are some of these).

The challenge now is to move beyond such regressive or disempowering approaches and articulate the connections at the level of the current dynamic reality of states, inter-state relations, non-state actors, and the array of political and social forces across Greater West Asia. Today, the assimilation of individual countries and events to a broader regional pattern is an emergent fact: events in Lebanon and Israel, Iraq and Afghanistan, Turkey and Libya are becoming comprehensible only in a broader regional and even global context (the latter includes both US policy and the shifting interests and power of Russia, India and China).

The linkage so frequently invoked has become a transparent, kaleidoscopic reality: a reality of states that look at their neighbours' nuclear and other programmes and react accordingly; a reality for the opposition and military groups who operate in different states of the region; a reality of public opinion, in an age of satellite TV; a reality of the outside world – particularly the United States and Europe, which are trying with almost no success to contain and manage the tensions in the region.

Today, this new reality is evident in a host of ways, including the new pan-Islamic consciousness that ties Arab with non-Arab causes and is evident among Muslims living in Europe as much as in the Arab world. It is also reflected by default in the selective language of US military and political strategy. George W. Bush has proposed a 'Greater Middle East Initiative' (one of the most pathetic projects of all time) but his conception of this area is revealing: it includes Afghanistan (as for the purposes of his 'War on Terror' it must), yet excludes the country more responsible than any other for spreading terrorism, Islamic fundamentalism, nuclear proliferation and corruption across the region, namely Pakistan.

The wider significance of the war between Israel and Hizbullah is part of this new reality. It is natural that many in the immediate region have viewed it as the sixth in the series of Arab–Israeli wars. There are indeed points of comparison: in the insecurity it has bred in Israeli cities, and in the connection between external intervention and more local resistance (1948–9); in the large-scale Israeli intervention in Lebanon (1982); in the involvement of the United Nations Security Council (1956, 1967 and 1973). But the deeper reality is different. It is not just the sixth Arab–Israeli war, a revival of the Lebanese civil war, an internationalisation of the second Palestinian intifada, or the latest outbreak of the 'War on Terror'; it is more than all of these – part of another broader and more protracted conflict with multiple centres and involving a rapidly shifting coalition of regional states with political and social movements. The key point of origin is 1979. With the benefit of a generation's hindsight, it is now clear that this conflict has been in train since the late 1970s – in particular, since the two strategic detonations of the last year of that decade, the Iranian revolution of February and the Soviet intervention in Afghanistan in December.

The shape of Greater West Asia and the establishment of linkages that were to produce such lethal effects were already evident in the era of those convulsions. The Israeli intervention in Lebanon in 1978 made its contribution, but it was the Iranian revolution and the sustained state support provided to the Lebanese Shi'a that helped both incubate Hizbullah and transform the Israeli–Lebanese confrontation of 1978 into protracted conflict. It was also in the Lebanese war of the 1980s that Iran and its Lebanese allies first engaged with Israel and the United States, with considerable military and political consequences. Meanwhile, to the east of the region, the young Islamic Republic state was being tested and hardened in the eight-year war with Iraq; and the US and its conservative Arab allies, with a little help from Israel, were encouraging the guerrillas and killers of the Afghan *mujahideen* from whom Osama bin Laden and his associates were to emerge.

These origins have grown diverse fruits. In light of the Lebanon war, two are particularly relevant. First, the major protagonist on the Arab side is not a state but an armed political group – and Hizbullah will, as a result, prove much more difficult to negotiate and reach agreement with than was the case in earlier wars. Second, insofar as states such as Syria and Iran are involved on the side of Hizbullah, they will pursue their involvement in a way that is quite different to Arab states in earlier conflicts. They are now not primarily interested in armistices, frontier delimitation or peace negotiations, but in using the Lebanon conflict to bargain with the US on other issues and to enhance their nationalist and radical legitimacy at home and regionally.

This Greater West Asian Crisis is more complex, multilayered and long-lasting than any of the individual crises, revolutions or wars that characterised the Middle East. The current West Asian wars involve a triangular conflict: Iran and its radical allies (Syria, Iraqi Shi'a parties, Hizbullah, Hamas); the forces of radical Sunni insurgency (in Iraq and in the al-Qa'ida network); and the US and its regional allies. In the case of Iran, there is no direct or immediate causal relation between Tehran's major role inside Iraq, its nuclear-enrichment plans and its support for Hizbullah – but all do form part of a broader Iranian drive for regional influence and for confrontation with the US and its major allies (Egypt, Saudi Arabia and Israel). In Lebanon, the Iran–US conflict is predominant; in Afghanistan or Saudi Arabia it is the Sunni–US dimension; in Iraq the conflict embraces all three points of the triangle, with the US pitted against both Shi'a and Sunni, even as members of these two groups kill and terrorise one other.

It is in this multidimensional context, rather than in the memory of earlier bilateral Arab–Israeli wars, that the current Israeli–Hizbullah conflict must be seen. In the perspective of a longer history it can be said to resemble the European war that began in 1914: another regional conflict long-planned even if suddenly, almost casually, detonated; one which once started, drew all the major states of the area into its wake, with dire consequences for all and catastrophic for many. It is a sobering comparison, but nothing in the current pattern of events across Greater West Asia makes it extreme. There may be possibilities for progress in the present moment, but currently it is the dangers that are far easier to see.

8. MAXIME RODINSON:
IN PRAISE OF A 'MARGINAL MAN'
8 September 2005

The role of French writers and intellectuals in shaping modern international debate on the Middle East and the Arab and Islamic worlds has been enormous. The concern of figures like Albert Camus, Pierre Bourdieu, Hélène Carrère d'Encausse, Olivier Roy and Michel Foucault has stretched from Algeria to Iran, and from political and ideological 'grand narratives' (colonialism, nationalism, revolution and Islam) to relationships of power and subjection (violence, torture and women).

Algeria, France's major Arab colony from 1830 to 1962, generated some of the sharpest commentaries and controversies among French writers; indeed the first three writers mentioned above (as well as Jacques Derrida) grew up there in the colonial period and were profoundly shaped by its conflicts. It was revelations of torture by French troops in counter-insurgency during the 1954–62 war that brought out the best of the French left – and the worst, as in Jean-Paul Sartre's dramatic and ill-judged support of the incitements to murder in Frantz Fanon's *The Wretched of the Earth*. (Sartre's characteristic opportunism and extreme callousness here significantly banalise the work of Fanon himself, whom David Macey's excellent biography reveals to be a much more subtle and important thinker than Sartre's endorsement indicates.)

Iran in revolution was another field of French argument, exemplified in Michel Foucault's indulgent reports of 1978–9. Foucault knew nothing about Iran and so made a fool of himself – whereas he had showed great courage and good judgement in his defence of human rights violations in Tunisia, where he had worked as a visiting academic. While the postmodern philosopher did get Iran wrong, the feminist Kate Millett got it absolutely right: the combination of solidarity and critique in her book *Going to Iran* (Coward McCann, 1979) was exemplary, and denounced as a result by Eastern Islamists and Western 'anti-imperialists' alike.

French discourse continues to produce some of the liveliest work of scholarship on the modern Middle East, backed by institutions that (so much in contrast to Britain and the United States) make it possible to study the languages and politics of the region and engage in public debate. The depth of understanding of journalist–diplomat Eric Rouleau and social historian André Raymond, and the research of the two most influential European commentators on political Islam, Olivier Roy and Gilles Kepel, make France's intellectual life – in contrast to its stagnant politics – still one of the liveliest in Europe.

The greatest of all French writers on the Middle East (and arguably the greatest *tout court*) is, however, less renowned today than he deserves to be. Maxime Rodinson (1915–2004) was certainly the formative influence on my own work. Rodinson's life-story fused scholarship and political commitment. He was born in Paris to a radical Jewish working class family, and worked his way to the Sorbonne where he studied Semitic languages, ethnography and sociology before teaching for seven years in a Muslim school in Lebanon. He returned to Paris to work in the Bibliothèque Nationale (in charge of oriental printed books) and later in the Sorbonne as Professor of Middle Eastern Ethnology and Old South Arabian Languages.

Throughout, his political engagement was consistent and profound. He spent two decades (1937–58) in the French Communist Party (PCF), but remained devoted to independence of mind and accuracy in research, traits that flowered in the decades he spent as a Marxist writer after he broke with the party. Alongside many articles in journals and encyclopaedias, he wrote several seminal books: among them *Mohammed* (Pantheon Books, 1961), *Islam and Capitalism* (Saqi Books, 2007) and *Marxism and the Muslim World* (Seuil, 1972).

I first met Rodinson in London in 1968 when he came over to discuss the translation of *Islam and Capitalism*, a learned and engaged rebuttal of the cultural reductionism of Max Weber and those other writers who tried to explain the Middle East by reference to some unchanging entity called 'Islam' (he was awarded the Isaac Deutscher Memorial Prize for this book in 1974). Against the stereotype of Islamic hostility to modern capitalism, Rodinson – using textual criticism, economic history and common sense – demonstrated that Muslims had never had any trouble in making money.

Rodinson was in a somewhat shaky state on that occasion: he had cut his head badly falling down the steps of 7 Carlisle Street, a dilapidated building in the Soho district whose old lino staircases led to the offices of the leading journal of the intellectual Left, *New Left Review*. His head swathed in bandages, Rodinson recalled the working-class left-wing Jewish milieu of his Paris childhood – an experience recounted in his autobiography, *Souvenirs d'un marginal* (Fayard, 2005). Maxime's father Moise came from Vitebsk, the same town as the painter Marc Chagall, and had played chess with Trotsky; a close family friend had played an important role, later much regretted, in persuading Nikolai Bukharin to return to Russia, where he was tried and shot by Stalin. Rodinson recalled going on a demonstration in 1927 to protest the execution in the United States of the Italian anarchists Nicola Sacco and Bartolomeo Vanzetti. He never lost the somewhat uneasy 'bad conscience of the ex-communist', and referred to the way he had both joined and left the PCF 'in the worst year' (during the Stalinist purges and after the Hungarian uprising respectively). But his years in the communist movement, and the relentlessly curious and measured Marxism he acquired, provided a perspective on the Middle East denied to many other observers.

At the same time, his opposition to Stalinism and to intellectual labelling made him especially sensitive to the dangers of unbalanced Western academic criticism. This was just one reason for his rather limited respect for Edward Said and his book *Orientalism* (Pantheon Books, 1978). Rodinson would not himself say what any comparison of the two works would demonstrate: that Rodinson's *Europe and the Mystique of Islam* (F. Maspero, 1980) is incomparably superior in its learning, regional depth and theoretical sophistication to Said's overvalued jeremiad. (Rodinson had no problem in being described as an 'orientalist' and remained a lifelong friend of Bernard Lewis, who – in Maxime's telling – had himself been a communist in his working-class Jewish East London youth.)

Maxime Rodinson wrote a number of recondite works – among them *Magic, Medicine and Possession in Ethiopia* (Walter de Gruyter, 1968) and a contribution to *Medieval Arab Cookery* (Prospect Books, 1998) – but his analytical reputation rests on his best-known works, *Islam and Capitalism* and *Mohammed*. The latter was for years a standard book in Arab countries but is now banned, following Islamic pressure, in Egypt and other Arab states.

His work on the Arab–Israeli question after the 1967 war is also seminal. The Six-Day War produced upheaval among the European and American Left as well as across the Middle East. Before 1967 leftist and socialist opinion had been solidly favourable to Israel, a reflection of two things: support for the socialist elements in the original Zionist project (then still evident in Israeli society), and the legacy of the Second World War and the genocide of the Jews (particularly potent in France). It was in this context that two Marxist writers of Jewish origin, whose relatives (in Rodinson's case, both his parents) died in the gas chambers, presented a fresh, independent and resilient analysis of the Middle East's central conflict – one which serves as a benchmark against which to judge later commentary on the Left, much of it partisan, short-sighted and lacking in comparative historical or internationalist perspective.

Rodinson's short, incisive *Israel and the Arabs* (Pelican Books, 1969) and Isaac Deutscher's famous interview with *New Left Review* (given in summer 1967, a few weeks before his death in Rome) proposed their solution to the question of Israel and the Palestinians. Its essence was an exemplary internationalism that recognised the rights of the two national groups, denounced the chauvinism and militarism of both sides, and (most important) rebutted in sharp, secular terms the religious rhetoric emanating from all quarters.

Rodinson and Deutscher strongly criticised both the political culture and the authoritarian politics of the Arab world (something today's solidarity movements seem unable to do) and the rabbinical, militaristic culture of Israel. Their committed secular stance is far removed from the totemic icons of 'identity', 'community', 'tradition' and 'feeling' that came to flourish in discussion of the region. It

remains of utmost relevance. Both writers were abused for this independent position; sometimes openly, sometimes by having parts of
their argument taken out of context and used for partisan purposes.
They were accused by supporters of Israel of being 'self-hating Jews' (a
nonsensical term that still enjoys excessive currency) and by Arabs of
being apologists for Zionism (because of their support for the existence of Israel).

In 1971 I interviewed Ghassan Kanafani, a leader of the Popular
Front for the Liberation of Palestine (PFLP), on the group's involvement in the airplane hijackings that precipitated the 'Black September'
conflict in Jordan in 1970. (Kanafani, one of Palestine's finest fiction
writers, although an unpersuasive politician, was assassinated in July
1972 by an Israeli car-bomb in Beirut.) When I proposed a two-state
solution to the Palestine question (as I continue to do), he was indig-
nant: 'But that is the Maxime Rodinson solution!' No more, it seemed,
needed to be said.

The tone and content of debate on the Palestine question have,
if anything, deteriorated since the early 1970s; nearly four decades
on, the simplistic and partisan positions of the 1960s have returned
to dominance. The position is even worse in that intransigence is reinforced with religious and communalist justification. European and
American supporters of Israel have switched terms, so that Palestinians
once denounced as 'Nazi' are now stigmatised as 'terrorist'; while the
Arab and now pan-Muslim side employs retrograde images of Israel
and Jews. Meanwhile, internationalist solidarity for Palestinians seems
weightless and void of political judgement – from the identification of
Zionism with racism (as if Arab nationalism itself is free of this) to the
short-sighted rejection of the 1993 Oslo Accords, the best chance the
Palestinians are ever likely to have to secure their own state.

The current debate on Palestine has travelled far from the calm, critical, genuinely internationalist observations of Maxime Rodinson and
Isaac Deutscher. Yet this too is a vista that they would have recognised
more than most. Deutscher's mordant Yiddish observation on the
Israeli victory of 1967, 'Man kann sich totsiegen' ('One can win oneself to
death') may still turn out, tragically, to be vindicated.

At the end of my own book *The Middle East in International
Relations* (Cambridge University Press, 2005), I cite Maxime
Rodinson's unceasing belief in universal values, in the need for

intellectual aspiration beyond what one is actually capable of, and for an enduring, unyielding scepticism towards the values and myths of one's own community. Amid a world scarred by state and terrorist violence and debased public debate (not least on the Palestine question) we need the wisdom and independence of Maxime Rodinson and Isaac Deutscher more than ever.

Four

Iran: Revolution in a 'Great Nation'

I. AHMADINEJAD AS PRESIDENT:
IRAN'S REVOLUTIONARY SPASM
30 June 2005

It is surprising that few inside or outside Iran predicted the victory of a populist and nationalist politician who acquired a national reputation only two months ago. Yet for all the charges of improper electoral practices (some of which may well be true), the scale of Ahmadinejad's victory speaks to an underlying mood of a significant part of the Iranian people. As much as the equally clear, nationalist and conservative voice of millions of American people in November 2004, it is a message the outside world should not ignore.

The result is dramatic in that it emphasises that Iran remains a country of powerful nationalist and popular forces, where the revolution of 1978–9 is far from forgotten. It also reveals that in a crucial respect this revolution is like many other upheavals in moving after twenty years not into a reform phase but a twenty-year spasm – a second reassertion of militancy and egalitarianism that rejects domestic elites and external pressure alike (as in Russia in the purge era of the late 1930s, China under the Cultural Revolution of the late 1960s and Cuba in the rectification campaign of the 1980s). It is dangerous on two counts: opponents of the Islamic regime may in their despair resort to violence; and Iran's enemies in both the Middle East and the West may be inspired to renew confrontation. These tendencies may develop even as the Tehran leadership itself risks falling prey to the illusions that have beset Iran's rulers (and many revolutionary regimes) across the past century.

The key to understanding Mahmoud Ahmadinejad's victory is popular resentment at the Islamist elite – the post-revolutionary ruling group of around 5,000 men, cleric and lay alike, a kind of Islamic nomenklatura. Over the last twenty-six years this elite has gradually consolidated its control of the state and exploitation of the economy. Any previous righteous revolutionary leader (Robespierre in 1790s France, Trotsky in his denunciation of the Soviet bureaucracy, Mao Zedong and Fidel Castro in their anti-bureaucratic mass mobilisations) would understand what happened. I encountered its reality some years ago when I visited the tomb of Imam Khomeini, an expansive conglomeration of mosques, apartments and restaurants in working-class south Tehran. (My secular friends were aghast that on my first day in the country in twenty-one years, I had chosen to go there. They assured me that the large crowds visiting the shrine were not Iranians but 'Afghans and Uzbeks' whom the mullahs had bribed to come with offers of free food and transport.)

The shrine administrator welcomed me and took me by the hand to enter the building where the tombs of Khomeini and his son Ahmad were located, in accordance with Shi'a tradition, inside a large rectangular cage. People were milling around, praying, sleeping, listening to tales of the seventh-century martyrdom of Imam Ali and his son Hussein. I got into conversation with a man in his late twenties, a person similar in background to the newly-elected president. He had spent several years in the army, and was now a driver in a ministry. I asked him what he thought about Khomeini and his reply echoed the views of many others: 'The imam was *sade* (pure – a word also used of a Turkish coffee drunk without sugar),' he said. 'He was straight. He did not lie.' And then: 'He was not like the others.'

The 'others' were not the Shah and his associates, ousted and exiled in 1979, but the entrepreneurs and wheeler-dealers, the privileged class of the Islamic Republic, symbolised by former president Hashemi Rafsanjani, whom Ahmadinejad defeated in the second round of the 2005 election. Rafsanjani's profile – a businessman with many commercial interests in Iran and lucrative connections in Europe, who as president (1989–97) had revealed little ability to address the economic or strategic problems of the country – was enough to discredit him in the eyes of regular Iranian citizens like the driver at Imam Khomeini's shrine. But in addition there was between him and the revolution's leader a vast moral difference. In domestic Iranian terms, the outcome in 2005 marks a victory for Ayatollah Khomeini's 1989 successor as *rahbar* (spiritual leader), Ayatollah Ali Khamenei. Ahmadinejad has lived his whole career under Khamenei's patronage, and is loyal to the alternative (non-elected) centre of political power that he embodies.

The conservative victory signals two things. First, there are very real policy differences within the Islamic leadership. Second, Ahmadinejad's triumph highlights a vital underlying factor in the formation of Iran's revolutionary regime: that the state, its ideology and its mentality were forged not in the years of Islamist struggle against the Shah (1963–78), nor during the course of the revolution itself (1978–9), but in the much more brutal and costly war with Iraq (1980–8).

This was the second longest inter-state war of the twentieth century, one in which as many as 750,000 Iranian soldiers died. It is the institutions created during that war – the *pasdaran* (Revolutionary Guards), the *basiji* (mobilisation militias) and the intelligence services – that are at the core of the Islamic Republic, not the clergy, the revolution's political leaders or the regular army. It is significant that most of the eight to ten key people around Khamenei owe their prominence to this conflict.

There is an important historical context that helps to explain the depth of Iranian national sentiment. Iran was invaded by Britain and Russia without provocation in both world wars; its ruler between the 1950s and the late 1970s was installed then sustained by the United States; and the invasion it endured by Saddam Hussein in Iraq in September 1980 was followed by Western refusal to allow the United Nations Security Council to condemn Iraq and order it to return to the pre-conflict frontiers. All Iranian political leaders can in principle draw on this historical background, but a figure like Mahmoud Ahmadinejad, who lived the experience of the devastating 1980s war, is especially well-placed to do so.

For reformers in Iran associated with Mohammad Khatami and with the student, women's and other civilian movements of recent years, Ahmadinejad's accession to power is a frightening moment. It also marks the third time in modern Iranian history – after the Constitutional Revolution of 1905–9 and the Islamic Revolution of 1978–9 itself – when progressive reformers' immense struggles against repressive regimes have been overwhelmed by another (popular, nationalist and authoritarian) movement. This, then, is a moment of truth for Iranian reformers about their own country. The reform movement indeed reflected important changes inside Iran; in the end, as has happened elsewhere, its programme of gradual secularisation, liberalisation and opening to the outside world will prevail when the revolution has exhausted itself.

But the movement itself was flawed: too divided to establish its own political authority, too naive about the tenacity of the authoritarian elite around Khamenei, and too inflexible to circumvent the ban on political parties in Iran by creating and sustaining alternative forms of mobilisation. Another impediment was the international context: it did not help Iranian reformers that George W. Bush denounced Iran in January 2002 as part of an 'axis of evil', four months after Iran had offered sympathy and support against al-Qa'ida over 9/11, and is now flirting with the most retrograde elements of the Iranian opposition in exile. While this handicapped the reformers, it only confirmed the conservative forces in their confrontational mentality.

In a broader perspective, the election outcome shows how much Iran – far from being an anomaly in modern politics – reflects general trends in the contemporary world. The nationalist response to globalisation among many Iranians has something in common with the reaction of many Europeans to the European Union constitution or Americans in face of economic and social dislocations. The populist anger at the misuse of oil revenues by Shah and mullahs alike – a recurrent theme for Ahmadinejad – is familiar to radical politicians like Evo Morales in Bolivia and Hugo Chávez in Venezuela; as Terry Lynn Karl notes in her excellent comparative study *The Paradox of Plenty: Oil Booms and Petro-States* (University of California Press, 1997), many developing states have experienced the political misuse of energy revenues.

Mahmoud Ahmadinejad, as much as George W. Bush, owes his electoral victory to popular mood and to the enduring strength within his society of the institutions born of earlier international conflicts. This mood and these institutions will define and constrain the way he addresses the fundamental problems he faces, from the economics of everyday life to Iran's nuclear programme.

Iran's new president will operate in a context where considerations of national prestige, regional influence and bargaining power are unavoidable. In this, as in its whole modern history of nationalism and revolution, Iran reflects the global context in which it finds itself. A country whose first revolution exactly a century ago surprised the world as much as did the contemporaneous one in Russia has once again staked its claim to be a focus of international attention. We can only hope that its new leaders, and its old foes, will check their illusions against reality.

2. MISCALCULATIONS IN TEHRAN
1 March 2007

A few years ago, during a visit to Tehran to give some lectures at the foreign ministry research and training institute, I was taken to lunch by a senior Iranian diplomat to a once fashionable Italian restaurant in the northern middle-class suburb of Tajrish. Educated as a scientist in the United States before the 1979 revolution, he had been an important figure in the post-revolutionary regime. I had met him at various conferences on European–Iranian relations and we had struck up something of a rapport. On this occasion, after the usual semi-official tour, we began talking about the early history of the Iranian revolution and of its foreign policy.

'We made three big mistakes,' he said: first, in holding the American diplomats hostage for a year and a half and thereby deeply antagonising the US; second, by not accepting the very favourable peace which Saddam Hussein offered in the summer of 1982 when Iran had the upper hand in the war, already two years old; and third – to me the most surprising of his points – in not supporting the communist regime that came to power in Afghanistan in 1978 and instead backing the pro-American guerrillas that (with eventual success) opposed them.

The reflections of this diplomat are of considerable relevance to the situation in which Iran finds itself today. For sure, the pressure being put on Iran by the US is arrogant and in many ways illegal. For Washington to protest about Iranian interference in Iraq when it is the US which invaded the country in 2003 and when it is Iranian allies (if not clients) who staff much of the government and armed forces of Iraq is also ridiculous. So too is the attempt to blame Iran for the spread of Sunni terrorism, including al-Qaʻida activities, in the region. No country has a greater interest in the stability of Iraq than Iran, a point that Washington has stupidly failed to note these four years past.

Yet there is another side to the US–Iranian polarisation that could prove dangerous not only to Washington but also to the Islamic Republic and which arises from the miscalculations of the Iranian leadership itself. Iran's President Ahmadinejad has made himself popular in much of the Arab world, and among Muslims more widely, for his outspoken denunciations of the US. He has also heartened many by his calls for the destruction of Israel (something he did indeed call for, despite claims by some inside and outside Iran that he was mistranslated: the words *mahv bayad bashad* [must be wiped out] leave no room for doubt).

Yet Mahmoud Ahmadinejad has also thrown caution, and a due evaluation of the enmity and strength of his enemies, to the wind. (Ayatollah Khomeini once rebuked Ali Akbar Velayati for following him in a violent denunciation of Saudi Arabia, reminding the long-standing foreign minister that it was his job to maintain relations with other states.) At the same time the president has indulged in a set of ill-conceived economic policies at home, squandering oil revenue to boost consumption, launching retrograde educational and cultural campaigns against secularism, while failing to meet the campaign promises to the poor that secured his surprise election in 2005. The failure of his candidates to prevail in the December 2006 elections to the Expediency Council, an important constitutional watchdog, and a growth of criticism even from conservatives and other clerics augurs ill for his future.

No one can tell where the current confrontation between Tehran and Washington will lead. Perhaps, as a result of impatience, miscalculation or innate risk-taking, Iran and the US will be at war in the near future. Or it may prove to be the case that both are playing for time: the Iranians want to spin out negotiations with the West over the nuclear issue until the US position in Iraq is even weaker; the US may want to stay its hand in the hope that domestic economic and social problems will further weaken the regime and allow them to precipitate political upheaval. Everything is possible.

In this context it is worth looking more closely at the way in which Iran formulates its foreign policy, and the roots of its high-risk policy. Much is made of the fact that Iran is an ancient imperial power. It may also be of some satisfaction to Iranian leaders that with their influence in Lebanon and Palestine, Iran now has a military emplacement on the shores of the Mediterranean for the first time since the Achaemenid empire (c. 550–350 BCE). Moreover, Iran's aspiration to nuclear capability, in whatever form, is as much due to the aspiration to be a major power as to military factors, just as is the retention of what are in practice useless and expensive weapons by Britain and France.

Certainly, Iranian official and popular attitudes towards nearly all neighbours (with the interesting exception of the Armenians) are replete with prejudice and a sense of superiority. 'You colonialists left your goat's droppings around the region, but sooner or later we will sweep them away,' one interlocutor in Tehran said to me. When I asked what these goat's droppings were, he replied: 'Pakistan, Iraq and Israel.'

It is in part this self-perception which explains one of the most constant features of Iranian foreign policy over the past century, one to which my diplomat companion was drawing attention during our lunch in Tehran: namely, the recurrent tendency of Iranian leaders to overplay their hand. Even a brief list is striking:

In the Second World War, Reza Shah, the first of the two Pahlavi monarchs, thought he could balance British and Russian pressure by maintaining relations with Germany, but in the end, as soon as Russia entered the war in 1941, Iran was invaded and Reza Shah sent off to exile in Mauritius.

In the early 1950s, the nationalist Prime Minister Mohammad Mossadeq thought he could nationalise Iranian oil (hitherto a monopoly of the Anglo-Iranian Oil Company, today's BP) on his own terms and avoid a compromise with Western governments: in the end, he was overthrown in the CIA and MI6 coup of August 1953.

During the Iran–Iraq war of the 1980s, Ayatollah Khomeini failed to grasp the Iraqi near-surrender of 1982, a consequence of his belief that Iranian forces could topple the Iraqi regime and impose a Shi'a substitute; the result was six more years of war, the deaths of hundreds of thousands of Iranians, the entry of the US navy into the war on the side of the Iraqis and (in August 1988) a far less favourable peace.

Much is made too of the fact that Iran is the most important Shi'a state and that the last great Persian dynasty, the Safavids (1502–1736), made Shi'ism a powerful political, military and cultural force in the region, a rival for centuries to the Sunni Ottoman empire to the west.

This Shiʻa identity, one that the mullahs have in any case overblown, has proved to be a mixed blessing for the Islamic Republic; for many outside the country – and even for Shiʻa in countries like Iraq, Saudi Arabia and Kuwait – Iran's projection of its Shiʻism has put them in a difficult situation, not least because of the implied claim of the superior authority of clergy and politicians, based inside Iran. Ayatollah Ali al-Sistani, the leading Shiʻa cleric in Iraq, and himself an Iranian, has long sought to limit such influence, as, in a much rougher way, has the rising Shiʻa leader, Muqtada al-Sadr.

Iran's imperial and nationalist past and its Shiʻa identity are not, however, enough to explain the noisy and risky policy being pursued today. Here two other factors need to be brought into account. The first is that Iran is an oil-producing country, a fact that, especially at a time of high oil prices, gives to state some leeway simultaneously to mollify the people and pursue expensive military programmes. The problem is that these expenditures do little to alleviate the long-term problems of the economy and are usually, in the Iranian case and also that of Venezuela, accompanied by much waste, corruption and factionalism. In this regard, Ahmadinejad and Hugo Chávez are two of a kind: intoxicated with their own rhetoric, insouciant about the longer-term economic development of their oil industries and economy as a whole, and wilfully provocative towards the United States and immediate neighbours alike in foreign policy.

The second and indeed the most important (and neglected) factor explaining contemporary Iran, however, is a fact evident in its historical origin, policy and rhetoric: that the Islamic Republic of Iran is a country that has emerged from a revolution and that this revolution is far from losing its dynamic at home or abroad. It is not in the imperial dreams of ancient Persia, or the global vision of Shiʻa clergy, but in the repetition by Iran of the same policies, aspirations and mistakes of previous revolutionary regimes, from France in the 1790s to Cuba in the 1960s and 1970s, that the underlying logic of its actions can be seen.

The Iranian revolution of 1978–9 was, as much as those of France, Russia, China or Cuba, one of the major social and political upheavals of modern history. Like its predecessors, it set out not only to transform its own internal system – at a high cost in repression, wastage and illusion – but to export revolution. And this Iran did: to Afghanistan, Iraq and Lebanon in the 1980s; and now to Palestine and, in much more favourable circumstances thanks to the US, to Iraq again. It can indeed be argued that it is the confrontation between internationalist revolutionary Iran on one side and the US and its regional allies on the other that has been the major axis of conflict in the Middle East this past quarter of a century. By comparison, America's war with Sunni al-Qa'ida-type militancy is a secondary affair.

Here, however, Iran has fallen into the same traps and illusions as others before. Like the French revolutionaries, the Iranians proclaim themselves to be at once the friend of all the oppressed and 'a great nation' (Khomeini's phrase echoed, whether wittingly or not, the Jacobins of 1793). Like the early Bolsheviks, the Islamic revolutionaries began their revolution thinking diplomacy was an oppression and should be swept aside – hence the detention of the US diplomats as hostages. Like the Cubans and Chinese, they have combined unofficial supplies of arms, training and finance to their revolutionary allies with the calculated intervention of their armed forces.

All of this has its cost. The gradual moderation of Iran under the presidency of Mohammad Khatami (1997–2005) reflected a sense of exhaustion after the eight-year war with Iraq and a desire for more normal external relations with the outside world, like the Girondin period in France in 1792–3 or the policies of Liu Shao-chi in China of the early 1960s: but as in those other cases, and as in the USSR of Stalin in the 1930s, there were those who wanted to go in a very different direction, who proceeded to tighten the screws of repression and raise confrontational rhetoric once again. One could indeed say that Iran under Ahmadinejad is now going through its third period or a mild replica of the Cultural Revolution.

How long this can continue is anyone's guess; but it is likely to be years before the Islamic revolution has run its course. Even Cuba, weak and exposed by comparison, has sustained its defiance and its model for well over four decades now. Yet even without war with the US, the risks and the costs are high, as many people in Iran realise only too well.

Here, again in a spirit of comparison, it is worth recalling the words of one of the wisest observers of modern revolutions, the now sadly deceased Polish writer Ryszard Kapuściński. His book *The Soccer War* contains a passage observing Algeria of the mid-1960s under Ahmad Ben Bella that applies to all revolutions, uncannily so in the case of Iran today:

Algeria became the pivotal Third World state, but the cost of its status – above all the financial cost – was staggering. It ate up millions of dollars for which the country had a crying need ... Gradually, the gap between Ben Bella's domestic and foreign policies grew wider. The contrast deepened. Algeria had earned an international reputation as a revolution state ... it was an example for the non-European continents, a model, bright and entrancing; while at home, the country was stagnating; the unemployed filled the square of every city; there was no investment; illiteracy ruled, bureaucracy, reaction, fanaticism ran riot; intrigues absorbed the attention of the government ... The country cannot carry the burden of these polices. It cannot afford to and it has no interest in them.[1]

Mahmoud Ahmadinejad and his advisers, and those of Hugo Chávez too, would do well to read and ponder these words.

3.   SUNNI, SHI'A AND THE 'TROTSKYISTS OF ISLAM'
9 February 2007

The conflict now besetting the Middle East is, like all major international conflicts, multidimensional. It involves not just one major axis of violence but several overlapping conflicts (Israel/Arabs, United States/terrorism, the West/Iran) that draw states and armed movements into their arena. The major concern of strategists and analysts remains the polarisation between the US and its foes in Iraq and, increasingly, in Iran. But there is another important, ominous conflict accompanying these that has little to do with the machinations of Washington or Israel, and is less likely to be contained by political compromise: the spread, in a way that is radically new for the Middle East, of direct conflict between Sunni and Shi'a Muslims.

Many generalisations and simplifications accompany the whole issue of Sunni and Shi'a Islam. In the aftermath of the Iranian revolution, when Ayatollah Khomeini produced a radical populist Third World rhetoric that denounced the West, the *taghut* (golden idols) and those who served imperialist interests in the region (among them the Shah of

---

1   Ryszard Kapuscinski. *The Soccer War*, London: Penguin, 1979, p. 110.

Iran, Anwar Sadat, Saddam Hussein and the Gulf rulers), it was claimed by many that Shi'ism, the belief of around 10 per cent of all Muslims, was inherently militant. Unlike the Sunni, who had historically accepted the legitimacy of the caliphs and who paid their clergy from state funds, thereby controlling them, the Shi'a refused to accept the Muslim credentials of their rulers and produced a clergy paid for by the subscriptions of the faithful that was closer to the people and so more radical.

I recall a conversation with Ibrahim Yazdi, the first foreign minister of the Islamic Republic of Iran (who spent years after Ayatollah Khomeini's death under virtual house arrest in Tehran). As he sat under the enormous chandeliers of what had been the Shah's foreign ministry, he exclaimed with pride: 'We are the Trotskyists of Islam!' The logic of Yazdi's characterisation – with its echoes of the Russian revolutionary leader's theory of permanent revolution – was to spread Iran's radical anti-imperialism across the region: a force far superior, in his view, to the then vacillating as well as pro-Soviet ideology of the secular Left.[1]

Much of this was simplistic and one-sided: like all bodies of religious text and tradition, Shi'a and Sunni beliefs are liable to many interpretations. Iran has chosen, however, to put a militant stamp on its beliefs and to promote these values across the Muslim world in a revolution that has far from run its course. Today, the international radicalism of the Iranian revolution has come to be an explosive force in the Middle East: directed on one side against the United States, but also, in a dangerous inflaming of communal relations, against Sunni Muslims as well.

This communal conflict is most evident in Iraq. What began in 2003 as a largely Sunni and former Ba'athist rising against the American forces and their Iraqi allies had by mid-2006 developed into a multi-sided conflict in which Sunni and Shi'a forces were in conflict with

---

1   Since the original publication of this article by openDemocracy, Mr Yazdi has written to me (25 February 2007) challenging this account of our meeting and arguing that in the years after the Islamic revolution he contested the view of those who were strong advocates of exporting the revolution, and accused them of being 'Trotskyists of Islam'. In particular he cites an article he published in the daily *Etela'at* of Azar 1364 (December 1985) on this issue. I am more than happy to record Mr Yazdi's views in this letter and to acknowledge that, in later debates, he did criticise the 'export of revolution': but my account of his remarks at that time, in August 1979, are accurate. It would appear that, in response to events, he changed his mind. What he did not contest is my account of our conversation as published in 1979 (*New Statesman*, August 1979) and later in book form (*Nation and Religion in the Middle East*, London: Saqi Books, 2000, p. 157), according to which he endorsed the campaign of repression against the liberal press.

the Americans but also increasingly with each other. In early 2007 it is estimated that up to 2 million people have been displaced by the war, equally divided between those fleeing to other parts of Iraq and those forced into exile.

The sectarian war in Iraq has echoes – if the consequences are as yet far less bloody – elsewhere in the region: in the Gulf states, notably Kuwait and Bahrain, where relations between the Shi'a and Sunni populations of these states (respectively a quarter and a half of the total population) have worsened; in Lebanon, where the forward advance of Hizbullah during and after the summer 2006 war led to worsened relations with the Sunni population, although not – even amid political tumult – to direct conflict; in Palestine, where there are no Shi'a, but where supporters of Fatah nonetheless took to denouncing the supporters of Hamas as 'Shi'a' on account of the movement's links to Iran.

In Syria matters are less overt, but it is no secret that for decades the Sunni majority have resented rule by an Alawi elite of Shi'a origin, represented by the Ba'ath Party which has controlled the country since 1963. The one direct challenge to the Ba'athists by the Sunni, in the form of a Muslim Brotherhood insurrection centred on the city of Hama, was crushed with great brutality by Hafez al-Assad's forces in 1982. Two decades later, the Muslim Brotherhood have regained considerable influence in the country, especially amongst the Sunni middle classes. The movement would be the main beneficiary of any fatal crisis of the Bashar al-Assad regime.

Against this background it was not surprising that some Arab leaders – notably those of Egypt, Jordan and Saudi Arabia – began to warn of the dangers of the advance of Iranian and Shi'a power and to present themselves as a 'moderate' Muslim bulwark against the advance of the revolutionary Shi'a alliance. At the level at which it has been developing in 2006 and early 2007, it is possible to envisage this conflict between Sunni and Shi'a as becoming the dominant regional fracture in the ensuing period – especially amidst a withdrawal, at whatever pace, of American forces from Iraq.

In such conditions, there are many analysts or propagandists who resort to the notion that this sectarianism is a 'deep structure', reflecting a latent atavism that has long underlain the politics of the region. The implication is that the overt violence of 2006–7 involves the emergence to the surface of deep and ever-present hatreds. (Similar arguments about 'ancient ethnic hatreds' were heard repeatedly in the context of the wars in Yugoslavia, Sri Lanka and Northern Ireland.)

However, another analysis is more persuasive. This sees the Sunni–Shi'a conflict as essentially a recent development, a product of the political crisis in the Middle East in recent decades and, in the case of Iraq, of the spiral of violence released by the United States invasion of 2003. In this perspective, the origins of the conflict – and more generally of the Arab–Persian conflict – lie not in ancient hostility and grievance but in the modern history of the region; in particular, the ways in which the twin revolutions of Iraq (1958) and Iran (1979) set in motion rivalry and insecurity between states and peoples that exploded first in the Iran–Iraq war of 1980–8, and again inside Iraq from 2003.

At the same time, two cautionary observations are in order. First, there is no deep divide in terms of religious belief because there is little to be divided about. The actual religious and theological distinctions between Sunni and Shi'a are small, far less than those between Catholics and Protestants within Christianity. They revolve not so much around questions of belief or even interpretation of holy texts, but around rival claims to legitimacy and succession in the aftermath of the Prophet Mohammed's death in 632 CE, with Sunni favouring the 'successors' or caliphs and Shi'a seeing succession in the Prophet's son-in-law Ali, the latter's son Hussein, and those who come after them.

The death of Hussein at the battle of Karbala (661) at the hands of the Umayyad caliph Yezid is taken as the founding moment of Shi'ism, to which all later historical legitimisation and annual mourning ceremonies refer. One of the major complaints of Sunni against Shi'a is that preachers in the latter's mosques curse the early successors of the Prophet, the caliphs revered by Sunni. But this seventh-century division does not account for the major conflicts of the Islamic world then or later in the same way that wars between Catholic and Protestant were to do in early modern Europe. There were, moreover, forms of coexistence and interaction between the two which find little parallel in Europe. These include widespread intermarriage (in Iraq as elsewhere) and the use even of places of worship associated with one sect by followers of the other. The Sayyidna al-Hussein mosque in Cairo, built by the Fatimid medieval Shi'a dynasty that ruled Egypt at the time, is also revered by Sunni; the Umayyad mosque in Damascus, the most historically important in the Sunni world, has a section devoted to the commemoration of Hussein to which Shi'a visitors from Iran regularly make pilgrimage.

Second, actual and direct conflict between Sunni and Shi'a (as distinct from suspicion and communal difference) has until recently been remarkable by its absence. What is more evident is differential political loyalty between the communities, in relation to (for example) Arab nationalism, secularism or the Iranian revolution. It has, moreover, been possible to identify particular Muslim ruling elites as either Sunni or Shi'a: Sunni in most cases, but Shi'a in Iran, Yemen and Syria.

Yet even here, where a sectarian element clearly entered into the distribution of power, it did not spark a revolt based on sectarianism itself. Thus the Kurds in Iran are mainly Sunni, a fact that no doubt contributed to their resistance to the Shi'a state created by Khomeini after 1979. In Iraq, the Shi'a rose up in 1991 against Saddam, but this was in conjunction with the Kurds on a mainly national political basis – even as Saddam replied by crushing the uprising under the slogan *La Shi'a ba'ad al-Yaum* (No Shi'a from Today). In the case of Iraq, the Sunni monopoly was partly broken once before 2003 in the person of the first president after the revolution of 1958, Abd al-Karim Qasim, who was half-Sunni, half-Shi'a, but seen as favouring the latter.

Where it has occurred in recent decades, overt conflict and sectarian violence between Sunni and Shi'a originated not in the Arab world or Iran, but further east, in Pakistan and Afghanistan. In the former, its encouragement became part of the ideology of militant Sunni groups associated with guerrilla action in Kashmir in the 1970s, and later in Afghanistan, to promote hostility to Shi'a; from the 1980s onwards there were regular attacks on Shi'a mosques in different parts of Pakistan. In the Afghan wars of the 1980s and 1990s, the militant Sunni groups who dominated the *mujahideen* came to attack the Shi'a community of Afghanistan as enemies of their cause. This radical Sunni rhetoric charged that, because they worshipped the shrines of imams and other holy men, the Shi'a were defectors from the monotheism of Islam, in effect 'polytheists'. Indeed, in some bizarre versions, the term for polytheist, *moshrik* (one who shares), came to be used as a synonym for 'communist', in the sense of someone who shared property in common.

The final twist in this saga involved the creation of a cult, by the Taliban in Afghanistan, of the tenth- and eleventh-century leader Sultan Mahmud, a man whose main claim to fame was that he had invaded India 'a hundred times': his grave in Ghazni was used as a shrine for young Taliban soldiers

being sent to fight Shi'a, where, they were told, Sultan Mahmud 'was killing communists, even in the time of the Prophet'. Such ideological invention and redefinition is central to the contemporary conflict of Sunni and
Shi'a. It involves the use on both sides of terms of abuse and historical
delegitimisation that, while they have historical precedent, have needed to
be recreated as bearers of modern identity and confrontation.

Modernity and the use of communal or religious differences for contemporary political ends are no barrier to the spread of hatred and violence. These fires, once lit, can destroy forms of coexistence that have
continued for centuries. This is clearly the case in the 'war of elimination' in Baghdad today (a city from which, it may be recalled, the Jewish
community who had lived there for over two millennia experienced a
mass exodus in the early 1950s). Moreover, while at the beginning states
may seek to control such sectarian loyalties, as both Iran and Saudi
Arabia have done, such control may not last: today Iran has much less
influence over the Iraqi Shi'a than it had three or ten years ago. How
far these flames will spread is anyone's guess, but it would seem that the
invasion of Iraq has set off a dangerous dynamic that could affect much
of the region. The US and its allies are certainly wondering which way
the Arab and Sunni world will jump in the event of an attack on Iran.

Some may take comfort from the dire warning that issued from a
conference of Sunni and Shi'a clergy recently held in Qatar. As representatives of each side promised to stop preaching suspicion of the other,
and Shi'a committed themselves to stop cursing the caliphs, a prominent
Iraqi cleric warned that if this conflict were to continue, the direst of all
consequences would follow: namely that young people in the Muslim
world would be tempted ... to turn to secularism.

4. IRAN'S REVOLUTION IN GLOBAL HISTORY
5 March 2009

The months of strikes and demonstrations that convulsed Iran in 1978–9
reached a dramatic culmination in the first eleven days of February 1979,
when an epic tide of revolutionary fervour brought the return to Iran
from exile of Ayatollah Ruhollah Khomeini and overthrew the hitherto powerful regime of Shah Mohammad Reza Pahlavi. In the ensuing

weeks, the victorious leaders of the popular wave established a new state, the Islamic Republic of Iran; this was proclaimed on 1 April and its constitution ratified in a national referendum on 2–3 December 1979. In consolidating power, as in executing their enemies, the mullahs and their political allies did not waste time.

Three decades is not a long period in the normal lifetime of a revolutionary regime – Cuba's celebrated its half-century in January 2009, China's will mark its sixtieth year in October, Russia's passed its seventieth before expiring. But it is an appropriate point to reconsider – in the perspective both of Iranian reality and of global history – events that were by any account among the most unexpected and influential of modern times.

Their scale was immense but their impact also individual and personal. In my own case, as someone who knew Iran in the time of the Shah and visited it in the early and heady post-revolutionary months, this was one of the most challenging periods of my political and intellectual life: both in understanding and engaging with these enormous and complex popular mobilisations, and in coming to terms with the repression, killing and exile to which many of my friends and comrades were later subjected.

The revolution of Iran can be seen as part of a series of such transformations that had overturned regimes in three continents in the previous two centuries: France (1789), Russia (1917), China (1949), Cuba (1959). What happened in Iran shares six broad points of comparison with these earlier moments.

First, a broad coalition of opposition forces came together to overthrow a dictatorial regime, building on long-standing social grievances but also energising nationalist sentiment against a state and ruler seen as too compliant with foreign interests. The coalition mobilised under Ayatollah Khomeini's leadership ranged from liberal and Marxist to conservative and religious forces: in effect a classic populist alliance.

Second, the victory of the revolution both required and was facilitated by the state's weakness of leadership and internal divisions. The Shah was ill, his advisers and generals were uncertain. The resemblance to other figures and regimes in a time of crisis – Louis XVI and Czar Nicholas II, as well as Charles I of England – is evident.

Third, the revolution possessed the quality that distinguishes mere coups d'état or rebellions from major revolutions: namely, it was not just political (in the sense of changing the political elite and the constitution or legitimating system of the country) but had profound and ongoing social and economic consequences. Because of it, Iran today has a new social order and a new set of social values – even as a new revolutionary elite, an Islamic nomenklatura, united by ties of power, business and marriage, controls state revenues.

Fourth, the revolution's core ideology may have propounded the need for a new, radical and egalitarian order; but it was supplemented by pre-existing ideas that were crucial to sustaining domestic support (above all, nationalism and a sense of the country's historic standing and mission). Ayatollah Khomeini at first refused to use the word *mihan* (fatherland) and denounced secular nationalism as an insult to Islam. But with the invasion by Saddam Hussein's Iraq in 1980 all this changed, and he and other leaders adopted the Iranian version of the term used by French revolutionaries in the 1790s, *la grande nation* – in Persian, *millat i bozorg*.

Fifth, the explosion of revolution at the centre of a multi-ethnic country – and driven especially from within its dominant ethnic component – had profound reverberations on the relations between Iran's different national components. In particular, it led not to the era of fraternal cooperation and solidarity anticipated in much of the political rhetoric of the time, but to conflict and war.

Here again, the pattern – a revolt at the heart of a plural country and the consolidation of a new authoritarian regime provoking contrary forces in the periphery – has rich historical precedents. The Young Turk revolution of 1908, the Bolshevik revolution of 1917 and the Ethiopian revolution of 1974 are prime examples; their echo in Iran concerned, above all, the Kurds. The hopes of this significant part of the population for an autonomous Kurdistan within a democratic Iran (and they knew the first was impossible without the second) were to be dashed.

Sixth, the revolution in Iran had explosive international consequences. There were persistent attempts to export the revolution to neighbouring countries, which intensified regional rivalries and fostered conditions that led to inter-state war. The Iranian revolution's efforts to promote its state interests and extend itself soon acquired resemblances to a reviving empire – with traces of France and Russia in particular, not least the contradictory trends whereby some forces in the region were inspired by the revolution while others drew on older antagonisms (such as Saddam Hussein's excoriation of Khomeini as a magus [Zoroastrian priest] and more recent concerns about a powerful new Shi'a 'crescent').

At the same time, the revolution's enduring influence was forged in these post-revolutionary conflicts. It was the international impacts of the 1979 revolution – above all the 1980–8 war with Iraq – that shaped the politics, defined the state institutions and steeled the will of the Islamic Republic (just as the civil war of 1919–21 was formative for the Bolshevik regime). The fact that many of those who went through the experience of that terrible war – such as President Mahmoud Ahmadinejad and his associates in the Revolutionary Guards – are now seeking to revive the revolutionary discipline and spirit of those years echoes similar attempts by Joseph Stalin in the 1930s, Mao Zedong in the 1960s Cultural Revolution, and Fidel Castro in his 1980s *rectificación* of the 1980s. All in the end failed, though the regimes themselves lasted.

The Iranian revolution thus bears comparison with its historic pre-decessors. But just as each earlier revolution can be seen in relation to others even as it displays its own singularity, this is true of Iran also. This is most obviously the case in regard to the leadership, ideology and goals of the revolution. For in the vanguard was not the secular radicalism of the inheritors of 1789, but a revolution under the banner of Islam; led by clerics, and ostensibly inspired by the goal not of advancing to a new and 'progressive' future but rather of returning to the model of Islam – defined as simple, puritanical and authentic – of the age of the Prophet. This form of ideology and leadership is all the more distinctive in that many other Islamist revolutionary movements before and since – such as those of Afghanistan, Egypt or Algeria (and, by extension, al-Qa'ida) – have had non-clerical leaders.

But in any event the 'religious' ideas of the Iranian revolution, and the application to modern politics of terms and images taken from the Qur'an, should not be taken entirely at face value. True, Islamic ideas (in regard to women, the law and the status of the clergy, for example) had a major impact on the social values of the Islamic Republic. But on closer examination, the programme and actions of Ayatollah Khomeini and his associates have much in common with other modern social upheav-als. Here are just five such affinities: the appeal to the mass of poor people (*mostazafin*) against the corrupt, foreign-linked, elite (*mostakba-rin*); the cult of the leader – Khomeini's official and entirely secular state title was *rahbar inqilab va bonyadgozar i jumhuri yi islami* (leader of the

revolution and founder of the Islamic Republic); mobilising nationalist sentiment in a country that had been unilaterally invaded, by Russia
and Britain, in both world wars; using, albeit in a chaotic and inefficient
way, the country's oil wealth for egalitarian social programmes in city
and countryside; and analysing the world in terms of a just struggle of
oppressed peoples against a dominant power – Khomeini cited those of
South Africa and Nicaragua, and though he did not often use the word
'imperialism' he deployed an apt Qur'anic term as substitute – *istikbar i
jahani* (global arrogance).

Above all, the Islamic revolutionaries of 1979 did what all
revolutionaries do – namely overthrow an oppressive government, seize
power for themselves and their allies, crush not only their opponents
but all dissidents within the regime, and then impose a new and even
more exacting and intrusive authoritarian regime. In summer 1979,
I was a witness of the brutal repression visited by the new state on its
former, now discarded, liberal and socialist allies. In this perspective,
the template followed by the Islamic Republic is not that of Mecca
and Medina in the seventh century but that of Paris in the 1790s and
Moscow and St Petersburg in the 1920s.

The common emphasis on the apparently unique religious character of the Iranian revolution may also mislead the analyst, in the sense
that it obscures other dimensions in which it was distinct. For in at least
three other ways the events of 1978–9 were indeed different from what
had gone before.

First, this revolution – more than any other in history – relied not on
force, military insurrection or guerrilla war but on politics. This is true
in particular with regard to the two instruments that European revolutionaries had themselves long dreamt of using – the mass mobilisation
of people in the streets (in the Iranian case, the largest such opposition
demonstrations ever recorded anywhere) and the political (as opposed
to industrial) general strike (which, from October 1978, paralysed the
economy and foreign trade). This, not the religious garb, was perhaps
the most paradoxical and original aspect of the Iranian revolution: in
its political form and process, and despite its religious and 'traditional'
guise, it was the first modern revolution.

Second, Iran's experience departed from the norm prescribed by
both historical precedent and textbooks of historical sociology: namely,
that a revolution's indispensable precondition is the weakening of the

state, usually as a result of foreign pressure – either defeat in war or by invasion, or via the withdrawal of support from an external patron (in the case of China and Cuba, this was the United States).

In Iran, none of this occurred. The Shah's regime was backed by the US (as also by China) to the end, while the Russians did not know what to do or think; no outside state gave any support to the revolutionaries; and the Shah's army had not been defeated in war. In another respect the Iranian revolution was almost unique in modern times, namely that it did not occasion rivalry between great powers: Russia, China, Europe and the US were united against it and supported Saddam Hussein's Iraq in its aggression of 1980.

Third, this was a revolution that was well organised, through a network of mosque and local committees – yet had no revolutionary party. It failed later, moreover – as the Cubans, for example, did – to consolidate one; the brief experiment with a ruling party after 1979, the Islamic Republican Party, soon petered out. Against this background, the Iran of today appears as another case of a revolution that approaches its middle years far from abandoned or defeated. In domestic terms, the post-revolutionary climate is far freer and more diverse than that seen in any other revolution; a wide range of opinions and interpretations of the revolution itself and its programme can be heard – even if violence, cruelty and intimidation are never far away. The presidential elections of June 2009 are even more important in this regard in signalling how Iran's past will influence its future course; though given the plurality of power-centres and opinions, even they will not be definitive.

In international terms, Iran – exactly like its other post-imperial counterparts, France, Russia and China – is pursuing a 'dual' foreign policy: one that combines aspirations to regional and military power with continued promotion of radicalism in neighbouring countries.

A thirty-year story is thus far from ended. No one involved in and affected by it – the region, the wider world, and above all the resourceful, sardonic and enduring people of Iran – has yet heard the last of the Islamic revolution and of this 'great nation'.

5. REFLECTIONS ON THE COUNTER-REVOLUTION IN IRAN
17 July 2009

One month after the outbreak of nationwide demonstrations in Iran in protest at the official handling of the 11 June presidential elections, and more generally at the domination of that country by a recalcitrant and demagogic clique, it appears at first sight as if the regime of Ayatollah Khamenei and Mahmoud Ahmadinejad, spritual leader and president respectively, has been able to contain and push back the challenge to its rule. Unanticipated by almost all internal and international observers, the mass movement of the Persian Spring seems to have been driven out of sight as suddenly as it burst upon the scene.

If past performance is anything to go on, this public display of state violence is only the beginning: as has occurred in earlier phases of the Islamic Republic, and also under the Shah's regime, opposition members will be brutalised and terrorised in prison and then forced to engage in televised 'confessions', acts of deliberately preposterous humiliation designed not to reveal the truth about 'foreign conspiracies' or whatever but to break the will of the regime's opponents. More ominously, once international attention has shifted away from Iran and foreign correspondents been expelled, an early phase of detention, mistreatment and public humiliation may be followed – as it was with the crushing of the liberal and Left opposition in 1979–81 – by the killing in prison of opposition members. In the past, such killings took the form of fake trials, where executions were justified under the catch-all charge of 'waging war on God', or by supposed attempts to escape.

The determination to repress and contempt for the peacefully and democratically expressed views of others which are evident in the recent events in Tehran were apparent in the first months of the Islamic Republic. I recall, in particular, an educative encounter in August 1979 with a Revolutionary Guard who had come with his colleagues to close down the offices of the independent newspaper *Ayandegan*. When I asked the *pasdar* what he was doing, he replied: 'We are defending the Revolution!' So why were they closing the paper? I asked. 'This newspaper is shit,' he declared. When I suggested that two million people read the paper, he replied, without reservation: 'All right, then these two million people are shit too!' Thus was my induction into the political culture of the Islamic Guards.

If this incident casts some light on the recent popular explosion in Iran, other analogies also suggest themselves, above all with challenges to communist rule in Eastern Europe after 1945. For in one sense, the Islamic Republic has, like communism, lost its original ideological credibility; in sociological terms, it has dug its own grave by educating people: the demonstrators in Iran did not carry posters of Shi'a Imams, Ali or Reza, or chant religious slogans, nor did they brandish pictures of Lenin, Mao or Che Guevara. They were, like the mass movements that challenged communism, part of a 'revolution of catching up', as Habermas described 1989, one that wanted to be part of the modern world and for their country to take its rightful and collaborative place in it. Their main cry was at once contemporary and resonant of the Constitutional Revolution of 1906: 'Death to the Dictator!' Their demand, reiterated by the presidential candidate Mir Hossein Mousavi in his statements since the demonstrations, is for a broad range of freedoms: of expression, of social behaviour, of media.

The greatest enigma, and also the most striking originality, of the recent Iranian crisis concerns the depth of divisions within the regime of the Islamic Republic itself. The success of Mir Hossein Mousavi in mobilising a mass movement in the weeks just prior and subsequent to the presidential election can indeed be understood and explained: a long-term growth of dissatisfaction with the social, economic and political actions of the Islamic Republic; a particular revulsion to the policies of President Ahmadinejad; a set of short-term factors in the days leading up to the election, including the success of mobilisation through new media, and the vulgarity of Ahmadinejad in his TV debates with Mousavi; and the creative and novel use by the opposition of SMS, Facebook and other communications.

What is much less clear is the schism that runs through the state, dividing the Islamic nomenklatura. Watching Iran in recent weeks has been like watching a stage where only some of the actors are in the light: there is another, equally important, process underway which remains in the shadows. This is the conflict within the clerical and political elite, indicated by the open defiance of former presidents Rafsanjani and Khatami, which has spread through the clerical city of Qom and much of the political elite. Whether it also runs through the armed forces, the Islamic Guards and the intelligence services we do not know: but it has to be taken as an initial premise that until there is evidence that these security bodies are indeed divided, the initiative will lie with the Khamenei–Ahmadinejad camp. Reports from Qom also indicate that the regime is doing all it can, using money and intimidation, to keep the majority of the clergy on their side.

What the recent demonstrations have most certainly achieved, and what may in the future form an important part of any more liberal Iranian political regime, is to demonstrate that the very history and legacy of the Islamic revolution are open to a range of different interpretations. For many years after 1979 it was the Marxist Left which claimed, with considerable exaggeration, to have 'made' the revolution, only to have had Khomeini and the clergy steal it from them.

What this argument obscured, however, is that there was another, much larger, constituency that the clerical elite usurped, which had in its nationalist opposition to the Shah and his alliance with the USA played a very significant role in the revolution, and which Khomeini had indeed robbed with his plan for an 'Islamic government'. Many of the demonstrators of 1979 did not want the Shah, but they did not want the dictatorship of the ayatollahs either: they wanted, as the slogans of the revolution indicated, 'Independence' and 'Freedom'. In a word, like the demonstrators who defied communism in Eastern Europe in 1988–9, they wanted to be part of the modern world.

With a heroism and lucidity that have commanded admiration the world over, the demonstrators in Tehran have shown a realisation of this programme. The slogans of the 1979 demonstrations, *marg bar fascism, marg bar irtija* ('Death to Fascism, Death to Reaction'), may come to join with that of the recent demonstrators, 'Death to the Dictator', to herald the end of the clique of usurpers who now rule Iran. The people of Iran and their friends and admirers the world over can only hope that this day comes sooner rather than later.

Five

Violence and Politics

1. TERRORISM IN HISTORICAL PERSPECTIVE
22 April 2004

The spring of 2004 has brought forth monsters. The Madrid bombings, Gaza assassinations, Kosovo killings, Ugandan massacres, Iraqi depredations, Sudanese persecutions: all remind the world (if it was ever tempted to forget) that a formative issue of the twenty-first century is the question of political violence and its causes. Much of this political violence can be categorised as 'terrorism', and all of it is a recognisable exemplar of that multi-layered and ultimately indispensable term. Its employment demands extreme care and discrimination, as well as awareness of its potential for misuse, but the pressing realities of our time force on us the responsibility to make it an instrument of enlightenment and understanding.

Terrorism is a complex issue that allows no easy resolution, intellectual or political. Probably no subject has been as important in international relations or as confused in its treatment. Yet never has clear exposition been more necessary; for since September 2001 it has been the shaping theme of American foreign policy, and by extension to much of the discussion of foreign policy in Europe, the Eurasian landmass, the Middle East and elsewhere.

Terrorism is not a specifically Middle Eastern or Islamic problem. Historically, the continent of Europe pioneered political violence on a world scale, developed modern industrial war and played the leading role in developing those particular instruments of modern political action and control: genocide, systematic state torture and terrorism. Today, Europeans are right to feel that their own lives, their psychological tranquillity and their flawed but nonetheless substantial liberal and democratic values are under threat, and will remain so for years to come. An age of innocence – born of the expanding prosperity of the European Union over five decades and the end of the Cold War – has come to an end, if not on 11 September 2001 then on 11 March 2004.

One can understand why so many politicians in Spain and beyond talk of the Madrid attacks as an attack on European values, and why the European parliament passed a resolution the day after the Madrid explosions for a 'European day against terrorism'. But these are partial, mistaken, responses: we who are Europeans also bear responsibility for such phenomena.

More importantly, it is not just Europeans, nor indeed Americans, who are the targets of terrorism, but also all those in the Middle East and elsewhere who stand against this totalitarian and fanatical but determined and patient enemy. The problem belongs, and will belong for a long time, to the entire world. We should frame our responses – security, political and moral – in these terms.

It is essential to grasp the global character of the terror problem for another reason: the darker side of globalisation that liberal optimism too easily forgets. Beyond the prosperous West, there is a world that is and feels itself to be deprived of the benefits of modern life. If there is one fact above all that informed Western opinion has to take into account it is what can be termed 'global rancour': the enormous and ever-expanding divide between the developed West and the large areas of crisis and anger that surround it, in the Middle East, Latin America, Africa and Asia.

The need to understand this point is highlighted by the first of successive assassinations in Gaza in recent weeks of leaders of the Palestinian militant group Hamas. Sheikh Ahmed Yassin was at war with Israel and had long accepted his fate. He was also a hero to his own people, and is now so to Muslims across the world for two reasons that go to the heart of the anger of poor people in the non-West. First, he resisted foreign occupation and arrogance. Second, he was a political leader who was personally honest. Like Ayatollah Khomeini and Fidel Castro, he had no villas in Geneva, no secret bank accounts, no bevy of attractive young women and no abstruse, alien, political rhetoric. For millions, he was a simple, honest, courageous man and respected as such, even if his tactics towards others were inhuman and criminal. Israel's action has made him a hero for Muslims worldwide, including those in the European diaspora, and the response will be terrible and sustained. The date of his assassination, 22 March 2004, may well in retrospect mark a more significant turning-point in the history of the Middle East, in particular of the now even more vulnerable Jewish state, than 11 September 2001.

We cannot yet know – just as we cannot be sure whether al-Qa'ida's Manhattan and Pentagon operation will in the course of time prove to have been a 'world-historical' but essentially one-off event, as were the 1929 financial crash, the 1945 atomic bombs and the 1962 Cuban missile crisis. But about 9/11 we can affirm one thing above all: this was a political event, not an act of providence, divine or fatal, nor an expression of irrationality or atavistic religion. The attacks on 11 September 2001 were, like the Madrid attacks and the other events mentioned at the start of this article, the product of particular, identifiable political factors – rooted in the recent history of the Middle East, of the Cold War and its aftermath, or a combination of both. And it is the interplay of these factors in the years to come that will determine the future. Whether there will be more dates codified as '9/11' or '11-M', whether the constellation of forces around al-Qa'ida will be able to sustain their campaign, and whether this event will come to define and poison the broader pattern of relations between the West and the Muslim world are questions capable of yielding to political calculation, judgement and choice.

In other words, part of their answer will lie where the political violence itself began, in the very contingency of politics – leadership, events, power struggles, and the longer-term consequences of actions by state and non-state forces alike. Behind this political determination of the future, however, lies the political disempowerment of ordinary citizens. To a far greater degree than in major wars – when citizens are mobilised on the front or behind the lines – most of the inhabitants and citizens of the world are reduced to mere spectators in the current wars on and by terror. They are unable to participate in any meaningful way in their outcomes.

Thus, they (we) are prisoners not just of their (our) individual powerlessness, the occasional vote or protest meeting aside, but of the very nature of this conflict. For it is not only a secret military battle. It is also one where feelings, myths and confused sentiments struggle to articulate themselves in public discourse, and where the sense of everyday security in the private lives of families and individuals is thwarted or undermined by large, impersonal forces they strain to understand.

It is precisely out of this 'universalisation' of the human condition in the age of terrorism and its wars, however, that some margin of participation, debate and critical reflection is not only made possible but becomes the active responsibility of those who have studied and reflected on the character of political violence in the current era. It is in this spirit – of belief in democratic political agency by citizens, even as serious, long-term challenges increasingly become the condition of all our existences – that I propose this brief mapping of terrorism and the lessons for the post-9/11 world.

'Terrorism' is too easily elided in contemporary political discussion with the general phenomenon of armed resistance to oppression by states. This latter activity has been a major feature of the modern world, especially in situations of domination by Western or colonial powers. In more recent times, it has included the activities of the African National Congress (ANC) against the apartheid regime in South Africa as well as the Palestine Liberation Organisation (PLO) in Palestine, the guerrillas in Afghanistan, and both the Sandinista Front for National Liberation (FSLN) and the Contras in Nicaragua.

The general right to resist, and, where extreme coercion exists, to take up arms, is generally recognised both in law and in modern political discourse: it was the basis for the Reaganite backing of revolt against communist Third World regimes (Angola, Grenada, Mozambique) in the 1980s as it was of communist backing for wars of national liberation in the 1950s and 1960s. This right is also a precious part of the legacy of political reflection in East and West over many centuries. The Christian legal and political tradition gave due respect to this principle. It was espoused by the English philosopher John Locke, the Founding Fathers in the United States of America, and currents of radical dissent in the age of empire and Enlightenment. It is equally present in Islamic discourse, where revolt – often referred to as *khuruj* (literally 'going out' against the tyrant), *dhalim*, *taghin* or *musta'bid* – is central to the tradition. In

the minds of hegemonic powers, and particularly in United States discussion after 9/11, the right to revolt has been generally omitted; many
non-Western states have been quick to take local advantage of a global
trend by crushing internal dissent (with indulgence from Washington)
on the grounds that it too is all 'terrorism'.

Terrorism is a distinct political and moral phenomenon, though of
course interlinked with the issue of revolt and opposition to oppression. Terrorism refers to a set of military tactics that are part of military
and political struggle, designed to force the enemy to submit by some
combination of killing and intimidation. As such, it is deemed to be a
violation of the rules and norms of warfare, in either of two senses: first,
where these are formally encoded, as in the Geneva Conventions of 1949
and their two Additional Protocols of 1977, the latter of which cover
irregular and terrorist actions, albeit inadequately; second, where they
exist informally, in relation to what are considered legitimate means of
waging war. These are notoriously vague and permit partisan interpretations, especially in situations of nationalist or religious fervour, but they
are also remarkably resilient and universal: the killings of women and
children, of prisoners or of groups of civilians are actions widely recognised in all cultures, religions and contexts as invalid in principle.

The first use of 'terrorism' was by the French revolutionaries, in an
exact reverse of the contemporary sense: to denote violence against a
people by the state. It was also used thus by the Bolshevik leader Leon
Trotsky in a book published in English as *In Defence of Terrorism*
(Labour Publishing Company and Allen & Unwin, 1921). This dimension should not be forgotten: in recent decades, states have killed and
tortured far more people and violated far more of the rules of war than
their non-state opponents. The recognition of the prevalence and crimi-
nality of 'state' terrorism should, however, be maintained in distinction
from two other issues: first, 'state-sponsored' terrorism, which has come
to denote the support for terrorist, and more broadly guerrilla, activity
by one state in the territory and/or against the officials and citizens of
another; second, the responsibility of opposition groups in revolt (legitimate or not) against dictatorial states themselves to respect the norms of
war – for their defenders all too easily resort to an (often justified) attack
on state terrorism to distract attention from the crimes of their own side.

The early history of terrorism, both as a term and a political phenomenon, casts some light on the present crisis and the 'war' against

terrorism. The rise of non-state terrorism espoused as a conscious political activity – for propaganda more than for actual state-challenging reasons – dates mainly from a century later; nationalist movements in Ireland, Armenia and Bengal are exemplary here. Russian anarchists also deployed this tactic.

In the post-1945 period, 'terrorism from below' came to be associated most with nationalist struggles against a colonial or quasi-colonial power deemed to be too powerful to confront on the battlefield alone, but which was politically vulnerable: the Zionist Irgun, the Algerian FLN, the Kenyan Mau Mau, the Cypriot EOKA, the Irish Republican Army (IRA) and the Basque Euskadi Ta Askatasuna (ETA) are examples – though Vietnam, significantly, is not. Only in the late 1960s did the main incidences of such activity shift to the Middle East, with guerrillas in Palestine, Iran and Eritrea resorting to attacks on civilians, hijacking of airlines, and kidnapping of politicians and ordinary civilians alike. But it is worth noting that these were groups inspired by secular, often radical or self-proclaimed Marxist-Leninist ideologies. Religious groups, like the Muslim Brotherhood in Egypt and Jordan, and the Fedayeen-i-Islam in Iran, did carry out selected assassinations of secular intellectuals or political opponents, but these were specifically targeted actions, not part of a broader social and political mobilisation to take power.

In light of 9/11, much has been made of the relationship between religion, in this case Islam, and acts of terror. But an element of robust and (in the proper sense, denoting a field of scholarship) orientalist comparison is pertinent here. All religions contain the bases of respect for general norms of behaviour in war, but they also contain elements that can be used for massacre, ethnic expulsion and the slaying of prisoners. The Judeo-Christian Bible, notably the books of Deuteronomy and Judges, provides good examples of this. It is indisputable that there are elements in the texts and traditions of Islamic peoples that can be assembled to make the modern device of political terrorism – but this is not a necessary, or singular, connection.

The key implication is that terrorism, as ideology and instrument of struggle, is a modern phenomenon, a product of the conflict between contemporary states and their restive societies. In rich and poor countries alike, it has developed as part of a transnational model of political engagement. Its roots are in modern secular politics; it has no specific regional or cultural attachment; it is an instrument, one among several, for those aspiring to challenge states and one day to take power themselves.

The ideology, strategy and tactics of al-Qaʻida certainly have distinct aspects, and are not a mere extension of this earlier history. Whether it is seen as a single act of 'terror from below', an extreme case of 'propaganda of the deed' or as a blow against a metropolitan First World city by a Third World movement, no action like 11 September 2001 was ever carried out before. It was, amazingly, the first time in five hundred years of unequal globalised North–South interaction and conflict that such an event has occurred. Al-Qaʻida itself is, moreover, not just another conventional modern terrorist organisation. Its ideology is an extreme case of hybridity, borrowing as it does some elements from Sunni Islam, others from Sunni sectarianism against Shiʻa Muslims; and mixing both with modern nihilism, the cult of extreme heroism, self-sacrifice and the gun, anti-globalisation rhetoric and, not least, nationalism. Like Nazism, it is an ideology that thrives on its inebriating incoherence.

In organisational terms, it clearly has a structure distinct from that of the Popular Front for the Liberation of Palestine (PFLP), the Liberation Tigers of Tamil Eelam (Tamil Tigers/LTTE) or ETA. At its core is a small conspiratorial group, led by Osama bin Laden and his Egyptian companion, Ayman al-Zawahiri; around them are small semi-independent groups, drawn from many different parts of the Muslim and non-Muslim world. Their approach is a result of two mutually reinforcing characteristics. First, a rational calculation that decentralised networks, active in fundraising and recruiting, are more resistant to penetration. Second, a cultural adaptation of the loose patterns of association, trust and commitment that characterise societies like those of Afghanistan and parts of the Arab world, where tribal patterns of behaviour to some degree still prevail.

The other key element in understanding al-Qaʻida, one that takes the focus right back to modernity and the historical context in which it emerged, is the Cold War, in particular its latter phase from the Soviet intervention in Afghanistan of 1979 onwards. Without the Cold War, and without lavish United States and Saudi support for the opposition guerrillas in Afghanistan, neither al-Qaʻida nor the whole transnational world of Islamic fighters would have come into existence. Years before al-Qaʻida started attacking Western targets in New York (1993) and Africa (1998), it was on the rampage in Afghanistan and Yemen, killing secular officials, intellectuals and opponents of its fundamentalist project. In challenging these two pro-Soviet Islamic Third World regimes, where (in a benighted way) reformist–communist states were trying to push through a secular modernising programme, the West and its regional allies turned too easily to the crazed counter-revolutionaries of the Islamic right. No historical analysis (indeed, no measured settling of moral accounts about 9/11 and what follows) can avoid this decisive earlier connection. Al-Qa'ida hates the West, but it is a creation – an ideological, militarised and organisational monster – of Western policy in the Cold War itself. On 11 September 2001 the sorcerer's apprentice hit back. Given a chance, it will hit back again.

No one can anticipate how the campaigns of al-Qa'ida or of those waging the 'War on Terror' will unfold. It will take years for this crisis to pass, and, in contrast to conventional wars, there will be no moment at which the war, or indeed the jihad, will clearly be over. Citizens in East and West will remain onlookers. But they (we) can take a stand, make judgements and attempt to influence policy.

In conclusion, then, here are four proposed guidelines for discussion by concerned citizens worldwide. First, terrorism of all kinds should be condemned. At the same time, a broader sense of proportion is needed. No discussion of terrorism from below, its history or its moral and legal dimensions can take place without parallel recognition of the role of states, past and present, in violating the rules of war with regard to the treatment of civilians and prisoners.

Second, we need to bear in mind, with some self-critical modesty, the fact that the major governments of the West have themselves in recent times supported groups that are on any objective standard 'terrorist'. Examples are legion, from UNITA in Angola, which killed hundreds of thousands in the wars that lasted from the mid-1970s to the late 1990s, to the Nicaraguan Contra, the right-wing governments of El Salvador and Guatemala in the 1980s, and above all the Afghan *mujahideen*. While the worst crimes have certainly been committed by radical regimes that were opposed to the West (Iraq, Syria, Iran), few states in the Middle East that have been allies of the West – not Israel or Turkey, Egypt or Saudi Arabia, not (in its earlier days) the Shah's Iran – have upheld standards of law and norms in regard to the treatment of civilians and subject peoples. In short, no discourse and no policy that casts al-Qa'ida as the sole, or main, violator of the rules of war in a conflict with something that calls itself without qualification 'the civilised world' is defensible.

Third, resistance to terror is not a prerogative of powerful Western states. Terror from below and above has been the experience of many peoples in the Third World for decades before 9/11 – be it in Lebanon or Israel, Sri Lanka or Pakistan, Indonesia or Cambodia, Sierra Leone or Rwanda, Argentina or Guatemala, or, not to be forgotten, Ireland or Spain. The victims who died in Manhattan fell in the shadow of thousands of others: intellectuals and peasants, priests and village leaders, trade unionists and student leaders, and (in Afghanistan in particular) proponents of women's rights; all had been slain, their families and friends terrorised and dispersed. This is a phenomenon with a very wide toll on every continent.

This does not preclude the citizens of the United States from expressing their grief and anger, but it should remind them that they exist in permanent relation to a worldwide movement that has deep roots, and that their country is part of this movement, not its singularised and unappointed master. Thus, the opposition to bin Laden cannot be based on some privilege of suffering on 11 September, any more than can the victims of a car accident or a violent theft claim a unique experience that entitles them to pursue vengeance in disregard of established norms. Nor is there any pure Western record in regard to the role of violence and terror over the past century: recall (for example) the millions killed by the Belgians in the Congo around 1900, or the millions slaughtered by France and the United States in Vietnam between 1945 and 1975 in the name of causes that were later abandoned.

Fourth, the fight against terrorism, on any continent and within any political or cultural context, involves a necessary security dimension. But it also involves historical perspective, political astuteness and the defence of those standards in the name of which the fight itself is being conducted. In other words, those who wage the fight must themselves respect law and show some element of historical modesty and perspective. This is all the more so because 'terrorism', like 'globalisation', 'human rights' and relations between 'civilisations' (not an analytic category I generally favour), is debated and understood through the nexus of existing world power relations.

No calm, level realm exists for the discussion of these topics. For this world is characterised by long-established and growing inequalities of power and wealth, against a background of centuries of colonial expansion, clientelist protection of oppressive regional regimes and Cold War intervention. So these topics have to be posed, debated and understood in a context where – put bluntly – the majority of the world's population, including its over one billion Muslims, regard the intentions and policies of the West, particularly the US, with deep distrust. This historical fact must inform, even if it does not completely alter, the formulation of policy towards the non-West today, including those countries where terrorism is said to be an issue. At the root of this phenomenon of globalised rancour lies an issue that also lies at the heart of terrorism: respect, or lack of it, for the views and humanity of others.

Here, across the violent canvas of modernity, imperialism and terrorism have joined hands; forcing their policies and views onto those unable to protect themselves, and proclaiming their virtue in the name of some political goal or project that they alone have defined. Terrorism can only be defeated if this central arrogance – one as evident in the subjugation of Asia, the Middle East and Africa around a century ago as it is in the cruel and deliberate blowing up of civilians in night clubs, restaurants and shops today – is overcome. This all has very little to do with different religions, or cultures, even if the issues can be phrased in various ways and languages.

The central challenge facing the world, in the face of 9/11 and all the other terrorist acts preceding and following it, is to create a global order that defends security while making real the aspirations to equality and mutual respect that modernity has aroused and proclaimed but spectacularly failed so far to fulfil. Terrorism, then, is a world problem in cause and in impact. It should be addressed in a global cosmopolitan context. Europe will probably again be its victim, but it is also historically and morally a contributor to this abuse of political opposition and an architect of political violence.

All human beings, European or not, are locked into a conflict that will endure for decades, the outcome of which is not certain. In engaging with it, citizens need five things: a clear sense of history; recognition of the reality of the danger; steady, intelligent political leadership; the building of mass support within European and global society for resistance to this new and major threat; and above all, our best defence, a commitment to liberal and democratic values. W. B. Yeats wrote in 'The Second Coming' (1921):

Things fall apart; the centre cannot hold;
Mere anarchy is loosed upon the world,
The blood-dimmed tide is loosed, and everywhere
The ceremony of innocence is drowned;
The best lack all conviction, while the worst
Are full of passionate intensity.

We must and can still prove him wrong. The future – just – remains open.

2.   A COMMEMORATION IN ATOCHA STATION
16 March 2005

To fly from Belfast to Madrid is to move between worlds. On a pale March morning, the grey roofs of Northern Ireland's capital and the wounded, often still barricaded and slogan-covered walls of its centre strike a dull note; what a contrast, half a day later, with the red tiles of Castile and the sunny expanses of the domain of Don Quixote. Few these days might note that the two locations have a special affinity: of all Western European cities, in the entirety of the post-1945 era, it is Belfast and Madrid which have borne the greatest toll of terrorist attack.

As sites of violence, they are not alone. Munich had its 1972 Olympic massacre of Israeli sportsmen, London was the target of more than a few IRA explosions (some with devastating economic consequences), the Paris metro was bombed by Islamists in the 1980s, Bologna saw its railway station attacked by right-wing extremists in 1980. But the terrorist experience of Belfast and Madrid is exceptional in its durability and scale.

For over three decades from 1969 Belfast was the site of sectarian violence, bombings and assassinations that claimed almost half of the 3,400 lives lost during the period. The killings in 1972 and the bombing of a fish and chip shop in 1993 were just two incidents (killing nineteen civilians) in a desolating catalogue of lost lives. Nor are the troubles definitively over; a climate of fear and intimidation still reigns in parts of the city, as indicated by the Irish Republican Army (IRA)-linked Northern Bank robbery in December 2004 and the gruesome pub killing of Robert McCartney in January 2005.

Madrid was a persistent target of the Basque separatist group Euskadi Ta Askatasuna (ETA) in its own long campaign from 1968, in which assassinations like that of Spanish Prime Minister Admiral Luis Carrero Blanco in 1973 mixed with targeting of civilians and security forces during the 1980s. Most recently, the 11 March 2004 attacks – which claimed 191 lives and wounded over 2,000 people, and in more subtle, insidious ways shattered the lives of thousands more – represented the terrible irruption of Islamist terrorism (and, in a twisted echo of ETA, irredentism) onto Spanish soil. In the anniversary week, Madrid was the scene of an international summit on democracy, terrorism and security, organised by the Club de Madrid and attended by dozens of politicians, civil society groups and activists, scholars and writers from around the world. Its core purpose was to contribute to evolving a response to terrorism that links the issue of security to the preservation and promotion of democracy.

The need for such a link is rooted in the historical and political cycle that began in the 'two hours that shook the world' of 9/11 and continued with the planting of bombs on commuter trains in Madrid on '11-M'. In this sense, the high-level gathering in Madrid represents one of the most searching explorations of the ideas underlying policy on terrorism to have been undertaken in this new era. At the summit's climax, King Juan Carlos of Spain and United Nations Secretary-General Kofi Annan were joined by NATO and European Union leaders and over forty heads of state or government in presenting the Madrid Agenda: 'a global democratic response to the global threat of terrorism'.

From these days and nights of intense discussion, plenary sessions, working groups and informal exchanges, three lessons and four questions emerge. The first lesson is that any response to terrorism must be international, based on United Nations and international law, and guided by discussion and cooperation between states. Kofi Annan appealed in Madrid for a stronger UN regime on terrorism, building on the twelve anti-terrorist conventions already in place. The contrast with the American approach – nationalist in tone, unilateralist in practice and contemptuous of the UN and international law (not least the Geneva Conventions) – could not be clearer.

The theme of democracy is one that goes to the heart of the terrorist issue: the second lesson is that democracy alone will not abolish terrorism, as the cases of the IRA and ETA make all too clear, but it does provide a context in which the phenomenon can be contained and in which negotiation can eventually take place (perhaps after a very long, gruelling period). But more important is the message which Spain along with several Latin American countries exemplifies, that it is possible to make a transition to democracy, and to reduce the role of the armed forces and the intelligence services in society, even while a terrorist campaign continues. This is what, with some aberrations such as the secret paramilitary forces known as the Grupos Antiterroristas de Liberación (GAL), the socialist government of Spain did in the 1980s.

Third, a gathering like that of Madrid highlights the need for discussion, questioning and even some doubt about how best to address the current Islamist challenge. There are two important lessons to be learned in this respect from earlier experiences of terrorism, as in Ireland and the Basque Country: that these Islamist groups are in essence political groups with political aims and calculations; and that the struggle to isolate and wear them down will be long and costly. Al-Qa'ida or some variant or offshoot thereof will probably be with us for decades to come.

Beyond these lessons are new and complex issues involving the 'Greater West Asian' crisis, the integration of Muslim immigrants in Western society, and the appropriate combination of military and legal measures needed to counter the terrorist threat within a constitutional framework. No one has all the answers to such questions, but the very openness of the Madrid event was another stark contrast to the thumping certainties and simplifications of current Washington orthodoxy.

Madrid's exhaustive exploration of how anti-terrorist and human rights agendas might be brought into a common frame still leaves four large questions unresolved.

First, there is as yet no effective coordinated international response to terrorism. The Anglo-American axis treats the conference with contempt: the United States representative is its new attorney general, Alberto Gonzales, the man who as White House counsel recommended the abandonment of legal guidelines preventing the torture of prisoners of the US after 9/11; the British sent no one at all. The Europeans make a show of unity but it is known that the EU anti-terrorism office set up after the Madrid attacks hardly functions at all, that states do not collaborate and in fact keep their specialist information to themselves.

Second, the dominant trend in dealing with terrorism is not the liberal multilateralism of Madrid but US unilateralism. This approach fails on two counts: it ignores the political and cultural dimensions of relations with the Muslim world, and it misleadingly confuses quite separate issues – the overthrow of the Iraqi dictatorship and Iran's regional policies – with the matter of terrorism.

Third, for all Madrid's discussion of the causes of terrorism, it seems impossible for the global public realm to register an inescapable fact: that al-Qa'ida is a product not of timeless Muslim or Arab mentalities but of the Cold War. Unless and until this central historical fact is recognised, there will be no understanding of the nature of the challenge al-Qa'ida and its cohorts now pose.

Fourth, the political divisions created by 9/11 and 11-M are still unresolved. The former split much of Europe from the US and (even if Donald Rumsfeld's notorious dichotomy between 'old' and 'new' was highly simplistic) smashed the unity of the EU itself; the latter left Spain's polity bitterly polarised, ending the virtually bipartisan policy on issues of violence and state legitimacy that had lasted since the end of the Franco dictatorship.

The conference ends on the evening of 10 March. The king and the United Nations secretary-general have spoken. The heads of state and government have repeated themselves. Bromides are duly recorded. The next day dawns cold. We head to the Atocha railway station where, at 7.37 am – the time of the first of the four train explosions – a dozen live TV broadcasts are positioned above the tracks. The 600-plus church bells of Madrid toll. Later, Spain's people observe a five-minute silence. At a ceremony in the Retiro park in central Madrid, at which no speeches are made, the king plants the first of what will be 192 trees (including one to commemorate a bomb disposal expert killed during the search for suspects) in a 'forest of the absent'. In Atocha itself, the red *cercanías* (commuter trains) immortalised in the photographs of mangled metal of a year ago come and go, disgorging passengers on what remains for them a normal working day. In Spain those who catch the train to central stations at this time of the morning are not the middle-class commuters of London or New York, but the dishevelled, the cold, the immigrants – those who, as Spaniards say, *no tienen coche* (are without a car to drive to work).

The faces in the waiting room say it all: they are in social terms replicas of the faces of the dead. The fact that those who died on 11 March 2004 were Madrid's ordinary workers, including immigrants from sixteen countries, symbolises the long retreat from any universalist or emancipatory concept of international political action. Here, brutally and from below, is the reverse of the nationalism, the particularism and the global narcissism that Washington so arrogantly proclaims from above.

3.   A VISIT TO 'GROUND ZERO'
25 May 2006

No special sign or warnings greet the traveller who seeks to visit the site of the World Trade Centre Twin Towers, destroyed in the epochal minutes of 11 September 2001. New Yorkers suggest taking the subway to Chambers Street station in Manhattan and then walking a few blocks, and this is what I do. Nothing marks the approaches to the site except one lone street vendor, who turns out to be from Cameroon, selling Twin Tower key rings, New York Fire Department T-shirts and a photographic album of the events from which all human victims are removed. Turning the corner into Cortlandt Street you run up against a large empty space, surrounded by a wire fence. Within its sixteen acres little movement can be seen: in effect, a building site where, between now and 2009, a new Freedom Tower and other smaller buildings are to be erected. Around the site apparent normality prevails: a temporary Port Authority train station was rapidly rebuilt; the Church of St Paul, where George Washington used to pray when New York was the US capital and where the fire-fighters and victims took refuge and rest on the day, stands unperturbed; hotels, cafes and offices continue as normal. No souvenirs, no plaques, as yet no memorial.

This apparent calm also applies to New York as a whole. In the immediate aftermath of 9/11 there were fears that businesses and residents would leave the city. Within a year or so, however, trends that had been in train before 9/11 began to reassert themselves: crime continued to fall; tourists came in increasing numbers; Broadway theatre enjoyed a boom; it was even said that New Yorkers were more polite to each other, and took more time to express interest in their neighbours. The same reassuring corrective applies to the world economy, another potential target of the attack on New York: it has, however, continued to grow strongly and has apparently been totally immune to increased security and transport concerns. The US airline industry was hit by 9/11 but it was already ailing.

History has a way of reducing, even banalising, the places where major events occur. The Sarajevo street where the Serbian nationalist assassin Gavrilo Princip killed Archduke Franz Ferdinand in June 1914 and where Serbian nationalists once erected a museum and venerated a replica of the assassin's footsteps has had its name changed from Princip to Ovala Street and the museum removed. A small plaque remains. The Polish guard post on the Danzig peninsula of Westersee where Hitler launched the Second World War at dawn on 1 September 1939 has a small museum and preserves some of the ruined buildings. The traces of the Berlin Wall are almost gone from the streets of Berlin and Checkpoint Charlie is marked only by a small museum.

In the case of New York – in effect, the launch of the Third World War – the historical significance of the site and of the events themselves is still disputed. Those who dispute the impact of what happened point out that Islamist transnational violence kills fewer people than car accidents, or AIDS, or lung cancer; the incidence of major incidents in Western cities has been relatively low. But over four years on, another argument can be made: that 9/11 was indeed a turning point in modern international history, unleashing processes that have far from run their course. That this is not reflected in the site as it is now may be trivial. That it is not going to be represented in the memorial or mainstream US discussion of the events that are set to prevail in years to come is much more serious. For the distortion in the way 9/11 has been represented and in the reactions it has occasioned lies not in alarmist exaggeration of this event, but in the abject failure of politicians and other leaders of opinion in the USA to understand the causes and hence the consequences of the al-Qa'ida attack.

The reasons for saying that 9/11 has had a major long-term impact on the world can be briefly rehearsed. First, it produced a huge change in US public opinion: a strengthening of nationalism and assertive patriotism; a massive increase in the public's sense of insecurity; greater suspicion towards people 'of Middle Eastern appearance'; and more overt hostility towards Arabs and Muslims, recently confirmed in the large-scale and ill-informed protests about a Dubai-based company acquiring interests in US ports, including New York. The political and intellectual climate in the USA, already moving in that direction, has shifted decisively to the right.

This has facilitated the second major change: in US foreign policy. We know enough from the vast array of literature on the subject that the neo-conservative lobby, festering and fretting through their exile from power in the 1990s, were keen to promote a more aggressive foreign policy, in particular to confront and attack both Iraq and Iran. Bush's weak 2000 election victory and the undecided nature of US public opinion made that impossible to achieve initially; 9/11 changed that, giving a pretext and support for the invasions of Afghanistan and Iraq. Anyone who doubts the impact of the attacks need look no further than the civil, nationalist and international war now raging in Iraq, which could have enormous consequences for the Middle East as a whole.

Third, 9/11 has produced a major shift in US relations with the rest of the world, be this in Europe or the Middle East: there is less support or sympathy for the US now than at any time since the Vietnam war era, even as those opposed to US power, from China, Iran and Russia to the new populist presidents of Latin America, take advance of Washington's distraction with Mesopotamia.

It is all the more grave, therefore, that the nature of these changes and the reasons for the 9/11 attack in the first place should be so little recognised at the place of their initial explosion: Ground Zero. What has happened here instead is a massive and successful denial of the international dimensions of this event, in the name of a simplistic and factional patriotism that is designed to prevent serious discussion of it. The rebuilding plans for the site have themselves been the subject of controversy: the New York Port Authority, the public body which owns the site, has been in conflict with the developer Larry Silverstein, who owns the commercial rental rights to the site.

Inevitably, money has prevailed over social and urban requirements. In order to receive the appropriate insurance payment, Silverstein, who is not a major New York developer, has pledged to reconstruct 16,000 feet of office space, even though there is already a glut of such space in Lower Manhattan: the whole World Trade Centre itself was a political showpiece, conceived by the then governor Nelson Rockefeller as a way of trying to rejuvenate that part of the island, and its construction involved the elimination of the Old Washington Market that had long been held in that area. Prior to 9/11 the World Trade Centre relied on large-scale leasing to public-sector bodies to remain occupied, and the same will probably occur again. Indeed, the involvement of official bodies in the Memorial Foundation set up to raise the $500 million needed to pay for it has meant that public subscription has been low, and that no significant contributions have been made in the past three months.

An immediate casualty has been the original design for the rebuilt tower by David Libeskind, who also built the Berlin Jewish Museum. But of more long-term political import have been two disputes about the nature of the memorial and of the museum that will be constructed on the site. The memorial was to list the names of all who died, i.e. office workers and fire-fighters, now reckoned at a more conservative total of somewhat over 2,000. But the New York Fire Department, which has made a great play of the heroic nature of its members on that day, with the implication that their members were greater figures than the passive office workers of the two towers, wanted to have the names of their members indicated by a special sign on the memorial. The families of the other victims have objected to that. The dispute over the contents of the museum has been even more serious. The original group set up to design the museum, and to meet the requirement that it relate to issues of human freedom, sought to include in it mention of other related questions of liberty and rights, such as the Civil Rights Movement, the Gulag and Abu Ghraib prison. This provoked an outburst from one of the family members involved, Debra Burlingame, sister of the pilot whose plane crashed into the Pentagon. In the name of her 'Take Back the Memorial' group, she denounced the 'un-American' character of the plans and was quickly supported by New York politicians in this claim.

Yet these are small questions compared to the much larger and wholly suppressed one of why it was that the al-Qa'ida squad attacked in the first place: the role of the USA in using and training such fundamentalists in the latter stages of the Cold War, the reasons for Middle Eastern hostility to US policy in the Middle East, the sources of anti-American sentiment the world over. Here, militaristic and nationalist bluster have prevailed totally.

It has become possible for the US public to face the events of that day in fictional form, as the recently released film *United 93*, about the plane that crashed in Pennsylvania, and a number of novels on the subject make clear. But recognition stops there: the denial and myopia found at Ground Zero are indeed part of a much wider failure of the

USA, its leaders and opinion-makers, to comprehend what hit them on that September day. Much of the discussion in Washington has centred on whether the CIA or FBI could and should have foreseen this event: but, as the final report of the National Commission on Terrorist Attacks showed, this investigation was misconceived from the start, treating 9/11 as a criminal event, looking for 'masterminds' and criminal networks, and completely ignoring the political causes and context of the attack.

Bush's purely military response to this phenomenon has compounded this initial failure of analysis. The distortion of the US response to 9/11 lies not, therefore, in some exaggeration of what occurred in Lower Manhattan that September morning, but in the failure to address and respond to the USA's role in helping to animate Islamist violence in the first place, and the political issues within the Middle East that fuelled, and after Iraq will continue to fuel, hostility to its politics and people across much of the world.

We can be sure that very little, if any, of this no doubt 'un-American' information will be vouchsafed to visitors to the World Trade Centre memorial and museum in the years to come. The result is that New Yorkers, and Americans in general, will never learn the reality of what smashed into them that September morning, let alone how and why their government has, if anything, made things worse in the ensuing years.

4. TWO DAYS WITH HIZBULLAH
20 July 2006

I had been in Beirut for two days in spring 2004 when I received an unexpected call from the international department of Hizbullah. Sheikh Naim Qassem, the deputy head of the party and its apparent political strategist, wished to see me to talk about the 'clash of civilisations'. He had read something I had written on the subject, a review of Samuel Huntington's book *The Clash of Civilisations and the Remaking of World Order* (Simon & Schuster, 1997), and wanted to discuss the matter further, in connection with a book on Hizbullah that he himself had written and was about to publish. Indeed, it was suggested, I might like to write the introduction to the English edition which was to be published in a few months' time (*Hizbullah: the Story from Within*, Saqi Books, 2005).

This was not exactly what I had intended for my days in the Lebanese capital. I had come to Beirut to lecture at the American University of Beirut (AUB) on the Yemeni revolutions of the 1960s and 1970s; but for all the enlivening tapes I played of revolutionary songs about peasant uprisings and the need to arm women, the topic seemed as remote to the students there as the wars of ancient Sumer. I also wanted to visit the Lebanese chapter of my publishers, Dar al Saqi. The company had issued several Arabic versions of books first published in English by its London counterparts, Saqi Books. Dar al Saqi's hospitality extended to sending a driver to buy me CDs of the latest Lebanese pop songs.

It was the first time I had been in Beirut since early 1971, a gap of more than thirty years that had encompassed the civil war of 1975–90. Lebanon may, before and even during the civil war, have been one of the most accessible of the twenty-five countries of the Middle East, yet it was not among those I worked on. Many other journalists and academics knew it well, whereas my own interests and priorities in those years lay elsewhere: principally Iran, Afghanistan, the Gulf states and Yemen.

My relations with the country and its Left intelligentsia were also complicated by the fact that my closest Arab friend, the Lebanese writer Fawwaz Trabulsi, with whom I had visited the guerrilla regions of Oman in 1970 and spent many a long evening of discussion with in London, refused to talk to me after we had differed on the Iraqi invasion of Kuwait in 1990. The only conversation I ever had with Fawwaz on the matter, a telephone exchange on 2 August 1990, the very night of the invasion, when I was in the home of the anti-Ba'athist writers Peter and Marion Sluglett, was to be our last-ever exchange – despite the efforts of several friends, American, British and Arab, to reconnect us. Much the same had happened with the prominent Arab intellectual and frequent visitor to Beirut, Edward Said. Evidently my own view of the world diverged somewhat from that of my Lebanese and Palestinian associates. It was not a place where I felt I would receive a warm welcome.

Even fourteen years after the civil war had ended, Beirut in spring 2004 was not in general an easy city, despite the beauties of its streets and waterfront, the delicacy of its food and the animating sensuality of its music. Every time a car with large men in leather jackets and large moustaches screeched to a halt near the cafe where I sat, I thought they had come for me (it was the season of kidnapping foreigners in Iraq). It remained too, as it would for months to come, a city under foreign occupation: the Syrians were encamped nearby and their tentacles were in every part, political and economic, of Lebanese life.

I decided this was not the place to spend the sabbatical year I was then approaching, and went instead to Barcelona, a city whose time of destruction, political murder and (for many Catalans) foreign occupation had passed some decades ago. Yet I had no inkling, as I passed the ornate residence of former premier Rafiq Hariri in the Hamra district of Beirut, that in February 2005 he would be spectacularly murdered, in what in Spanish is termed a *magnicidio*, an act with regional repercussions that continue to this day.

My sense of reluctance about revisiting the city was owed not only to the terrible carnage it had witnessed, but to memories of the number of friends and acquaintances who had lost their lives there: Abdul Wahhab al-Kayyali, a Palestinian academic with whom I had studied in London in the late 1960s, had used the newly-opened British archives on Palestine to write a thesis on the 1936 Palestinian revolt, then returned to the region and tried to set up his own guerrilla group only to be murdered, probably by the Syrians; Ghassan Kanafani, the Palestinian novelist and spokesmen for the Popular Front for the Liberation of Palestine (whom I had interviewed at length for the *New Left Review*), who was killed by an Israeli car-bomb; Salim al-Lawzi, the Lebanese journalist who had moved his weekly *al-Hawadith* to London when the war began, returned for his mother's funeral and was captured by the Syrians, who smashed his writing hand before they killed him; Nasser Said, the head of the Saudi left-wing nationalist party, with whom I had lunched on the sunlit Beirut Corniche, was kidnapped by Yasser Arafat's security forces in 1979, handed over to the Saudis and never seen again; Malcolm Kerr, the American academic and author of some of the best books on inter-Arab politics, killed in his office at the American University of Beirut (AUB) in 1983; Leigh Douglas, one of the few fellow British academics who had worked on modern Yemen, killed by supporters or agents of Libya as he left a nightclub in April 1986 a few days after the United States bombing of Tripoli (for which Muammar al-Gaddafi blamed Margaret Thatcher as well as the Americans). All these, and in addition the lengthy but miraculously ended ordeal of my good friend the journalist Charles Glass, who managed to escape from his imprisonment by Shi'a militia in Beirut's southern suburbs.

The trip with a Hizbullah driver to the Shi'a heartland of Haret Hriek in southern Beirut was in one sense familiar, given prolific television footage of the war and of the kidnap locations of Western hostages in that district. The first impression was paradoxical: huge posters of bearded Lebanese and Iranian radical clerics rose by the roadside, beneath which many of the young women who passed by wore no headscarves. At the Hizbullah headquarters – one of the buildings destroyed by Israeli planes in the bombing of July 2006 – I was ushered through various security checks into the office of Sheikh ('clergyman' in the Lebanese context) Naim Qassem, who sat in a leather armchair under portraits of Iranian spiritual leaders Ayatollah Khomeini and his successor Ayatollah Ali Khamenei.

Sheikh Qassem and his associates were in confident mood: the party had just won considerable success in the Lebanese local elections, and international attention was focused on the fresh revelations about torture and abuse by American forces in Iraq at Abu Ghraib prison. Hizbullah's decision in 1992 to participate in national political life meant that the group now had seats in the Lebanese parliament; it was about to commit itself to accepting ministerial seats in the Lebanese cabinet. This growing presence in Lebanese politics had led to increased international recognition: Hizbullah, through Sheikh Qassem and the international department of the party, had for some time been meeting European diplomats based in Beirut, and the European Union was trying to persuade the US to do the same.

Born in 1953, Sheikh Qassem acquired degrees in religious studies and chemistry; he taught the latter subject for many years. In 1991 he became deputy secretary-general of Hizbullah under its leader, Sheikh Hassan Nasrallah. Both men had studied in Iran; like many Hizbullah personnel I met, Sheikh Qassem spoke good Persian and was happy to converse in the language. Indeed, he made a point of stressing the close relationship which Hizbullah had with the Islamic Republic; these were evident enough in the two portraits hanging above him, but are also embodied in the centuries-old ties between centres of Shi'a teaching and religious training in Lebanon and Iran. The dramatic political events of the late 1970s and early 1980s – including the Iranian revolution and the Israeli invasions of Lebanon – had both created the environment in which Hizbullah emerged and nurtured a relationship that had deep cultural and religious as well as political roots.

My discussion with Sheikh Naim Qassem was in some ways different from many other interviews I had conducted with Middle Eastern political figures over the years. The sheikh remained calm and succinct throughout the conversation, and avoided long historical excursions of the kind most radical politicians in this region (as elsewhere) regularly indulge in. The British were not blamed for too much. We began by discussing the history of Hizbullah. In the interview and at much greater length in his book, Sheikh Naim Qassem described the situation in the late 1970s and early 1980s: on the one hand, the 'disappearance' and apparent murder of then Shi'a leader Imam Musa Sadr while on a visit to Libya, presumably because he had objected to the Libyan attempt to hegemonise the Shi'a community in Lebanon.

With the first Israeli military intervention in 1978 and then the triumph of the Islamic revolution in Iran in early 1979, a number of radical Shi'a groups were formed, with the aim of promoting the place of the Shi'a in Lebanon, a country where they had been the least favoured religious group – despised by Christians and Sunni Muslims, but abused also by the Palestinians, who tried to take over southern Lebanon in the 1970s, creating their own 'Fatahland' near the Israeli frontier. At the same time, these radicals were inspired by the Iranian revolution's call for an 'Islamic government' along the lines propounded by Khomeini, and sought initially to replicate this in Lebanon. By the early 1980s, and with the large-scale Israeli invasion of 1982, Hizbullah was fully formed as a coherent military and political group, aiming above all to drive the invaders out of their country and in so doing to lend support to their goal of representing the Shi'a community and promoting an Islamic government in Lebanon.

Hizbullah played the leading role in fighting Israeli forces and those of their Lebanese Christian allies, the South Lebanese Army, based along the frontier in the south. The final Israeli pull-out in May 2000 came as as much of a surprise to Hizbullah as to anyone else, but was widely perceived in Lebanon and the Arab world as a whole as the group's (and Iran's) victory: within days of the Israeli pull-out, the Iranian foreign minister Ali Akbar Velayati embarked on a triumphal tour of southern Lebanon.

On the matter of political relations with Iran, the sheikh was absolutely clear. Hizbullah regards the Iranian spiritual leader, in this case Khamenei, as its ultimate authority; all major political decisions regarding Hizbullah are referred to – when not actually taken in – Iran. He gave the example of the decision taken in 1992 to enter Lebanese national politics: Hizbullah set up a commission, which prepared a report, with various options; this report was sent to Iran; it was Ayatollah Khamenei himself who took the final decision, in favour of participation.

The sheikh obviously believed in the political role of the clergy; there was no trace in his rhetoric of the fine old Arabic radical term *kahnutia* (clericalism), so often denounced in the speeches of the Yemeni revolution. Sheikh Qassem did not, however, wish to imitate the Iranian Islamic model in Lebanon too closely. Hizbullah itself accepted that Lebanon was a multi-confessional society and that what was appropriate for Iran was not suitable for Lebanon. Qassem had indeed developed relations with leaders of the Maronite Christian community in the country and saw the future as one in which each party and group sought to preserve this pluralistic model. This was all the more rational in that for a Shi'a group like Hizbullah, the most immediate enemies within its own society were not Christians but radical Sunnis of the kind inspired by Saudi Arabia, for whom Shi'a are apostates and polytheists who (as in Iraq, Pakistan and formerly in Afghanistan) can be attacked and killed without compunction. Hence Hizbullah's hostility to Osama bin Laden and al-Qa'ida, including their adoption of the theory of the 'clash of civilisations'.

This tone of tolerance and flexibility did not, however, extend to the discussion of Israel or of Jews in general. The military struggle of Hizbullah against Israel was officially confined to their expulsion from Lebanon and was incomplete only because of Israel's continued occupation of a small part of southern Lebanon, the Shebaa Farms, near the Syrian frontier. Sheikh Qassem, and military commanders of Hizbullah I later met, confirmed that they were helping Hamas and Islamic Jihad inside Israel and Palestine; but they appeared to want to limit their own (at that time sporadic) armed activities to the Shebaa issue. However, there was no margin of doubt in the sheikh's view that Israel was an illegitimate state and that it should be abolished. This position was bolstered, as evident in his book, by the deployment of quotes from the Qur'an denouncing Jews and calling for a struggle against them. I put it to the sheikh that this use of the Islamic tradition in a context of modern political conflict was racist, a point he evidently did not accept.

An alternative, open and respectful attitude to Jews can also be derived from other parts of the Islamic tradition, but this, like the racist reading, depends on contemporary political choice.

The discussion with Sheikh Qassem concluded, and I made it clear that my lack of credibility in the study of Lebanon meant it was probably not appropriate for me to write the introduction to his book. I was then ushered by Ibrahim Moussawi, the head of the Hizbullah international department, to nearby al-Manar TV studios (another building targeted by recent Israeli attacks, though the attempt to stop the station from broadcasting has not been successful). There I took part in a one-hour discussion of the Abu Ghraib tortures, centred on the interesting question of why it was that members of the United States armed forces were torturing Iraqis in this way. Against the view of the other discussants that this treatment reflected particular hostility to Muslims, I argued that it reflected a more general contempt among armed forces in the West for people of colour, and indeed for any subaltern or subjugated people (in Vietnam as much as in Iraq).

The next day I was taken on an intense field-trip by one of the Hizbullah military commanders to the key installations and battle sites of the Lebanese South. Beyond a certain stage, there was no sign of the Lebanese army or police, only Hizbullah roadblocks with the yellow flag of the organisation fluttering above. The Hizbullah flag was also much in evidence at Chateau Beaufort, the crusader castle long occupied by the Israelis, as it was at Khiam, the abandoned prison used by the South Lebanese Army to detain Lebanese and Palestinian prisoners in terrible conditions. Khiam was abandoned in Israel's final departure in May 2000, with several thousand SLA taking refuge with their families in Israel.

Amid all these sites of killing and heroism, and the massed heaps of detonated Israeli military fortifications that dot the South, there was at first sight an air of near-normality, even optimism: in Marjayoun, the Christian district from which many SLA had come, shops and hairdressers were open and people strolled easily in the streets; some of the Hizbullah people were building homes near the frontier. We lunched in an outdoor country cafe by a river, within a short distance of the Israeli lines. 'They will never dare to return here,' was the refrain of my militant guide. Towards the end of the day, my guides took me to a hill overlooking the Israeli frontier, and the town of Metulla. There, I sensed that another perspective and another future were equally contained within these seemingly peaceful hills.

From one roadside vantage-point, they had pointed to the still unresolved Shebaa area to the south-east. As we looked over to this Israeli town, with people clearly visible walking in the streets, the chief guide turned to me with an unambiguous message: 'It took us twenty-two years to drive them out of here [Lebanon], and it may take us up to forty years to drive them out of there [occupied Palestine].'

I decided long ago, in dealing with revolutionaries and with their enemies in the Middle East and elsewhere, to question their motives and sense of reality, but to take seriously what they stated to be their true intentions. Those words, spoken on the hill overlooking Metulla in 2004, were sincerely meant, and carried within them a long history of fighting, sacrifice and killing. In light of recent events, it would be prudent to assume that much more is to come.

5. REASON AMID ROCKETS:
MORAL JUDGEMENT IN TIME OF WAR
10 August 2006

The cycles of memory work in unexpected ways. The current war involving Israel, the Hizbullah movement and Lebanon provokes a recollection of the first time I came face to face with the Arab–Israeli dispute. It was in October 1964 at a debate in the Oxford Union, only days after that momentous 15–16 October on which Nikita Khrushchev fell in Moscow, the Chinese exploded their first atom bomb, in Xinjiang, and (more parochially) the Labour Party won the British general election, ending thirteen years of Conservative rule.

It takes an effort of imagination to recall now how different then was the balance of public attention and sympathy between Israel and the Palestinians compared to today. Israel enjoyed enormous authority – not so much as a close ally of the West, which at that time it was not (the alliance with the United States took shape only after 1967) but as the site of an experiment in socialist economics and living which the kibbutz system epitomised. By contrast, nearly everyone in the West who thought about the matter, on left or right, regarded the Palestinian

issue as being one of 'the refugees' and the obstacles to their resettlement – as if they were a late, post-Second World War residue of the
millions of 'displaced persons' whom the great European conflict had
shunted across frontiers.

The Palestinian guerrilla movement emerged only with the formation of the Palestine Liberation Organisation (PLO) in Cairo in January
1964. It was initially under the control of the Arab states, and of Egypt
in particular; its first armed action – an attack on a power station near
Galilee – occurred in January 1965. Any sympathy for such 'Arab' causes
on the Left at that time focused more on the experiment in 'Arab socialism' under Gamal Abdel Nasser in Egypt and on the experiences of
workers' control and peasant cooperatives that had arisen out of the
Algerian revolutionary war of 1954–62; perhaps also, a few were dimly
aware and supportive of the remote but reputedly resolute imamate of
Oman (which had, in fact, ceased to exist).

All of this was to change after the Six-Day War of June 1967, with
the emergence of the Palestinian resistance movement in the West Bank
and in Jordan, and the gradual loss of sympathy for Israel across much of
the world. This latter process did not take place overnight: Cuba, for example, maintained relations with, and admiration for, Israel until after
the war of 1973.

The Oxford debate of October 1964 thus took place before the enormous shifts of sentiment and solidarity, evident today in relation to
Lebanon and the Hizbullah movement, towards Arab causes and away
from Israel. I was then a student in my first weeks at university, with
the general interest in Third World struggles characteristic of that time,
but with no knowledge of this particular question. I sat in the balcony
and watched the two main speakers make their respective cases: on the
Israeli side, the urbane silver-haired Labour MP (and part-time novelist)
Maurice Edelman; on the Arab side, the Lebanese writer and longstand-
ing pro-Palestinian campaigner Edward Attiyah.

The debate was conducted along already (and still) familiar lines: on
one side, evocation of the genocide of Jews in Europe under Nazism (the
term 'holocaust' came into general use only later), the Arab refusal to
accept the 1947 United Nations partition plan, and the Arab responsibility for the flight of the Palestinian population in the war of 1947–9;
on the other, the violence of the Zionist acquisition and conquest of
Arab land, the betrayal by Britain of its many promises to the Arabs up

to its unilateral backdoor scuttle from Palestine in May 1948, and the hypocrisy and passivity of the international community thereafter.

As it continued, however, the atmosphere became more disputatious. Edward Attiyah's speech was interrupted by the shouts, way beyond normal heckling, of a group of young supporters of Israel who rose to their feet in unison, seeking to silence the speaker by accusing him of being a Nazi and raising their arms in mock-Hitler salute. This must have been hard to take for the author of the elegiac autobiography of a Lebanese upbringing, *Having Been an Arab*, who (in common with other modern Arab intellectuals such as George Antonius, Albert Hourani, Hanan Ashrawi and Edward Said) was brought up as a Protestant, and in his case had identified England as his spiritual home. I was never to find out. Attiyah battled on, his voice rising intermittently above the din, before a sudden pause. A throttled sound came from his throat, and he fell to the floor, victim of a heart attack. He was dead. I shall never forget the sound of his body hitting the Union's wooden floor.

The next few years were (in another phrase not yet current) a steep learning curve for a young student. A watershed moment in the redrawing of intellectual and political battle lines was June 1967, when Israel conquered all of mandate Palestine in a lightning war. In its wake, the strategic relationship between Israel and the United States began to be forged, and an international left-wing movement of solidarity with the Palestinian people grew. The Six-Day War precipitated a new phase of political alignment and argument in and about the Middle East. In their essentials, the controversies, issues and even the language of the thirty-nine years that have followed have remained constant. This indeed is confirmed by the familiarity of so much of the mass of material published and broadcast since the outbreak of the Hizbullah–Israeli conflict on 12 July 2006 that is now consuming Lebanon.

Hence, at least for those of my generation formed in the 1960s, the arguments of those times remain often bitterly relevant. Amid the unconscionable violence, targeting of civilians, and appeals to unreason and ethnic identification that such modern wars entail, it is all the more necessary to retrieve the example of those who sought to defend core values that crossed boundaries of prejudice and narrow partisanship. I have already honoured one of those in this collection: the great French scholar of the Muslim world, Maxime Rodinson (see 'Maxime

Rodinson: In Praise of a "Marginal Man"'). Two more such figures were formative in articulating an internationalist position – one (Isaac Deutscher) within a Marxist framework, the other (Hannah Arendt) within a broadly liberal perspective.

Isaac Deutscher, the son of a rabbi in Poland and a committed socialist political activist there in the late 1930s, survived Nazism and Stalinism to write path-breaking biographies of Joseph Stalin and Leon Trotsky. Soon after the 1967 war, Deutscher gave an interview to three editors of the London-based Marxist intellectual journal *New Left Review*: Tom Wengraf, Peter Wollen and Alexander Cockburn. In it, Deutscher struck a note that has diminished to near-invisibility in more recent debates, where claims of identity prevail over universal principle, where identification with one side or the other predominates, and where the atrocities and callous political blunders of each combatant readily find their intellectual defenders.

Deutscher's approach rested on three clear and courageous premises: that both leaderships, Arab and Israeli, were guilty of demagogy and misleading their own people, above all by promising a victory that was unattainable and by stoking hatred of other peoples and religions; that the antecedent histories of both peoples (genocide in Europe for the Jews, and denial of national rights for the Palestinians) could not be deployed to legitimate the maximal current claims of either side; and that   a principle Deutscher resolutely adhered to – the Israelis and Palestinians were peoples with legitimate claims, which should be recognised on a sensible, and lasting, territorial and political basis. He built on these premises an argument – couched in tones of anti-clerical, universalist disdain, something all too lacking in these days of grovelling before 'identity', 'tradition' and 'faith communities' – that was clear in its rejection of the invocation of the sacred, the God-given, in political debate. Deutscher rejected Talmudic obscurantism and bloodthirsty Arab calls for vengeance alike.

The work of the German philosopher Hannah Arendt (who had found refuge in the United States by the time the Second World War broke out) was not directly related to the Arab–Israeli question, but her liberal internationalist outlook does have immense relevance to it. This is especially true of *Eichmann in Jerusalem*, her 1963 book on the trial of the Nazi war criminal Adolf Eichmann. This is best known for its controversial phrase, born of watching this shifty and apparently normal

man in the glass dock, 'the banality of evil'. The controversy it has generated is something of a distraction, as the vast literature on killing in
other dictatorships and massacres across the world suggests: the archi-
tects of Stalin's gulag or the Serb massacres in Bosnia were no less banal.

Much more controversial (and neglected) is Arendt's critique of the
legal and moral case made by the Israeli prosecutors against Eichmann.
For, whereas the Nuremberg trials of the Nazi war criminals had been
conducted under what at least purported to be some form of international law – the precursor of later codes of universal jurisdiction,
crimes against humanity and the International Criminal Court – Adolf
Eichmann was prosecuted for the taking of Jewish lives in a Jewish court.

A case that in 1946 had been (if weak in some points of principle)
confident in its universalist aspirations had by the early 1960s been
converted into something derived from the ethnicity of the victims.
And this ethnicisation of the victims was, at the same time, deemed to
convey a particular right, if not responsibility, to the state that lay claim
to representing those victims, namely Israel. This was what Hannah
Arendt identified.

What Isaac Deutscher and Hannah Arendt noted contains truths
that the contemporary Middle East, and the world, sorely need. Their
relevance is to much more than the Arab–Israeli question; it applies
in principle to any of the numerous other national or inter-ethnic conflicts across the world where local rhetoric and partisan solidarity from
outsiders have reinforced each other in a dance of death, as if one side
were angels and the other devils – Cyprus, ex-Yugoslavia, Nagorno-
Karabakh, Sri Lanka, Northern Ireland. In regard to the Middle East,
Muslims and Arabs across the world identify with the Palestinians (and
more recently, Hizbullah) on ethnic, religious and communitarian lines;
Jews do the same, in support of Israel. Even many of those Jews who
oppose the policies of the state of Israel speak as Jews ('not in my name').

There is an enormous historical regression involved here. It involves
seeing membership of a particular community, or claims of affinity,
ethnicity or religious association with others, as conveying particular
rights (or particular moral clarity) on those making such claims. In purely
rational terms, this is nonsense: the crimes of the Israelis in wantonly
destroying Lebanon's infrastructure and the crimes of Hizbullah and
Hamas in killing civilians and placing the lives and security of their
peoples recklessly at risk do not require particularist denunciation.

They are crimes on the basis of universal principles – of law, decency, humanity – and should be identified as such.

(In this regard, ethnic and religious diasporas are among the last people who can offer rational explanation or moral compass in regard to such events. Recently, when interviewed by a BBC panel set up to consider accusations of bias in regard to the Arab–Israeli dispute, I was given a list of the British-based groups the panel had consulted – Muslim and Arab on one side, Jewish and Zionist on the other. My recommendation to the panel was to ignore completely what any of them said and to question whether they should have any standing in the matter.)

In such times, the moral clarity of Isaac Deutscher and Hannah Arendt is essential, even where subsequent history and philosophical debate have moved arguments on. Any hope, for example, that a solution to inter-ethnic conflict could be found on the basis of proletarian solidarity must be dispelled as ineffectual at best, dangerous at worst: proletarian solidarity did not save the Jews of Europe in the 1940s and has not reconciled Arabs and Jews thereafter. Equally, a condemnation of the actions of militarised states and guerrilla groups must be based on more than a rejection of their demagogy and chauvinism; it requires a quality that has been long neglected (including by the Left, as is evident in much discussion of the war in Iraq), namely respect for the laws and norms of war, as in the Geneva Conventions (1949), the Additional Protocols (1977) and related documents. Across the world there are movements of solidarity – including with Hamas, Hizbullah or the Iraqi resistance – that, while invoking universal principles of war against Israel, fail completely to apply the same principles to the behaviour of the guerrillas and other groups, even though many have committed terrible acts of barbarism, murder, intimidation of civilians and fostering of inter-communal hatred.

This is vividly apparent in the way that esteemed voices of the British Left, high on anti-imperialist rectitude, revel in the slaughter of civilian United Nations officials in Iraq (in the bomb of 19 August 2003 which killed Sergio Vieira de Mello and twenty-one others, including the human rights scholar and openDemocracy columnist, Arthur Helton); while they and others finesse or condone the killing of civilians in Israel, and the wanton sacrificing of the security of the whole population of Lebanon in the name of a self-proclaimed 'national resistance'. Much of this rhetoric comes from groups in Palestine and Lebanon that for years sought to destroy the one real chance for coexistence and peace between Israelis and Palestinians, namely the 1993 Oslo accords. In opposing the accords and then trampling them into the ground, they were at all times vigorously supported by fellow intellectual acolytes in the West who are relentless in a rhetorical 'solidarity' which does so much disservice to those it ostensibly champions.

Isaac Deutscher and Hannah Arendt were intellectuals of their time, whose ideas were forged in the war against fascism and the critique of Western and Soviet narratives of the Cold War. Their inheritors may be found today in the work of the best non-governmental organisations as much as among their intellectual inheritors: among them, human rights organisations such as Amnesty International and Human Rights Watch that resolutely, with as much accuracy as war and propaganda allow, document and condemn the crimes and violations of all sides.

The sustained independence of mind and clarity of principle of figures such as Deutscher and Arendt should guide judgement and commentary on the latest war in the Middle East. The alternative is more missed opportunities for peace, and more debates (like that I witnessed in October 1964) where vitriol and the refusal to listen replace the deliberation, understanding and reason that the public sphere, global as well as national, desperately needs.

6. THE ATTORNEY GENERAL COMES TO TOWN
27 March 2006

Alberto Gonzales, the attorney general of the United States, is all that the modern state would wish to have as its representative: detached in the fulfilment of his bureaucratic obligations; obedient to, if not obsequious towards, his boss; wordy and word-twisting in matters of legal definition; stonewalling on matters of substance; and, above all, distinctly cold in matters of human concern.

When he took the stage at the International Institute for Strategic Studies in London on 7 March 2006 to speak on anti-terrorism policy and the need for international cooperation, Gonzales – the highest legal authority in the executive branch of the world's leading democracy – did not immediately command attention. Yet the attorney general, a former

White House counsel, is the man who presided over (and to a considerable degree served to authorise) a range of contentious US detention policies: from Guantanamo to Abu Ghraib, from 'rendition' to 'stress positions'. Gonzales was evasive on matters of substance, jocular in response to questions touching on matters of human suffering. Asked if he thought that setting dogs on naked prisoners was a form of torture, he said he did not give opinions on individual detention practices. When it suited him, he shifted responsibility – and hence blame – from the Department of Justice to the Department of Defense. Above all, he was apparently oblivious and indifferent to the consternation, rage and concern which recent US policies – enacted following the 11 September 2001 attacks in New York and Washington – have occasioned.

There is nearly always something slightly chilling when groups of mid-Atlantic government officials, arrayed in phalanxes of grey suits, get together to discuss their security concerns. But never, in more than thirty years of observing such occasions, have I seen such an appalling, collusive, complacent and – in its own understated way – evil performance as this. That the US – its officials and citizens – has been, and will continue to be for a long time, the object of violent attacks, at home and abroad, is not in question. Nor is the right and responsibility of any state to protect itself as it can, including by taking anticipatory measures abroad. The issue, and what has become a matter of worldwide alarm and criticism, is the flouting of international law, the laws and norms of combat and international opinion, as well as the disdain in which the George W. Bush administration, from the president downwards, continues to hold international law and the institutions in which it is embodied. In this regard, Gonzales's performance on a sunny morning in London was true to form.

On matters of US policy, Gonzales argues for increased international cooperation while acknowledging differences on matters of 'rendition' (secret kidnapping and deportation to third countries of terror suspects) and on 'treatment of foreign fighters' (such as denial of prisoner-of-war status to captured opponents). He makes no apology for the use of the term 'War on Terror'. We are at war, he argues, and are using the methods of war. The enemies of the US have attacked embassies, blown up ships, attacked civilian offices and tourist centres as well as the American financial and administrative capitals. Sixty-seven United Kingdom citizens died in the attack on the World Trade Centre in New York, he reminded his British audience. At the same time, he praised the UK for increased cooperation on 'data exchange', including DNA material and fingerprints, and listed a number of incidents in 2003–4 when such exchanges of information between officials of the two countries had thwarted attacks and saved lives.

Department of Justice officials are now attached to the US embassy in London, and British police officials to the country's embassy in Washington. Resorting, in what must be the most tired of transatlantic tropes, to a quote from Winston Churchill, Gonzales made an appeal 'to all freedom-loving peoples'. His qualities as an apologist were evident in his response to questions. When asked by a senior British military historian what the West could do to reverse the alienation of moderate Islamic opinion across the world, as a result of revelations about Guantanamo and Abu Ghraib, the attorney general had nothing of substance to say. Asked by the representative of the BBC whether the interrogation practice of 'waterboarding' – in which water is poured onto a prone prisoner's covered face, making the captive feel that he or she is about to drown – should be permitted, Gonzales made a joke.

In response to questions about torture, he quoted from a Congressional definition, according to which torture involved the infliction of 'severe mental or physical suffering'. It had not been US government practice to allow torture, he said: US legal standards were being upheld, while cases of reported abuse were investigated. Asked by the CNN correspondent about Council of Europe and Amnesty International documentation and criticism of the rendition programme, Gonzales saw no reason for second thoughts, and reminded his audience that unpublicised flights by US military planes had been authorised by European states for decades. When would the US close the centre at Guantanamo? All detention policies were under constant review, he said, but the US had the right to hold detainees 'for the duration of hostilities'. That claim is even more ominous than it may first appear: current US military doctrine talks of a 'long war', implying the conflict may last for decades.

Alberto Gonzales's performance was also remarkable for what he did not say. The title of his London talk included a reference to international cooperation, but this appeared to be very much a one-way street: not only did he make no mention of the most obvious existing international bodies for dealing with cases of transnational criminal behaviour, the United Nations tribunal in The Hague and the new International

Criminal Court – the second of which the US flatly opposes – but at no point did he make even the most cursory reference to international law. While vaunting the US campaign against terrorism, he saw no need to acknowledge that many other countries – in Europe and in Latin America – had longer experience of reconciling democracy with anti-terrorism than had the US, or that huge effort had gone into trying to get a common policy on terrorism formulated within the United Nations.

Of equal importance – and in striking testimony to the blinkered when not catatonic nature of current US government thinking – no one mentioned the role played by the British–American presence in Iraq in generating hostility to West. Whether or not the US and European countries share values on matters of detention and interrogation, Washington's policies have put all of its allies and friends, from the militarily engaged British and Poles to the cartoonists of provincial Denmark, on the same frontline.

The most striking response to the insouciance of Gonzales had come a day before he spoke, with the publication on 6 March of an Amnesty International report on the treatment of prisoners in Iraq (what is now, in an odious euphemism, routinely referred to as 'prisoner abuse', but which is, in many cases and by any normal standards, torture). The Amnesty report, *Beyond Abu Ghraib: Detention and Torture in Iraq*, showed how the mistreatment, beating, humiliation and prolonged and illegal detention of Iraqis was taking place not only in the notorious Baghdad prison, but in even larger numbers in the British-administered Camp Bucca in Basra and in another centre in the northern city of Sulaimaniya. Some of the estimated 14,000 prisoners had been in detention for over two years and had no remedy or recourse. In all of this, Iraqi forces, formally invested with detention powers since June 2004, have played an active role – including mass killings by interior ministry officials in Baghdad. But British and US forces, in overall command, have also set a standard of barbarism by their actions and, perhaps more importantly, by their failure to take effective and exemplary action against those responsible.

Among the broader issues raised by this terrible story – which will harm Western policy and any associated democratising aspirations for the Middle East for decades – there is one that perhaps is most relevant here. This is that the levels of abuse, beating, humiliation and torture practised by the US and British armies in Iraq reflect not some aberrant behaviour, nor the stress of battle, nor the actions of 'rotten apples';

rather, they reflect the deeply embedded, officially sanctioned and officially covered-up racism and brutality that lie at the core of the culture of the armed forces of these two states.

In the case of the US forces – and perhaps to a lesser extent in the case of the British – they also reflect the prison culture which these countries permit at home. In a moment of exceptional objectivity, a US prisoner being released from years of detention in North Vietnam, a man who had suffered abuse at the hands of the Hanoi government, once observed: 'No country puts its best people into its prison service.' That may be so, but such prison services are sanctioned and protected by political and state officials.

However, the pervasive, institutional and sanctioned misconduct witnessed in Iraq goes further than this, and speaks to the endurance of the mentalities that the US and Britain have inherited from their history of military conduct worldwide. A similar attitude lies in the British response, from Prime Minister Tony Blair downwards, to the fatal police shooting of an unarmed Brazilian worker, Jean Charles de Menezes, in the London underground in July 2005.

That event, following the 7/7 bomb attacks on four underground trains, revealed much of the unchallenged nastiness within the British state, including the culture of cover-up that pervades it, and the energetic use of fake leaks and innuendo by the police in controversial cases (in which the London press is so collusive). Even the phrase used, 'shoot to kill', is a euphemism, since the man was shot while being held on the ground, not while running away. The real name of the policy should be 'murder to deter'.

It is much discussed, in regard to former dictatorships of southern Europe or Latin America, whether there has been 'security service reform', whether the former generals and police chiefs have been reeducated in democratic norms and the rule of law. But as Iraq has shown, the armed forces of Britain and the US are as much in need of such a thorough and ruthless purging of both personnel and attitude as those of Spain or Chile – and are even less likely to be subjected to it. The US military's propensity to brutality and institutional cruelty, given official sanction from the top by Gonzales and his chief, George W. Bush, will remain for a long time to come.

The conduct and defence of such practices by the United States government, and the kind of ritualised stalling engaged in by the British state, have hit hard at any regime based on international law and on the

universalist assumption, legal as well as moral, of equal worth and treatment of human beings. Indeed, the whole language of the US government rejects universalism. It does so in its appeal to 'US values', its focus
on the protection of US citizens, its disdain for the United Nations and
its refusal to see how US policies past and present have contributed to
fuelling hostility around the world.

On the matter of the universality of torture, a good friend of mine
– a wry Turkish intellectual who has had reason over the years to reflect
on such matters in his own country – suggested a simple test: if Alberto
Gonzales is in any doubt as to whether setting dogs on a naked and
shackled man is torture, he should himself volunteer to undergo this
form of interrogation. It might be the route to a quick, direct and, in its
own way, universal answer.

Six

Profane Agenda: Politics and Profit in the Lands of Islam

I.   A TRANSNATIONAL *UMMA*: REALITY OR MYTH?
6 October 2005

In the four years since 9/11 much has been written in the West and in the Islamic world about the emergence of a new 'transnational' and militant Islam, a community of jihadis who operate independently of states, recruit from many countries, and whose operations are not confined to any particular state. Al-Qa'ida, for example, has had fighters from dozens of countries – from Saudi Arabia, Yemen, Egypt and Morocco, to Bosnia, Chechnya, the Philippines and Pakistan (and, on occasion, Britain, France and Australia also).

In one sense, there is nothing particularly Muslim about this phenomenon. The facility of virtual and physical movement today means that many ideas, symbols and causes are transmitted globally and near-instantaneously. British surprise that the bombers who attacked London on 7 July 2005 were 'home-grown' missed the fact that there are very few purely home-grown things left – and that, in any case, at least one of the bombers had been exposed to Pakistani Islamist, if not al-Qa'ida, influence. Yet there is clearly some truth in the claim that the present form of Islamic militancy has distinct and novel features. The decentred structure of al-Qa'ida is very different from the hierarchical system of inter-war world communism or from traditional guerrilla groups such as Ireland's IRA, the Kurdish PKK, Lebanon's Hizbullah or Palestine's Hamas; and its ability and willingness to hit targets in the United States, Western Europe, the Middle East, Africa and South-East Asia all seem to reinforce this transnational model.

Moreover, and despite the activities of transnational militants like Che Guevara, no other guerrilla, insurrectionary or group in history has been able to recruit as widely as al-Qa'ida now does. No other national-ist or revolutionary group has hit targets in such a wide range of coun-tries and within the ambit of what appears to be a coherent, if demented, global strategy. The organisational flexibility of this phenomenon is also remarkable – hence the search for words to describe this original-ity: *mouvance*, a French fusion of 'movement' and 'tendency', originally used of the non-party 'new social movements' of the 1970s and 1980s in Western Europe; or 'franchise'; or 'affiliates'.

Something evidently new is operating here, which is confirmed by the difficulty in establishing clear links of organisation, recruitment or com-mand between (say) Madrid's 11-M, London's 7/7 and al-Qa'ida leaders in Pakistan or Afghanistan. The prison sentences given in Madrid to alleged al-Qa'ida activists, including the Al Jazeera journalist Tayser Alouni – for far lesser periods than the prosecution and investigating Judge Baltasar Garzón had requested – reflect scepticism in Spain about the degree to which the accused had in any real sense been part of al-Qa'ida prepara-tions for the 9/11 attacks. The same problem bedevils attempts by Italy, Germany and Britain to pin specific charges on Islamists in detention.

There is enough contemporary evidence, then, to make Islamic trans-nationalism worthy of attention. Moreover, the idea is reinforced by the way it draws on two elements, historical and doctrinal, of the Islamic world. First, transnational activities – of a commercial and financial as well as a political and religious kind – have been common in the Muslim world for centuries. If anything, it is the recently created modern state, with its frontiers, centralised tax systems and bureaucratic adminis-trations, which broke ties of scholarship, mystical orders and trading groups that had existed for centuries.

In terms of political ideas, the whole history of the Islamic countries from around the second half of the nineteenth century has been one of ideologies and doctrines produced in one country and then being applied in very different ones. The nineteenth-century reformer Jamal al-Din al-Afghani, for example, at various times influenced Ottoman Turkey, Iran and (via his follower Mohammad Abduh) Egypt. A more recent and striking case of cross-boundary and cross-national fertilisation was the use made by the Egyptian fundamentalist thinker Sayyid Qutb, the spiritual father of al-Qa'ida, of the writings of the Pakistani writer Maududi.

What may appear as recent and artificial roots in the Islamic world are often historically deeper. For example, the influence of the Iranian clergy in Iraq and Lebanon does not derive from some new conspiratorial activism by the Islamic Republic, but a continuation of ties that have existed for centuries between the clergy and Shi'a communities of the three countries.

Second, Islam as a doctrinal system also favours transnational ties. Islam set out – like Christianity, but unlike Judaism or Hinduism – to be a world religion. The claim of some Islamists that the Prophet Mohammed invented globalisation is exaggerated but contains some truth. In modern times, Islamists have repeatedly portrayed the division of the Muslim world into separate nations as the product of imported Western ideas of nationalism and imperialism. Ayatollah Khomeini once said: 'Islam has been slapped in the face by nationalism.'

There are also countervailing trends to the transnational view. Muslims do proclaim one faith and one God, and feel in some respects (as on the *hajj* to Mecca and Medina) a sense of common history and community. But this religious internationalism has always coexisted with multiple other identities. Muslims can also feel that they are Egyptians, Pakistanis, Indonesians, Nigerians and Palestinians. Doctrinal claims that Islam as a religion prohibits nationalism are of little value, for two reasons: nationalism (identification with a particular state and people) is a universal phenomenon; and the textual sources available to a Muslim allow for national loyalties. A verse in the Qur'an proclaims that Allah has created different 'tribes and peoples, so that they should get to know each other', and the Prophet Mohammed is accredited with saying that with 'love of homeland comes faith'. The Muslim Brotherhood established in Egypt in 1928 – the nearest Islamic equivalent to the Communist International – significantly never imposed centralist control of the Bolshevik kind on its members.

The world today contains more than fifty Muslim-majority countries, in which strong nationalist and patriotic sentiments flourish – often directed against fellow Muslim peoples (Iranians, Iraqis, Sudanese, Egyptians, Uzbeks, Tajiks, to name a few). This adherence to national as opposed to Islamic identities is reflected in the way that Middle Eastern Muslim states (except Saudi Arabia) invoke elements of the pre-Islamic past as a form of legitimization; this, even though Islam formally denounces the pre-Islamic period as one of *jahiliya* (ignorance). Thus Egypt celebrates the Pharaohs, Tunisia the Phoenicians, Iran the ancient Persian empires, and Yemen the kingdoms of Saba and Himyar.

These considerations are relevant to Osama bin Laden's transnational project; research on jihadi documents and interviews with former or imprisoned members reveal strong inter-ethnic tensions within the movement. The excellent new book by Fawaz Gerges, *The Far Enemy: Why Jihad Went Global* (Cambridge University Press, 2005), shows that although al-Qa'ida's footsoldiers come from many countries, its leadership is drawn from two only: Egypt and Saudi Arabia. This raises the issue of the precise meaning of 'transnational'. A business does not merit the term merely because it sells, has factories or shareholders from several countries: most so-called 'multinational' corporations are, in large measure, national corporations that operate internationally. Such companies and their senior management almost always have direct institutional and cultural associations with a single, predominant, national state.

The same routinely applies to groups resisting or seeking independence from the grip of a state or system of states. The Cold War echoed to noisy rhetoric from East and West about the degree of state sponsorship of guerrilla, terrorist or national liberation movements. In reality, the picture was mixed: South Vietnam's NLF was always more controlled by Hanoi than was claimed at the time; the Nicaraguan Sandinistas were closer to the Cubans; while the Palestine Liberation Organisation was less controlled by either Arab states or Moscow than it seemed. In the 'War on Terror', a similar confusion operates. Washington's attempts to link al-Qa'ida to Saddam Hussein (before his 2003 overthrow) or Iran are bogus, while the current Sunni Islamist insurrection in Iraq does indeed receive some covert support from neighbouring states concerned to protect their options in the future.

Al-Qa'ida's current status as an apparently free-floating and stateless group, it must be recalled, is for Osama bin Laden and his cohorts very much a second best. Al-Qa'ida began life and long continued its operations with the support of states: 1980s, phase one: activity in Pakistan,

Saudi Arabia and the United States; 1990–6, phase two: work alongside the Islamist revolutionary regime in Sudan to export revolution to
Egypt, Algeria, Saudi Arabia and Eritrea; 1996–2001, phase three: operations from Afghanistan as an ally of the Taliban government. Al-Qaʿida
is a state-centred group in a further, highly important sense: its goal is to
take power in specific Islamic states and establish a new form of authoritarian government, a caliphate. The preferred option and long-term goal
of al-Qaʿida is therefore not something different from transnationalism.

The Muslim world is not, nor ever has been, defined wholly or
mainly in terms of the *umma* or transnational linkages and identities. To
be sure, forms of solidarity over Muslim-related political conflicts and
issues – such as Palestine, Kashmir and now Iraq – do exert a hold on
many people, and inspire some to radical activism. But just as the international communist movement after 1917 masked sharp internal differences of culture, politics and interest, so today's global jihadi movement
contains such fissures. The *umma* may not be as stateless, fluid or international as it appears.

2.   FAITH AS BUSINESS: ISLAM, LAW AND FINANCE
   12 February 2008

A controversy over the relationship of what is termed Sharia, or Islamic
law, to wider legal systems was ignited on 7 February 2008 by an
unlikely source: an academic lecture by the spiritual head of England's
established Church. The Archbishop of Canterbury's address explored
the landscape of plural jurisdiction in Britain and considered with sympathy 'what degree of accommodation the law of the land can and should
give to minority communities with their own strongly entrenched legal
and moral codes'. The message conveyed from a text replete with caveats
and circumlocutions was (in the words of Rowan Williams's preceding
BBC radio interview) that 'certain provisions of Sharia are already recognised' in society and law, and that their application is 'unavoidable'.

The media furore that has ensued is as predictable as it is founded on
widespread ignorance of the ostensible substance of the argument. In this
it is part of a wider pattern whereby news stories about aspects of Islamic
activity and social practice – 'Islamic law', 'Islamic banking' or 'Islamic

dress', for example – come to prominence and are circulated without a proper examination of the provenance and meaning of these terms.

In many European countries (the Netherlands, France, Denmark and Germany, as well as Britain), 'Islam'-related issues connected to the veil, medical hygiene or religious imagery become the trigger for entrenching opinion, drawing battle-lines and fomenting indignation. If the pattern is to be broken and a more constructive form of public discourse conducted, it can only be done by informed reason, including historical and linguistic clarification.

A vital step is to note what lies beneath the surface of controversy and what is seldom taken into account. In this case, to pose the question as being in favour of or opposed to something called 'Islamic law' is to start from the wrong place. The assumption of both sides of the argument is that Sharia – for or against it – is a given text, a code available in set form to which jurists and believers may or may not relate.

This assumption of fixity is, on closer examination, quite false on three accounts. First, Islamic law – or more properly, legal practice in the fifty-seven Muslim countries – is, like any other system, plural and multivocal: the result of centuries of inherited practice and precedent, allowing of many different interpretations. There is no fixed legal code, and never has been. Second, the interpretation of law, and the selection of which precedents or past cases to invoke – including which bits of a supposedly sacred text to use – are a function of contemporary power relations (whether of class, state or religious establishment). Third and most important of all, the very term so often fought over – Sharia – is a misnomer, for it is not a legal or sacred code at all, but a political slogan and modern invention of nineteenth-century neo-Wahhabi reformers. In fact, Sharia is no more specific than the terms 'British way of life', 'the Italian way' or 'American values'. The scholarly authority Aziz al-Azmeh has noted that Sharia is more akin to generic terms like *nomos* or *dharma*: it cannot serve as the basis for any decisions on legal codes or practices.

What do the texts say? The Qur'an, the only part of the Muslim tradition that is divinely sanctioned, contains around 6,000 verses, of which less than a hundred are concerned with matters of a legal nature; nearly all relate to personal and family matters. In no way can this legacy, supposedly immutable and definitive, form the basis for a modern legal code. The word Sharia occurs only four times in the Qur'an; it denominates, in a general way, 'the right path' (indeed each community, be it Muslim, Jewish or Christian, is to have its own such 'path').

A common confusion is made between Sharia and *fiqh* (Islamic jurisprudence) – the corpus of law which has arisen over centuries and which forms the basis for law in many Muslim countries, and is obliged like any modern legal system to pronounce on all matters from the personal to the commercial. This is not divinely sanctioned. Indeed the only parts of Islam that have such sanction are classified as *deen* (religion). *Fiqh*, therefore, is a system of conventional law, without divine sanction and allowing of many interpretations. Beyond the fact that the Sunni world has four main schools of *fiqh* – Maleki, Shafi'i, Hanbali and Hanafi – each reflecting developments in medieval Islamic society and politics, the Shi'a have their own, distinct, system. Where the confusion has arisen – and where both Islamic fundamentalists and well-meaning but ill-informed Western observers like the Archbishop of Canterbury have contributed to the problem – is in pretending that there is one single legal text (Sharia) and that this supposedly univocal code carries divine authority. Nothing could be further from the truth.

A similar ideological slippage, and abandonment of a comparative common sense, arise in regard to the issue of Islamic 'economic principles' and in particular of 'Islamic banking'. A dose of economic realism, and first-hand knowledge of the region, may also help to dispel some of the effusions that have been circulated in recent years about a supposedly different basis for conducting economic life in the Muslim world (from the 'Islamic economics' of the Iranian revolution, to the current vogue for 'Islamic banking'). These fashions reveal – as much as do the straight exercise of political power or the subjugation of women – the way that supposedly religious or cultural values are used to rebrand or disguise what are on closer examination universal forms of resource and power manipulation.

The Iranian revolution of 1979 proclaimed a new set of 'Islamic economic principles', based on some vague extrapolation of the principle of *zakat* (charity), one of the five duties of the Muslim. It succeeded, however, only in creating a perfectly recognisable ramshackle rentier economy, laced with corruption and inefficiency; in short, a conventional product of 'development' in what was known as the Third World, and little different from its oil-producing counterparts Nigeria, Venezuela and Indonesia.

The resurgence of 'Islamic banking' – a practice and idea that has spread from Malaysia to Turkey, Egypt and the Gulf – is now expected to account for assets reaching $1 trillion by the year 2010. Such Western institutions as HSBC, Dow Jones, Citibank, BNP Paris and others have all signed up to this parade of corporate piety. The financial press of the Middle East is full of articles concerned about the shortage of 'experts' and 'appropriately qualified scholars' in Islamic finance. But all this needs to be taken with a pinch of salt, good secular salt at that. Anyone who has studied the economic history of the Muslim world – from the trading activities of the Prophet Mohammed in Mecca and Medina in the seventh century to the banks and finance houses of the Arab Gulf today – will know that business is conducted as it is everywhere, on sound capitalist principles.

There is no basis for the supposed textual or canonical theory of 'Islamic banking'. The late Maxime Rodinson – the greatest authority on this matter – showed in his great work *Islam and Capitalism* that there is, in fact, no Qur'anic or authoritative prohibition on the taking of interest; there is only (as in most religions) a condemnation of *riba'* (excess, or profiteering). Muslim writers have long differed on what *riba'* means; some confine it to profiteering in essentials like foodstuffs. Nor, in the end, do the supposedly 'Islamic' banks of today provide a fundamentally different service. They do two things: first, offer a degree of local affiliation or allegiance to investors (much as does in principle the Bradford & Bingley Building Society or the Chase Manhattan Bank); and, second, serve as a more friendly recipient for investors with cash (especially in the sense of asking fewer questions about the origin of the funds than do many other financial institutions in the West in this era of client identification and post-9/11 controls). Islamic banking is capitalist banking with a different cover: a way in the end to ensure that more money – whether it comes from the exports of the oil producers, drug production in Afghanistan, or the hard-earned toil of minimum-wage service workers in Europe's cities – is put into circulation. It is, as the British ambassador to one Gulf state put it to me, 'a means of getting the money out from underneath the bed'. Its relation to tradition, sanctity, the Qur'an and all that is purely presentational.

Moreover, the supposedly compulsory ban on profiteering does not apply when interests of state are involved: if Islamic authority and what is often misleadingly called 'Sharia' prohibit excess profits, then where are the voices of criticism when it comes to exorbitant and (in terms of production costs) wholly unjustified increases in the price of oil? If ever there was a case of *riba*, one to which all Islamic oil-producers subscribe, it is the rent that OPEC extracts from the sale of oil. Here, as in so many other matters, it is religious text and tradition that serve capital (when not greed) and not the other way around.

Much of the controversy about Islamic law, as in the current British uproar over the remarks of the Archbishop of Canterbury, leads those proposing a compromise with Sharia to allow some elements of it, but to condemn its inhuman or barbarous (to cite two familiar adjectives of choice) side such as stoning, or denial of the legal equality of women. But this is not the fundamental issue, which is respect for tradition itself (and, a closely related factor, the official obsequiousness towards bearded patriarchs of all religions who today claim to own and be able to interpret it).

The supposed authority of Islamic text and tradition is the greatest of all fallacies underlying this moving theatre of Islamic banking and finance, as of the misconceived debate on Sharia. Similar sleights of authoritarian hand occur in Judaism and Christianity in regard to such issues as the status of women, the rights of gays and the celibacy of the clergy. A lot of forgetting is necessary to uphold reverence for such traditions, which are based often on medieval practice (e.g. the principle of a celibate clergy must suppress the fact that St Peter and many of his successors were married). In any event, the reverence for tradition is only the other side of power interests seeking expression and consolidation. The word 'tradition' should alert a person to the very modern forces it connotes and often conceals.

3.   FINANCE IN THE GULF:
     THE CHIMERA OF 'SOVEREIGN WEALTH FUNDS'
     5 March 2008

The world's financial press has a new obsession to succeed the 'sub-prime mortgage' craze of autumn 2007: 'sovereign wealth funds', those state-backed investment bodies whose accumulating assets (often fuelled by the high energy prices of the 2000s) are roaming the globe in search of businesses to invest in, partner and perhaps devour.

The enormous capital assets of these funds, and their potential influence on Western markets and business, make the focus (and to a degree the fear) understandable; but some at least of the reporting and discussion about these new behemoths in the Western media has a bias towards misunderstanding.

The world's sovereign wealth funds (SWFs) are believed already to command assets worth around $3 trillion ($3,000,000,000,000), a figure higher than the GDP of the United Kingdom. But the SWF phenomenon represents a major change in the world's financial and investment markets in a way that goes beyond even considerations of this epic (and often suddenly acquired) scale of riches. For its significance lies also in the intellectual and policy context of its emergence: namely, that after three decades of policy, propaganda and hype about 'freeing up markets', 'reducing the role of the state' and 'promoting the private sector', the SWFs embody a massive and unstoppable shift of influence back to what are in effect state-owned entities. Take that, neo-liberalism! The cunning of history has done it again.

The power the SWFs have been suddenly seen to wield has panicked the world's older financial elites into flailing responses: an attempt at the World Economic Forum in Davos to negotiate a code of conduct with representatives of SWFs; Australia's consideration of stricter disclosure requirements; and the European Commission's proposed 'code of practice' (released on 27 February 2008), designed to guide investments from SWF countries in European and United States markets. A closer look at the last of these in particular highlights how far there is to go before a strong, democratic response to the rise of the SWFs is developed.

The European Commission's code enjoins the SWFs annually to declare the origin and disposal of their assets; to abstain from using investments for political purposes; and to make their management structures transparent. The Commission – keen to show that Europe believes in 'open' capital markets, concerned to avert possible controls on capital inflow by key European states, and faced with the refusal of SWFs to sign a firm undertaking on these matters – thus opted for a 'wish list'. The code appears naive and unworkable at best, deceitful (designed to fool domestic political audiences into thinking that something is being done) or complicit with unaccountable entities of enormous power at worst.

But it is worse: for the European Commission, and Western governments in general, are in no position to lecture the rest of the world on correct behaviour in such matters. The European Union itself proclaims open markets yet practises protection in regard both to agriculture and significant areas of European trade and industry; over airlines, or France and Germany's gas and electricity giants, for example, open markets are forgotten.

As for the 'good practice' now recommended to the SWFs – of not using their economic power for political purposes – this is something that Western states have been doing from time immemorial. Economic activity and state interest have, after all, permeated the international market for as long as it has existed; the policy of sanctions against Cuba by the United States or Iran by the United Nations are current examples, while the history of oil companies in Latin America and the Middle East in the past century is replete with many more.

Moreover, the European Commission's proposals suggest a lack of awareness of the kinds of states and societies from which the SWFs are emerging. A state-owned investment fund will behave no differently to the states of which it is an appendix. Where there is no clear distinction between state and private interests and (a very condition of authoritarian and secretive political control) no clear evidence on who takes decisions within these SWFs or on what criteria – as is the case to a great extent in Russia, the Arab Gulf states and China – it is not clear what the value of such a 'code of practice' can possibly be.

The Gulf states in particular remain – for all the superhighways, skyscrapers, 'knowledge cities' and glitzy conferences – controlled by secretive ruling families whose members regard the state and its revenue as theirs. An Arab ambassador recently put it to me that the minister of finance is, in effect, the private accountant of the ruler. No one knows what the state's (or ruler's) income is. Oil revenues provide the basis of an informed guess; but when it comes to the often equally large income from capital invested abroad and who controls it, not even broad estimates exist.

The new power of state corporations is most obvious in the energy market. The control by the state and its associated companies of production and distribution of key energy resources is a key source of state power in the Middle East, as in Russia and China. In this environment, the rise of the SWFs has international implications for inter-state as well as business relationships.

A powerful state may establish a degree of order in business and state affairs. But in the Middle East and Russia (to name only these areas) the very nature of the originating state guarantees that there will be problems, for three basic market and regulatory preconditions for a sustainable working model are absent: there is no free press, hence no independent investigation or reporting on economic matters – the least that would happen if a Gulf Arab or Russian paper did print independent reports is that the advertising would dry up; there is no rule of law, hence those with power in such countries are free to break contracts, renege on commitments, re-appropriate assets and even pilfer state funds as they see fit. This is not going to change in the near future – indeed, the availability of new oil and gas revenues may only make it worse. In addition, there is no independent parliament or political structure. The Russian elections of December 2007 (parliamentary) and March 2008 (presidential) show that legislatures count for little; of what remains, intimidation, forcible exile, imprisonment, or, more congenially, bribery, solve the rest. As for the Gulf states, all talk of a transition to democracy is nonsense: the rulers and their associates continue to make all the major decisions.

The requirements of the European Commission's code include the publication of statistics and data. Many Western accounting practices are far from perfect in this respect, but in the Middle East the situation is on another level of unreality: it is no exaggeration to say that no official and business statistics – on oil output or revenue, on state income or expenditure – are reliable.

The idea that a code of practice can address such systemic conditions is unreal. The kinds of practice Russia has engaged in – tearing up contracts with foreign firms, appropriating the businesses of figures like Mikhail Khodorkovsky of Yukos Oil – is evidence of the state's controlling ambition; while the conduct of Saudi Arabia in relation to the al-Yamamah arms deal with Britain in the late 1980s – and the investigation into the bribery associated with this deal, which was abandoned in 2006 – reveal the way the House of Saud is used to doing business. The ideas of 'transparency' and 'accountability' beloved of Western NGOs and progressive business advocates look irrelevant in this context.

The notion of Western-style controls regulating the policy and behaviour of, for example, Arab Gulf states is revealed too in the irrelevance of the idea of 'insider trading' in the region. Such a concept has no purchase – trading, contracts and deals are based not on public accounts or commercial law (let alone on transparency) but on personal contacts. This was emphasised to me over three decades ago by the wise Iraqi economist, Mohammad Salman Hassan: 'In the Arab world no contracts are institution to institution, state to state, or enterprise to enterprise. All are person to person. On this they rely.'

For some Western banks and businesses starved of funds, and facing the credit crunch sparked in autumn 2007 by the sub-prime mortgage crisis in the United States, all this may appear good news. Their balance sheets have (as the financial journalists say) 'lots of holes to be filled'. But these institutions – and Western governments – which wish or are obliged to deal with SWFs have a clear choice. They can enter agreements with SWFs (and other economic and political bodies in authoritarian states) with their eyes open, aware of the arbitrary administrative practices, occult financial sources and political interests involved. Such an approach is possible; many have followed it over the years. They can also choose to leave the SWFs to invest elsewhere; and to wait for the time – on present showing, a pretty long way away – when both the SWFs and the wider political and financial systems of these countries are more able to meet Western criteria.

This is the choice. What Western banks, businesses and governments should not do is to fool their publics, and possibly even themselves, about the realities of business, politics and influence in authoritarian states. The indulgence (or worse) towards money laundering and fake accounting in the West, as well as the venality of many of those involved at the highest levels of business and power, may give a clear signal as to which path is the more likely. But at some point a dysfunctional global financial system needs bold action based on principle with long-term purchase, not mere calculation of short-term benefit. The SWFs are not going away. It is time to relearn the old phrase about speaking truth to power.

4. A STATE OF ROBBERS: THE JAMAHIRIYAH AT 40
9 September 2009

The celebration of the fortieth anniversary of the Libyan 'revolution' of 1969, in effect a coup d'état by Colonel Gaddafi and some of his associates and relatives, brings to mind a conversation I had just after that event with a friend of mine, who is a senior Algerian diplomat. The Algerian government had been as surprised and bemused as any other at the emergence of this bizarre, radical and eccentric regime in a fellow North African state. Houari Boumedienne, the Algerian president, had asked my friend to visit Tripoli and assess the new leadership there. When he returned to London, I asked him how he had found the Libyan leaders, at that time Colonel Gaddafi and his close associate Major Jalloud, a relative of the Colonel's who was subsequently expelled from power. The diplomat's answer, in elegant French, was unforgettable: '*Ils ont un niveau intellectuel plutôt modeste.*' In more Anglo-Saxon terms, 'They were pretty stupid.'

In the ensuing four decades or so, little, indeed nothing, has occurred to alter that judgement. One of the most costly aspects of the Libyan revolution, one that comes from Gaddafi himself, is administrative chaos. I recall on a visit in 2002 to Libya that officials and academics – those who did not treat us to lengthy disquisitions on *The Green Book* – would, in an embarrassed and reserved sort of way, say that their country had 'management problems', an indirect reference to Gaddafi's style. With many of the elite educated in the West (one professor took me aside to ask me nostalgically about a pub in Durham), and with access to Italian television, people were evidently fed up but resigned. During that visit, I got an insight into the chaotic management system prevailing in that country: it was announced that on a particular Sunday there would be a meeting of ministers, in effect a cabinet meeting: however, since Libya officially has no 'capital', no one knew where this would be and so senior officials and their advisers were driving around the desert from one place to another, trying to find out where they were supposed to meet.

Since the international rehabilitation of Libya after 9/11, it has become common to argue that Libya is changing, is 'not the country it was a decade ago' and so forth. Libya has certainly changed its foreign and defence policies: many countries do, even Stalin's Russia or Kim Jong-il's North Korea. Some small changes in the human rights situation have also occurred, but arbitrary arrest, detention, torture and disappearances still take place. In addition, as every Libyan is aware, for all the rhetoric about 'revolution' and the 'state of the masses', this leadership has squandered the country's wealth on foolish projects at home and costly adventures abroad: with a per capita oil output roughly equal to that of Saudi Arabia, it has none of the urban and transport development, or any of the educational and health facilities, that that country and other oil-producers in the Gulf can boast. Tripoli, the unofficial 'capital', retains the impressive white buildings and squares of Italian colonial rule, as reportedly does its Eritrean counterpart Asmara: but these are in a state of extreme dilapidation – Tripoli is the Arab equivalent of Havana, not a North African Dubai or Doha.

Libya has emphatically not introduced significant changes in its political system, especially not with regard to human rights or governance. In 2009 the Jamahiriyah remains one of the most dictatorial and opaque of Arab regimes. Its population of 6 million enjoys no significant freedoms at all: anyone who cares to read the annual reports by Amnesty International or Human Rights Watch on Libya will get a glimpse of the real situation, one of continued abuse of human rights on a systematic scale. Under Law 71, those who opposed the ideology of the 1969 Gaddafi revolution may be arrested and even executed. Migrant labourers continue to be treated abominably and were in the past subject to cruel and arbitrary mass expulsions (to Egypt and Tunisia). To date, Libya has refused to sign the 1951 Refugee Convention and does not collaborate with the UNHCR. Migrants returned from Italy under an obscure and brutal treaty signed between Gaddafi and Silvio Berlusconi are granted no rights. There is not even the flicker of diversity found in such neighbouring dictatorships as Egypt or Sudan.

Among the most prominent guests at the 1 September celebrations in Tripoli, apart from Robert Mugabe and the internationally indicted President Bashir of Sudan, was Mohammad Abdi Hasan Hayr, an illiterate Somali fisherman believed to be the leader of the pirates operating off the Horn of Africa. Libya's friends in Europe tell a tale of their own: Silvio Berlusconi, a frequent visitor, and Giulio Andreotti, the Italian foreign minister who tipped the Libyans off to the 1986 American raid, himself accused of a long-term association with the Mafia. For my part, I do not forget the fate of my fellow student of Yemeni affairs, the British academic Leigh Douglas: in 1986, when he was teaching in Beirut, he was kidnapped by Libyan supporters and, together with another British colleague, shot.

Nor – and this is most relevant to the question of reputation – is the damage Libya wrought solely a matter of the West, of Lockerbie, the IRA and ETA: Libya's reputation among other Arab states and peoples is abysmal. Western businessmen and politicians and the inevitable intellectual fellow-travellers may take Libya seriously, but I have never met anyone in the Arab world who does. Libya has over the years interfered with and helped make more difficult the situations in Egypt, Sudan, Yemen, Saudi Arabia, Lebanon and Palestine. To take the case of Lebanon: it was the murder of the Lebanese Shi'a leader Musa Sadr while on a visit to Libya in 1978 that opened the door for the rise of Hizbullah.

As someone who has lived and worked in Yemen, I can testify to the damage wrought by Libya in that part of the world in the 1970s and 1980s: inciting a war between the two states of North and South Yemen in 1972, then promising large-scale aid to the left-wing regime in South Yemen in the 1980s, only to cut off this aid abruptly when the Yemenis disagreed with Libya over events in Ethiopia. One of the most striking buildings in Aden in the early 1980s was the shell of the unfinished Libyan hospital in Khormaksar – its funding arbitrarily cut from one day to the next.

On Palestine, Libya has been a wrecker, neither helping the Palestinians to organise themselves effectively in order to negotiate from a stronger position with Israel, nor promoting a reasonable peace with Israel itself. It long created division within the Palestinian nationalist movement, at one time backing the Abu Nidal faction which sought to assassinate PLO officials who negotiated with Israel and was involved in some of the worst terrorist acts. Libya may be marginal to the Arab–Israeli question, but it has at the same time continued to emit extreme anti-Israeli views: indeed, on the eve of the fortieth anniversary celebrations in September 2009, Colonel Gaddafi told a meeting of African leaders that Israel was responsible for all the conflicts and problems in the continent. The official Libyan position is that Israel should be abolished and merged into one state, termed 'Isratina': innovative as this may sound, this is just another way of trying to eliminate the state of Israel.

In sum: today, few, if any, in the Arab world show any respect towards this regime. For reasons that are not entirely clear, but may have to do with Iran displacing Libya as the patron of radicals in Lebanon, Tripoli has also long championed chauvinist anti-Iranian and anti-Shi'a rhetoric: during my 2002 visit I endured a long rant from the then Libyan ambassador to Tehran, denouncing the Shi'a as, in effect, accomplices of Western imperialism.

Libya is by no means the most brutal regime in the world: compared to Sudan, Iraq and Syria, it has less blood on its hands. But the state of the Jamahiriyah remains a grotesque entity; a contemporary example of the early modern European state; a protection racket run by a group of people, their relatives and friends, who have wrested control of a state, its economy and its people by force. In forty years no attempt has been made to secure popular legitimisation. Libya cannot even point to the achievements that some of the other Arab oil-producers claim. The outside world may be compelled by considerations of security, energy and investment to deal with this state: there is no reason, however, to indulge its fantasies or the fictions that are constantly promoted within the country and abroad about its political and social character. The Jamahiriyah is not a 'state of the masses': it is a state of robbers, in formal terms a 'kleptocracy'. The sooner it is consigned to the dustbin of history, and the Libyan people allowed to determine their own leaders and political system, and not least, to benefit from the oil and gas deals that the West is now so keen to promote, the better.

Seven

Universalism Imperilled

I. THE CRISIS OF UNIVERSALISM: AMERICA AND RADICAL ISLAM AFTER 9/11
15 September 2004

Three years after the most spectacular guerrilla action of modern history, the coordinated events of 11 September 2001 in the United States, the world appears further away than ever from addressing the fundamental issues confronting it, moving ever more deeply into a phase of confrontation, violence and exaggerated cultural difference. The response to 9/11 on both sides has been, in essence, a rejection of universalism: of the belief, gradually built up over the twentieth century, in shared moral and legal principles and in the ability of states and international bodies successfully to resolve conflicts through multilateral action.

On the militant Islamic side, the worldwide military challenge to US power is framed in particularist, religious, nationalist and historical language; it rejects any sense of global solidarity against oppression. On the Western side, state policies have equally fallen back on particularist rhetoric and practice – whether in the appeals of the US president after 9/11 to 'American values', the Russian invocation of a right to a worldwide attack on its enemies after the Beslan assault of September 2004, or the instinctive appeal to 'European values' by European Union states in the aftermath of the 11 March 2004 bombings in Madrid.

All this has struck a serious blow at what had been a growing world consensus prior to 11 September 2001, namely the belief in international institutions, international norms and international law (not least with regard to human rights and the conduct of armed conflict). The regression is apparent on both sides. The United States under George W. Bush has openly rejected the claims of international law, for example those of the four Geneva Conventions of 1949 on the treatment of prisoners of war. The rhetoric of al-Qa'ida is even more anti-universalist; it is laced with Arab nationalist motifs, virulent attacks on fellow Muslims who are Shi'a and a total contempt – celebrated in bloodthirsty proclamations and macabre videos – for general principles in relation to the conduct of armed conflict in the modern age.

This rejection of universalism has been supported by a widespread growth in nationalism in both the developed and underdeveloped worlds. Anatol Lieven's *America Right or Wrong: An Anatomy of American Nationalism* (Oxford University Press, 2004) acutely analyses this trend in the context of the United States, where the current presidential election campaign is marked by affirmations of national greatness and the glorification of past imperial wars.

But it is not just American nationalism. Around the world, the constraints of law and general moral decency that once restrained nationalism seem to have been eroded. In Israel, the public mood has shifted further towards aggressive action; across Europe, advocates of immigration and multiculturalism are under attack; in many former Soviet republics and in Eastern Europe, nationalist demagogues hold sway; in Japan, a revived rhetoric of national assertiveness is taking hold. This ideological shift was underway before 9/11. It was given intellectual support by the spread of a vapid relativism, sometimes termed 'postmodernism', that had – in response to the collapse of forms of rigid political rationalism – gained considerable influence across the developed world in the 1980s and 1990s.

9/11 compounded this process in the generalised and pervasive fear that those events caused, and in the superficial and ranting responses it occasioned in much of the West. There is another reaction not to be underestimated among many people in America and Europe: a retreat from engagement with the political world and international events – even if this lacked a clear public expression by dint of its very private and socially atomised character.

A crucial part of these responses is the fact that this armed conflict, between established states and a hidden but global insurrectionary movement, leaves the great mass of the people feeling there is nothing they can do. The huge worldwide demonstrations of 15 February 2003 leave the majority of citizens in the position of reluctant spectators in the conflict itself, deprived even of that form of minimally meaningful participation that the war effort of, for example, 1939–45 in Europe permitted.

The other side of post-9/11 confusion is a worldwide crisis of the state. In one sense, the state system of three years ago has largely held: only in Afghanistan and Iraq has there been significant regime change. Numerous other elites, what may be termed the 'crackdown states', have taken advantage of US appeals for solidarity in the fight against terrorism to impose more authoritarian control over their own societies, and particularly over those calling for greater recognition of minority rights: Uzbekistan, Russia, China, Egypt, Israel. Two important US allies, Pakistan and Saudi Arabia, are themselves the sites of significant anti-Western and pro-al-Qa'ida feeling. The US has for its part openly vaunted its military power and increased its defence budget to $400 billion.

Yet this enhancement of state military power has been offset by an even greater demonstration of state weakness. The United States' military power has not eliminated al-Qa'ida in any state, despite the despatch of marines, intelligence operatives and much more; it has failed to crush opposition in either of the two states it has invaded, Afghanistan or Iraq. The use of the US military and the blustering and arrogant words that accompany it have instead provoked a new level of anti-American and by extension anti-Western feeling across the Muslim world and beyond. This process was taken to new heights by the revelations of torture and sadistic abuse of Iraqi prisoners in Abu Ghraib prison in Baghdad. In Europe, the American response to 9/11 has provoked such anger that transatlantic relations and public attitudes on both sides of the divide are now more distant and antagonistic than ever.

The US has, in essence, no diplomatic policy left – a fact exemplified by the indefatigable ignorance of the US president and the timidly inadequate conduct of his secretary of state. They and the wider US political elite are bereft of understanding of the crisis the world confronts, and of the need for a response that combines military with political and cultural initiatives. The United States is dragging the Western world, and all who are opposed to fundamentalist violence and its accompanying social programme, towards a global abyss. This weakness of the state is evident even within the US itself. Three years after 9/11, not a single successful prosecution for al-Qa'ida activity within the US has occurred; nor has a single person been arrested, let alone convicted, of the anthrax attacks that followed the plane hijackings.

The now lengthily investigated intelligence failures prior to 9/11 could probably not have been avoided, given the multiplicity of data involved. The record of the intelligence services after the attacks is more striking: of more than 590 people detained at Guantanamo Bay in Cuba, not one it seems is a significant member of al-Qa'ida or has been the source of any valuable information on that group. Furthermore, the financial controls established to check the financing of fundamentalism after 9/11 seem to have been ineffective. Some guerrilla attacks may have been prevented, notably in Britain, but al-Qa'ida and its allies have still been able to conduct their worldwide campaign with a large measure of impunity; political targets over the last three years include Indonesia, Yemen, Spain, Saudi Arabia and Turkey. Al-Qa'ida, not the US administration, took and has so far retained the global military and political initiative.

Taken together, the crisis of universalism, the weakness of the traditional nation-states and the militarised character of world politics today mean that the major issues already confronting the world before 9/11, none of which have become easier since then, are being increasingly neglected. The existence of specific transnational problems like the spread of HIV/AIDS and narco-trafficking is sufficient evidence of this. Moreover, none of the inter-ethnic conflicts that fuel public support for Osama bin Laden have been resolved, most notably the Palestine question.

The most important of all these issues is the profound inequality in global conditions of wealth and life between the rich elites of the OECD states and the rest of the world. This polarisation lies at the heart of the pressure to migrate to the richer states of the world, of the corrupt character of many states and of the rising world resentment of the West and especially of the United States. It is this issue, not some exaggerated or invented 'clash of civilisations' or conflict between Islam and the West, that has created sympathy for Osama bin Laden in the Middle East. The Western response to 9/11, based on the vaunting of American power and interests and a reliance on the use of force, has only made this worse. The efficiency of the United States as a bureaucratic, logistic and military administration, combined with the utter inability of the US government to comprehend – let alone adequately respond to – the attacks of 11 September 2001, make vividly clear the 'failed' nature of the US state.

The events of 9/11 would in any circumstances have been a great challenge – political, intellectual and cultural – to all thinking people in the United States, Europe, the Middle East and beyond. They dramatically highlighted a conflict that had already been developing for some years and which promises to dominate at least the first part of the twenty-first century. But the response of the United States of America to the attack on its territory has made any serious, effective and considered course of action even more difficult. The world is being dragged towards disaster by two arrogant militarised leaderships. We must do all we can to persuade people to shift in the other direction, the better to address the issues that predated 9/11 – issues that remain very much alive and pressing, and which, if left unresolved, will lead to more spectacular and ghastly confrontations.

2.   LETTER FROM EUSKADI
   3 August 2007

The association of the Basque Country with political and often violent conflict is at first sight belied by the sense of tranquil prosperity exuded by its capital, Vitoria. Yet as soon as the visitor begins to make sense of the city's basic geographic and historical coordinates, it is impossible to avoid being confronted by the intractable nationalist dispute that has wracked the region, and Spain at large, for almost forty years.

This city of 250,000 people is known in the Basque language as Gasteiz, just as the Basque Country as a whole is Euskadi. It is capital too of Álava, the largest of the three Basque provinces; Guipúzcoa and Vizcaya (Biscay) are the others, though Basque nationalists also include within the historic (and imagined) nation the neighbouring province of Navarra and an area of south-west France, both home to Euskera (Basque-speakers). This wider territory comprises the entirety of Hegoalde (the four provinces of southern Euskadi) and Iparralde (the northern French area). In the weather reports of the local nationalist press, for example, this aspirational Euskadi is represented as a separate geographic unit.

Vitoria is a long-established manufacturing centre which has expanded since it was named as Euskadi's capital under the system of regional 'autonomy' (in British terms, 'devolution') that was introduced in 1978 as part of the transition to democracy after the death of General Franco in November 1975. The choice of Vitoria was in part by default: the other obvious candidates were excluded either for reasons of political sensitivity – Guernica (Gernika), the historic capital, was devastated by the German air-force attack in May 1937; or due to reluctance to grant disproportionate influence to the largest cities – the ports of San Sebastián (Donostia) and Bilbao (Bilbo).

Vitoria's layout is clear from any high point around the city: on a slight hill stand the churches and narrow streets of the old walled town, established far from the Arab armies to the south in 1181 by Sancho the Wise, King of Navarra; beyond lies the urban civility of modern Spain that in turn gives way to the arid hills that lie between the cereal-growing plateau of Álava and the Bay of Biscay. The vast Cathedral of Mary Immaculate (only completed in 1973, and one of two cathedrals in Vitoria) exists among a variety of churches, the most prominent of which are floodlit at night.

The main square, named 'The White Virgin' after the city's patron saint, hosts a large memorial to the victory of the Duke of Wellington in the battle of Vitoria of 21 June 1813, a decisive moment in what for Spaniards is the 'war of independence' (and for some others the 'peninsular war'). In August the same square is the site of a curious local custom, whereby everyone in the crowd lights a cigar as an angel 'descends' from the belfry of the fourteenth-century St Michael's Church.

The summer is a time of regional festivals, and the papers are full of their attractions, from the annual San Fermín bull run in Pamplona, capital of Navarra, to musical performances by Norah Jones and Ornette Coleman. This is also the season when the University of the Basque Country runs its summer school, generously supported by local and provincial Basque authorities, at which I have been invited to give a series of lectures.

I duly begin each talk with a few words in Basque: *egún on doóri* (good day, everyone). The welcome is warm, and on my second night in Vitoria – accompanied by the other teachers and students of the school – we are invited to walk a short distance along a sunny tree-lined avenue to the house of the *lehendakari* (president of the Basque Country), Juan José Ibarretxe.

After the customary mass photograph in front of the presidential residence, Ibarretxe welcomes us with an introduction of judicious nationalist affirmation to the place of the Basque Country in today's world. The notes he strikes are familiar enough, if no doubt heartfelt, and are immediately comprehensible to the motley collection of visitors (students from elsewhere in Spain and from Latin America, as well as two academics from Turkey): the Basque nation speaks the oldest language in Europe; it is part of Europe and of the globalising world (Ibarretxe never mentions the word 'Spain'); its future rests on the skills and education of its peoples; it is open for visitors and business alike.

Juan José Ibarretxe is an economist who has been *lehendakari* since 1998, and it shows: he exudes a strong and well-polished confidence. His party, the centre-right Eusko Alderdi Jeltzalea/Partido Nacionalista Vasco (Basque Nationalist Party/PNV), which long predates the Spanish civil war of 1936–9, has been the ruling party in Euskadi since the late 1970s. In recent years it has governed in coalition with two smaller left-wing, more overtly nationalist parties.

Yet all is not well in the PNV, or in the Basque Country or, indeed, in Vitoria's relations with the rest of Spain. Vitoria itself is far from being the bucolic urban space that it at can first appear: in the days after I was there, police discovered a house in which a military commander of Euskadi Ta Askatasuna (Basque Homeland and Freedom/ETA) – the armed opposition group that has been waging a guerrilla war for Basque independence since the late 1960s – had been based until recently; its streets are regularly convulsed by the Basque practice of *kale borroka*, a form of street violence in which crowds of young people armed with Molotov cocktails attack government and commercial buildings, intimidate the general population and attack, in a clearly targeted way, the homes of those who do not support the nationalist cause. Much as ETA and its friends claim that all of this is spontaneous, a 'natural' response to Madrid's repression, it is an open secret that the *kale borroka* is controlled and switched on or off by ETA and its allies.

In the Spanish provincial and municipal elections of May 2007 the PNV's share of the vote in the Basque provinces fell significantly, in a sign of general tiredness with the party's long period in office, as well as of punishment for corruption. A few weeks earlier, ETA had announced it was ending a ceasefire it had declared in March 2006 with the expectation of negotiating with the Spanish government: arrests and discoveries of substantial supplies of weapons have followed, in Spain and France. The Basque Country, if not all of Spain, is on alert for a new wave of ETA attacks, possibly coinciding with the summer tourist season. The morning after Ibarretxe welcomed us, the press carried reports of an attempt by right-wing politicians to prosecute him for illegal contacts with ETA; meanwhile the moderate chairman of his party, Josu Jon Imaz, has opposed Ibarretxe's plan to hold a referendum by the end of 2007 on Basque sovereignty.

Thirty years after the reintroduction of democracy to Spain, and the granting of substantial autonomy to the Basque provinces, the central problem in the politics of Euskadi remains what it was three decades ago: the armed campaign waged by ETA. ETA has continued to call for the full independence of Euskadi and persists in maintaining the claim to Navarra, despite the fact that everyone knows that the great majority in that province do not consider themselves Basques. As with Sinn Féin and the IRA in Northern Ireland, ETA historically mobilised political support through an allied political party, Herri Batasuna, which (again like Sinn Féin) regularly won 15–20 per cent of the vote: more than enough to sustain a mass political base and provide flexible and compliant political cover for the armed movement.

Herri Batasuna (HB) was banned before the last municipal elections, but much of its support went to another party, the Acción Nacionalista Vasca (ANV), until then a relic of a split from the PNV of the 1930s, but recently strengthened by the award of €700,000 in compensation for property seized during the civil war. It is hard accurately to read the results of the May regional and municipal elections in terms of ANV support, because of a high level of abstention and disqualification of candidates (for being associated with HB); but it would seem that the pro-ETA vote largely held up. In some municipalities, the ANV is now the governing party.

Ibarretxe's problem is that while ETA is condemned by most Basques, and has suffered major blows as a result of arrests in Spain and France, the underground nationalist group continues to be able to dominate if not control the political agenda, not only in the Basque Country but on the national level. His own party is split at least three ways: one wing (without saying so too loudly) favours Basque independence, achieved by democratic means; another, led by Imaz, is opposed to independence; while Ibarretxe, himself inclined against independence, believes the best way to weaken ETA is to put the question of independence to the vote, something the Imaz wing believes will only legitimate ETA's intransigence.

This, however, is only part of the problem: for the question of ETA and the related issue of Navarra are at the centre of national – Spanish – controversy and denunciation. Even more than the other 'hot' questions of contemporary Spanish politics – compulsory citizenship education in schools, gay marriage and the 'law on historical memory' relating to the Franco-era repression – the issue of ETA is the one that the opposition Partido Popular (Popular Party/PP) uses to berate the government.

Although the José María Aznar government did hold talks with ETA during an earlier 441-day ceasefire in 1998–9, the position of the PP now is to denounce all negotiation and to mobilise right-wing opinion and the families of ETA victims to oppose any such talks. At the tenth anniversary commemoration of the killing by ETA of Miguel Ángel Blanco, a PP local councillor in the Basque town of Ermus, the PP sought to exclude representatives of the government and to use the ceremony to stake a partisan position.

On his side, Spain's prime minister José Luis Rodríguez Zapatero took a risk in June 2006 when he followed his cautious welcome of ETA's March ceasefire announcement with a pledge to open discussions with the organisation's representatives; Madrid's emissaries are reported to have met five times with ETA in Geneva in ensuing months. But a bomb in the Terminal 4 car park at Madrid's Barajas international airport on 30 December 2006, in which two immigrant Ecuadorian workers were killed, as well as ETA's continuation of recruitment, training, reconnaissance and intimidation, suggest that the organisation was, at best, divided on the wisdom of the ceasefire.

The announcement of an end to the supposedly 'permanent' ceasefire, laced with mendacious and self-serving attacks on the Zapatero government, was timed for 6 June 2007 – a week after the municipal elections, but two days short of the 441 days of the 'indefinite' ceasefire of 1998–9. From what can be made out of the murky internal politics of the *abertzale* (the pro-ETA political world), those who genuinely wanted an exploratory dialogue with the Socialist government have been overruled by a new, younger and harder generation of militants. The latter holds the democratic process, the tolerance of other parties and the massive social protests that their actions have occasioned within the Basque Country in contempt.

Against this background, and with the polarisation of Spanish politics as a whole, it would appear that the Basque question is once again at an impasse. Far from having learnt the lessons of the past, or come to accept that any campaign for independence should be conducted by peaceful and constitutional means, ETA would seem to have set itself on a course of non-negotiable confrontation with Madrid.

Allusions are often made in Spain to a possible knock-on effect of the peace agreement in Northern Ireland, and Sinn Féin has, while continuing to indulge Basque nationalism, called for such a repetition. In some senses there are analogies: the majority of the population in the province concerned clearly oppose violence and most probably do not want independence; any sense of the legitimacy of armed opposition ended with the death of Franco in 1975. Instead, an underground armed group has hijacked the imagination of a significant part of the younger generation, maintaining its hold through intimidation, extortion, street violence and the systematic abuse of the autonomous linguistic and education rights acquired in the late 1970s. An article in the weekly supplement to *El País* on the town of Hernani, where the ANV runs the local council, gives a chilling and entirely convincing portrait of a world where intimidation, fear and silence are the order of the day.

However, the differences with Ireland are also significant. Five in particular deserve emphasis: first, Spanish opinion as a whole is agitated by the Basque question and would not tolerate the loss of the Basque provinces, whereas since the 1970s at least, the mass of British opinion would have been happy to see all of Northern Ireland disappear into the Atlantic; secondly, there is no equivalent in Basque politics of the US Irish lobby, an influential but external nationalist grouping that while indulgent of Catholic nationalism, sought a compromise and was willing to give political and financial backing; thirdly, the fundamental axis of the Northern

Irish conflict from 1968 onwards was – 'anti-imperialist' and nationalist rhetoric notwithstanding – between two communities within Northern Ireland whose more extreme representatives finally made a deal, not between extreme Catholic/Irish nationalism and Westminster; fourthly, after the Provisional IRA leadership broke with the leftist Official IRA in 1969 and established hegemony over the Republican movement, there was a continuity of leadership over the ensuing decades – such that, once it became evident in the course of the 1980s that a complete victory was impossible, this leadership was able, in agonisingly slow and crab-like manner, to bring Sinn Féin and the IRA into negotiation; fifthly, while in Ireland, the political wing more or less controlled the military wing, in Euskadi it would seem to be the other way around.

On the last evening of my stay in Vitoria I walked to the Basque parliament, a three-storey building on the other side of Florida Park that once housed an educational institute. In front of this democratic and constitutional edifice, with the word *Legebiltzarra* (which I guess to be the Basque for 'Legislature') inscribed above the entrance, I recalled my first visit to Euskadi in 1966, and a ride on a country bus from Bilbao to visit – in effect to pay homage to – Guernica. At that time, it was still forbidden to use or display the Basque language in public, and local officers of the Guardia Civil, Franco's thuggish police force, were all from other provinces of Spain.

In a little bookshop down a side-street, in response to my inquiry about the Basque language, the owner surreptitiously produced a little booklet, *Apuntos del Idioma Vasco*, a book I still possess. In Guernica, I visited the famous tree, one of four in the Basque Country, under which in medieval times the newly created Lords of Biscay would come to swear to protect the *fueros* (rights) of the Basques. In 1483, Queen Isabel, clad in Basque national costume, visited the town.

In 1966 some of the ruins of the 1937 attack were still visible, while the walls of the town were covered with slogans calling for the restoration of the *fueros*: these had, in fact, been lost in the 1870s, when the Basques sided with the insurrection of the right-wing rebel Carlists. In 1966 the *fueros* were above all a symbol of constitutional and legal resistance to Francoism. However, the outbreak of the ETA military campaign two years later changed the nature of Basque nationalism, from one demanding the restoration of historic and constitutional rights to one in which the most vocal and intransigent were claiming independence.

Standing outside the Basque legislature in Vitoria in 2007, it was not unreasonable to conclude that, in large measure at least, the *fueros* have indeed been restored by a sorely tried and increasingly exasperated Spanish democratic system. One of my Turkish companions observed: 'If the Kurds had 20 per cent of what the Basques now have, they would be happy indeed.' Such proportion and self-restraint are not, however, the mark of modern nationalism, in Euskadi or anywhere else.

3. POST-COLONIAL SEQUESTRATION SYNDROME: TIBET, PALESTINE AND THE POLITICS OF FAILURE
13 May 2008

Two current and high-profile events – the crisis in and around Tibet following the Lhasa riots of 14 March 2008 and the sixtieth anniversary of the establishment on 14 May 1948 of the State of Israel – have more in common than it may first appear. Indeed, their commonalities are shared to a degree by other political and ethnic disputes across the world, to the extent that they compose a distinct phenomenon which may be termed 'the syndrome of post-colonial sequestration'.

The category may sound abstract but the lived experience it denotes is real and multiple: that is, the cases where countries or peoples have at a decisive moment of international change, amid the retreat of imperial or hegemonic powers, failed (through bad timing and/or bad leadership) to establish their independence. Tibet and Palestine (Israel's 'other') are classic examples of the syndrome. The contrast is with other countries or peoples that have, as it were, managed 'to get out in time'. Kuwait is one such: a country that is (more than most) artificial and invented, yet which was able to receive widespread international support when invaded by Saddam Hussein's Iraq in 1990 precisely because it had acquired independence in 1961 and had long been a member of the Arab League and of the United Nations.

The victims of 'post-colonial sequestration', by contrast, failed to make it past the barrier of independence and international recognition. Instead they fell into a state of half-recognised but contested existence. After the war of 1948–9 the 'Palestine question' disappeared almost entirely from the international scene, only to re-emerge with the defeat of the Arab armies in the six-day war of 1967. Tibet too has undergone long years of neglect in the international arena, punctuated by periodic (and notably near half century) reincarnations of interest. the bloody British occupation of Lhasa in 1904–5, the insurrection against Chinese rule and the flight of the Dalai Lama in 1959 and now the uprising of March 2008.

An essential element in understanding this syndrome, both from 'within' (the people or country concerned) and 'outside' (the international order), is to abandon the idea that the division of the world into today's nation-states corresponds to any fundamental principles. The map of the world, now containing close to two hundred independent entities, is not drawn according to ideas of natural justice, divine or even historic entitlement, nor even of the democratic and liberal self-realisation of 'nations'. It is, rather – as scholars of nationalism from Ernest Gellner to Tom Nairn have pointed out – also arbitrary and contingent: a result of power politics; accidents; wars; state crises; and hegemonic, colonial (in the case of the Central Asian republics of the former Soviet Union) ideology.

In this haphazard context, the chances of failure or success in achieving international recognition can be equally contingent. The arbitrary nature of states and frontiers in Africa, the Middle East, Central Asia and Latin America testifies to this, as do in Europe the examples of Belgium, Switzerland, and most recently Kosovo. Some entities gain established existence and recognition, others do not: there is no natural order in deciding their fate, even if larger political trends and dynamics may in some eras offer a more propitious context. In each case, however, it is usually international politics that plays the decisive role. In particular, the key moment of possibility – and danger – is the convulsive change that occurs when wars end or colonial powers prepare to withdraw. The end of the two world wars in the Middle East is emblematic of the process.

In the aftermath of the Great War of 1914–8, the Ottoman retreat was accompanied by the emergence of various de facto states and movements claiming independence. The Kurds of Turkey and Iraq were promised consultation on independence in the Treaty of Sèvres (1920); the former Ottoman province of the Hijaz, whose ruler Sharif Hussein had supported the British in their campaign against the Turks, and the western Arabian state of Asir, also proffered their claims. But newly assertive states – Kemalist Turkey, British-ruled Iraq and the newly expanding Kingdom of Najd (later Saudi Arabia) – occupied and annexed these territories, crushing the aspirations of the time.

A similar process occurred after the Second World War. The British had ruled the administrative entity called 'Palestine' since 1920, in effect transposing an imagined, biblical and nineteenth-century romantic term onto a slice of territory that had hitherto been divided up between three Ottoman provinces. A similar process of arbitrary delineation and nomenclature occurred with Lebanon, Syria, Jordan and Iraq.

Yet if the colonial creation was arbitrary, the development inside the colonial box of two ethnic communities and two corresponding nationalist movements – Jewish/Zionist and Arab/Palestinian respectively – was real. The unilateral (and profoundly irresponsible) British retreat in 1948 was followed by war, in which the Zionists successfully fought to achieve their independence and the Palestinians (earlier defeated in the 1936–9 insurrection) failed to secure theirs and were occupied by the armies of neighbouring Arab states, Egypt and Jordan. The result by 1949 was the sequestration by Israeli and Arab states of the former British colony.

For two decades, until Israel expelled the Arab states in the 1967 war, Palestine was divided between three regional powers. Since 1967 the unity of the British colonial artefact has been re-established and, in effect, a civil war within that territory has continued. In the face of Israeli power on one side, and the weakness and accommodations of Arab states on the other, Palestine failed to make it.

For all the differences of region and political context, a comparable process was taking place at that time over Tibet, where aspirations to independence were crushed as the forces of the victorious Chinese revolution of 1949 subordinated and incorporated the territory into the People's Republic of China. Here, much of the energetic debate about Tibet's 'historical status' – whether (as Tibetan nationalists and their supporters claim) it was an independent state before China occupied it in 1950–1 or (in Chinese nationalist terminology) an 'inalienable part' of historic China – is based on a dubious premise. For 'history' and its associations is not the unarguable source of judgement that both sides see it as.

Even if Tibet had been an integral part of China for centuries, this would not gainsay its contemporary right to claim independence as a territory with a clearly distinct language and culture, and with several decades of de facto and modern sovereignty before 1950. After all, Ireland was long ruled by England, Norway by Sweden, and Finland, Ukraine and the Baltic countries by Russia, without this contradicting their right to independence in the twentieth century.

It is not essential to this line of argument, but worth saying anyway, that even on historical grounds the Tibetans have as good or better case for independence as these other lands. Chinese armies have certainly occupied Tibet on various occasions in past centuries, as English armies occupied much of France. But from the mid-eighteenth century, Tibet was in practice independent under its Dalai Lama rulers based in their capital, Lhasa. The few European travellers who reached this 'forbidden city' in the 1840s (such as the French priests Père Huc and Père Gabet) noted that the Chinese presence was purely formal, the two *ambans* (Beijing officials) posted there having no more power than, say, a British high commissioner has in independent Australia or India.

The Tibetans were able to achieve and sustain this de facto independence for two reasons: the weakness of the Manchu empire in Beijing (which in the course of the nineteenth century lost control of parts of Mongolia, Korea and Taiwan); and the fact that Tibet came, again in the nineteenth century, to be part of a string of independent but virtually unexplored Asian states which acquired neutral 'buffer' status between the British and Russian empires.

In a swathe of countries – from Persia in the west through Afghanistan to Tibet – this was a period of Anglo-Russian rivalry, scheming and exaggeration of threat. The occasional military incursions by the British (against Persia over Herat in 1856, in the Afghanistan wars of the 1840s and 1870s, and in the Younghusband expedition to Lhasa in 1904) were designed not to annex these states to the Raj but to re-establish a strategic status quo, often on the basis of grossly inflated reports of Russian influence.

The problem for Tibet was that its leaders preferred – in a judgement that was good in the short term and catastrophic in the long – to avoid international diplomatic contact, in some cases even recognition. Even in the 1940s there was no direct radio contact between the authorities in Lhasa and the outside world. This approach was shared by some other aristocratic states which remained free of colonisation well into the twentieth century (Haile Selassie's Ethiopia, the imams of Yemen, the sultan of Muscat, the kings of Afghanistan). But when international circumstances changed, their remoteness turned from protection into danger: the ending of the 1939–45 war transformed the world around Tibet, with Britain's departure from India in 1947 and the Chinese communist triumph of 1949.

A newly independent India, mindful of the dangers of fragmentary forces within its own territory, did not adopt the Tibetan cause; this served further to alter the strategic situation to Tibet's disadvantage. The Lhasa government, presided over by an inexperienced teenage Dalai Lama and riven with internal conflicts, made a belated attempt to turn de facto pre-modern independence into international recognition by despatching a mission to the United Nations. It was too late: Tibet, like Palestine, was crushed by the shifts in regional power and imperial readjustment of the post-1945 world. The Tibetan uprising of March 1959 attracted international sympathy, and some CIA support, but to no avail.

This 'sequestration syndrome' applies in other more recent cases: Eritrea and East Timor, respectively post-colonial victims of Ethiopia and Indonesia. They did manage after bloody wars to secure independence, Eritrea's in 1993 and East Timor's in 1999 – but only when the oppressor state's regime (Mengistu's Derg and Suharto's New Order) had fallen. An example on the other side is the former Spanish colony of Western Sahara, seized by Morocco at the moment of decolonisation in 1975. The gathering of such diverse places under one rubric may seem forced, even preposterous – particularly to hegemonic nationalists from Tel Aviv, Beijing, Ankara, Rabat, Moscow, Belgrade and many other capitals (which is not to ignore the fact that the leaderships of independent and often small states that have 'got out in time' can be among the most virulent of nationalists, and distinctly hegemonic towards their own minorities and/or colonial components). But it speaks to the realities of the modern world, and indeed suggests a realistic pessimism about the possibility today of resolving many of these disputes. If the concept of 'post-colonial sequestration' holds, then it carries a vital lesson: only if there is a major political shift in the hegemonic state that has committed the sequestration, and which has secured some international indulgence for it, is there a realistic prospect of post-colonial annexation being reversed.

This implies that the granting of – or even, in the end, the demand for – independence is in the short and medium term less important than respect for regional and cultural rights within a democratic frame-work. The reason why such entities as Bavaria, Catalonia, Crete and California (among others) do not in their majority favour independence is less because they lack a good case in principle and precedence, and more because their major goals (including democracy, respect and economic prosperity) are deemed by the great majority of their citizens to be better realised by remaining part of the larger entity. The same may apply, in the end, to Scotland.

Hence the solution to the problems of Palestine, Kurdistan, Western Sahara and Tibet needs to do two things: discard sterile and polemical (thus exclusionary to those with independent minds and those not directly involved) disputes about historic claims – as opposed to objective, grounded, careful and respectful historical argument; and focus on the attempt to secure a measure of democratic (including federal) freedoms for subject peoples and territories.

The first is self-explanatory, except to nationalist partisans and political sectarians. The second requires a larger change in the whole political system of the country of which aspirants to autonomy, sovereignty and recognition (and possibly, in the end, independence) are a part. If Israel were prepared to grant democratic rights and freedoms to the Palestinians whose lives it controls, and China to permit the same to its citizens (including Tibetan and Uyghur), then all options – negotiated independence, democratic federalism, new states or refounded states – could be freely placed on the table. The current inclinations of these dominant states and their publics and the foreseeable international distribution of power suggest that the prospect of 'de-sequestration' is at present dim. The time for a realistic optimism, for Tibet and Palestine at least, is not yet at hand.

4. GEORGIA'S WAR:
ON THE MISCALCULATIONS OF SMALL NATIONS
26 August 2008

The brief and vicious war between Georgia and Russia over South Ossetia has killed an untold number of people and displaced and traumatised many thousands more; promised a lengthy and abrasive aftermath; postponed even further the prospects of a settlement over this and Abkhazia, the region's other territory lost to Georgia's control in the early 1990s; created new enmities as well as poisoning existing ones; and planted seeds of yet further conflict.

In the wake of the disaster, the urgent need is to assist and protect the civilian victims from its continuing ravages via an intense effort of humanitarian mobilisation and sensitive diplomacy. Beyond that, a survey of the freshly ruined landscape is needed to assess how the region, the continent and the notional 'international community' can begin to pick up the pieces. But between the immediate and the strategic, an interim political assessment of this war suggests a lesson that relates both to Georgia itself and to the political leaderships of other local actors (especially 'small nations') who have found themselves – or chosen to be – involved in military contest with bigger neighbours.

Where Georgia itself is concerned, the lesson can be summed up in a phrase: pity (and of course help) the Georgians, but condemn their leaders. For if most Western governments and commentators have focused on the high politics and historical echoes of the conflict – from Russia's excessive military response to the implications for Georgia's entry into NATO; from the role of the United States to echoes of Czechoslovakia in 1938 and 1968 – less attention than is warranted has been paid to Tbilisi's contribution to the disaster.

In strict terms, the chief responsibility belongs to Georgia's reckless and demagogic president, Mikheil Saakashvili. His precipitous launch of a brutal assault on the South Ossetian capital of Tskhinvali on the night of 7–8 August 2008 is worse than a crime: it is a terrible blunder. More broadly, however, the responsibility devolves onto the self-inflating nationalist ideology which traps Saakashvili and Georgians who think like him. Here, indeed, is a local manifestation of a universal problem. For while the particular circumstances of the latest Caucasian war have been ably analysed, it is important to broaden the discussion by exploring the role that the nationalist ideology of Saakashvili's type – with its heady mix of vanity, presumption and miscalculation – has played in the modern world.

There is still reluctance among many analysts of international relations to believe that local and/or 'small' actors in a political situation – in this case the Georgian leadership – have their own agency, freedom of manoeuvre and responsibility. (This flaw is shared by that particular

kind of American and of course 'anti-American' leftist for whom everything that happens in the world must by definition be the responsibility
of the United States: an understudied genre of vulgar imperialism.)

In fact, it is routinely impossible to make sense of almost any conflict or region without registering that local states, opposition groups or
minority movements can act with considerable autonomy in pursuit of
their own interests – even to the extent of manipulating (and on occasion deceiving) distant and more powerful 'allies'. There are many cases
during the Cold War, for example, where Third World states attacked
their neighbours on their own accord yet were widely characterised
as having acted on orders – as 'clients', 'proxies', 'agents', 'pawns'. They
include: Israel in attacking Egypt in 1967 and Lebanon in 1982; Turkey
in invading Cyprus in 1974; Egypt in attacking Israel in 1973; Cuba in
sending troops to Angola in 1975; Iraq in attacking Iran in 1980 and
Kuwait in 1990.

The international context matters, but it is not determinant: what is
determinant is the reading of that international situation and the calculation of risks and opportunities which the local leaders and political forces
make. Sometimes they get it right. Cuba's judgements that Washington,
battered by defeat in Vietnam, would not stop its forces crossing the
Atlantic to Angola in 1975, was one such – yet before he took that decision, Fidel Castro asked for a detailed analysis of opinion in the US
Congress. More frequently, the leaders concerned are not so careful.

If the supreme responsibility of democratic leaders is indeed to protect their own peoples, then the briefest of comparative overviews can
show just how pernicious is the impact of the kind of nationalist delusion displayed by Mikheil Saakashvili. His blundering into war over
South Ossetia is but the latest example of how the nationalist obsession
with the fetish of 'territorial integrity' corrupts the Georgians' worldview: for it entails a multiple refusal to look at reasonable, humane compromises; a misreading of international political realities; and a resort to
destructive and often useless violence.

Here, the flaws of nationalism can match or exceed those of
religion, in a way that offers a sidelight on the much-vaunted catch-all
ascription of responsibility for modern conflicts to a supposed 'clash
of civilisations' (by which is usually meant 'Islam'). But South Ossetia
and its neighbours share a history where Christianity intermingles with
empire (Georgian, Ottoman, Russian and Soviet) in the experience of

its peoples. The chief agent of destruction is not to be found in 'culture' (in the guise of religion or some other vague source of identity) but in the arrogance, recklessness and ignorance born of nationalist excess – which, to be sure, often uses religion and associated 'cultural' offerings as part of its packaging. The problem is a political one; and where 'cultural' differences are small – as in Transcaucasia, parts of the Balkans and Northern Ireland – the political conflicts can more than compensate.

The case of Cyprus is illustrative in this regard. In July 1974 a group of right-wing Greek Cypriots toppled the elected (and more moderate) government of Archbishop Makarios with the support of the junta in Athens. At first it seemed that the world, even Turkey, had accepted it. I was in Cyprus at the time, and well recall conversations with Greek Cypriots to the effect that: 'The Turks will never invade. The Russians will stop them.' So it went until the sky north of Nicosia was filled with the transport planes despatched by Turkish Prime Minister Bülent Ecevit, out of which floated the Turkish paratroops coming to occupy the north of the city and of the island – where they remain today.

Ever since, the Greek Cypriots have blamed everyone but themselves for this debacle: the Americans (who encouraged the Turks to invade because they wanted a base in northern Cyprus, at Kyrenia); the British (committed under a 1960 treaty to defending the integrity of Cyprus and with two bases on the island, who did nothing and so showed their historic 'pro-Turkish' bias); the European Union and the United Nations (who have sought to impose unwanted solutions).

Similar miscalculations have dominated in the Palestine conflict. Few nationalist leaderships have shown such little strategic sense; ever since the re-emergence of a nationalist movement in the 1960s, policy has been led by militaristic rhetoric, misjudgement of the regional and international situation, and a misconceived sense of how friends and foes alike would react. On two occasions the Palestinians, led by Yasser Arafat's Palestine Liberation Organisation, found themselves with forces and considerable political support in neighbouring Arab states: Jordan (1967–70) and Lebanon (1970–82). On each occasion the movement was carried away by delusions of power and of allied support far in excess of the reality, which led them needlessly to provoke local political forces and armed groups; the result was the destruction of their local bases and their expulsion from the country. In 2000 Arafat, faced with the failure of peace talks with Ehud Barak, agreed to support and promote a 'spontaneous' uprising (the second intifada). He apparently imagined that in so doing, he could break Barak's political will and obtain more concessions: instead he got Ariel Sharon, who had his own ideas about how to provoke a spontaneous uprising, and did a far better job of it in September 2000.

The Israelis themselves are possessed of a military efficiency, a strong international ally and a historic self-righteousness that at times has served them ill; but they too have repeatedly overplayed their hand. They missed the historic opportunity to resolve the Palestinian issue in the aftermath of the 1967 war by withdrawing promptly from the territories they had occupied by force. In 1982 they blundered into a war in Lebanon, where they failed either to destroy their enemies or to install a client regime, and ended up eighteen years later in unconditional flight from a ferocious Hizbullah enemy on their tail. For years the Israelis boasted that they had achieved complete control of Gaza, only to pull out in the end, leaving the terrain open for Hamas. Many citizens of the Israeli state must wonder what the costs of long-term intransigence and settlement expansion will be; and indeed if such a posture may, in the end, not produce the very dire consequences that Israel seeks to avoid.

The blunders brought on by nationalist (and associated revolutionary) delusions in the twentieth century are indeed global. There was North Korean president Kim Il-sung's disastrous attempt in June 1950 to seize South Korea in a sudden attack, which was repulsed by a rapidly mobilised United States expeditionary force. Only the massive intervention of Chinese 'volunteers' saved the communist regime from annihilation. The inhabitants of Baghdad may also recall the miscalculations of Saddam Hussein in his invasions of Iran (1980) and Kuwait (1990). These comparatively more recent examples were long preceded by the classic such miscalculation of the 1916 Easter uprising in Dublin. On that occasion a poorly armed insurrectionary force was defeated and part of the city destroyed by a British riposte as rapid and predictable as that of the Russians in Tskhinvali.

True, such miscalculations about the capabilities of one's own forces and the reactions of others are not confined to small nations. Most major nations have many and larger blunders to their name: the Americans in Korea, Vietnam and Iraq; the British in Suez; the French in Vietnam, Suez and Algeria; the Russians in Afghanistan; the Italians and Germans in the 1930s and 1940s. The difference is that except in the most extreme of cases – notably Nazi Germany – these large states have been able to recuperate their losses and in large measure continue to inhabit their illusions of grandeur. Smaller peoples pay a higher price.

It is said that when he took over from veteran Georgian leader Eduard Shevardnadze in 2004, Mikheil Saakashvili told the older man – known in Georgian as *tetri melia* (the white fox) – that he had had the chance to be the great founder of a new Georgia, but that he had missed the opportunity. Saakashvili's entrapment in nationalist delusion was always going to backfire. In the moment of Georgia's latest agony, it will be little consolation that he has brought his country into the modern world in a very different way.

5.   LETTER FROM YEREVAN:
ARMENIA'S MIXED MESSAGES
15 October 2008

Armenia should be smiling. After many years of conflict, poverty and isolation, the trend of events in this south Caucasus region might seem at last to be going in favour of the small, landlocked republic. The short war between Georgia and Russia in August 2008 has humbled its sometimes difficult neighbour while leaving intact its friendship with the northern giant; it maintains control of the disputed territory of Nagorno-Karabakh against any attempts by its hostile neighbour Azerbaijan to reclaim it, with Moscow's victory over Tbilisi helping to counter – for the moment – the threat of renewed war with Baku; and it has hosted without serious incident the president of Turkey, a neighbour from whom it has long been divided by the bitter, unresolved past.

These developments can plausibly be seen as making Armenia more secure than it has been since it gained post-Soviet independence in 1991 (or, more accurately, the restoration of an independence first proclaimed in 1918). Yet to officials in the country's foreign ministry – working in the imposing russet stone buildings overlooking Republic Square in Yerevan – the outlook is more sombre than sunny.

The deeper realities of present-day Armenia help explain why. The freedom of manoeuvre of Armenian politicians and officials is as constrained as the country's geopolitical position itself: the events of August

2008 have also highlighted that fact. Strong relations with Russia to the north and Iran to the south are a given. Both have long displeased the George W. Bush administration. An American ambassador has taken up residence in the heavily fortified embassy compound near the airport, but only after an interruption of three years; and it is notable that United States vice-president Dick Cheney failed to include Armenia in his post-war tour through Azerbaijan, Georgia and Ukraine. Indeed, there is no significant public voice in Armenia in favour of entry to NATO or the European Union,

Yerevan may have been a beneficiary of the Georgia–Russia war, though in fact it has limited direct interest in their conflict. The economic and political situation in Georgia does affect the approximately 200,000 Armenians who still live in the Javakheti region of southern Georgia, who were traditionally involved in servicing the former Soviet bases there. In recent years, they have been hit both by considerable poverty and by the rise in Georgian nationalist sentiment. At the same time, Armenia faces the world with its frontiers to Azerbaijan and Turkey closed, reliant for its trading connections on the land route through Georgia to the port of Poti or the one through Iran to distant Tehran.

Just as important is that the assertion of Russian power may (according to influential voices in Yerevan) have acted as a deterrent to Armenia's rival Azerbaijan, whose rising oil-revenues and self-confidence might otherwise have propelled it to try to reoccupy the areas of its country seized by Armenia in the war of 1992–4. This prospect remains far from unthinkable – and no one expects the Russians to send combat troops to help Armenia. But there are several thousand Russian soldiers in the country already, in bases along the frontier with Turkey, only 40 kilometres from the capital. Moreover, large quantities of Russian military equipment have been pre-positioned: in the event of a new war with Azerbaijan, the assumption is that these weapons would be made available to the Armenian forces.

There are also signs that the war in Georgia has led to a rethinking of policy in Armenia's powerful western neighbour, Turkey. Armenians cannot forget the terrible killings – by any normal criteria, a genocide – of Armenians in Turkey during 1915 and afterwards. Above Yerevan stands the great memorial named *Tsitsernakaberd* (Swallow Castle), which commemorates the tragic, defiantly unforgotten event. It consists of a dignified stone esplanade leading to a pointed tower, and to a sunken chamber with an eternal flame. Twelve columns commemorate the provinces of 'western Armenia', today's eastern Turkey, from which Armenians were expelled in the midst of the Great War and its aftermath.

The issue of the Turkish refusal to acknowledge the genocide has long poisoned, and will probably continue to poison, Armenian–Turkish relations. My impression in Yerevan is that since the victims of the genocide were part of what is now the Republic of Turkey – hence the ancestors of today's diaspora in Europe, the United States and parts of the Arab world – a settlement that is not acceptable to these descendants would not pass in Yerevan. But there is some movement on both sides. For those in Turkey, Armenia and the diaspora who wish to arrive at a considered and shared historical judgement – admittedly still few, though their number is growing – the materials for arriving at a reasoned judgement are there.

A more immediate concern is the blockade imposed by Turkey since the early 1990s war between Armenia and Azerbaijan. Armenia desperately needs to open its frontiers to expand its trade links. Some recent developments – among them the announcement by Ankara of a new South Caucasus Initiative, and the historic visit of Turkey's president on 6 September 2008 to watch an Armenia vs. Turkey football match in Yerevan – suggest that a shift in attitudes may be occurring. But the lesson of other conflicts, such as the Arab–Israeli dispute, is that broad declarations and symbolic gestures are not enough: it is not clear (so my interlocutors at Armenia's foreign ministry told me) that Abdullah Gül's expression of goodwill is being translated into policy detail lower down the bureaucratic scale. For anyone familiar with the contemporary state of public opinion in Armenia and Turkey, the chances of a major breakthrough still appear slim.

The Armenians shared the surprise of the rest of the world about the events of August 2008. The summary judgement of one informed observer sums up the reaction: 'Misha blew it.' No one I met believes the Russian claim that Washington encouraged Tbilisi to attack South Ossetia and Abkhazia; but most voiced severe criticism of NATO's vague and apparently open-ended commitment to Georgia. An astute Mediterranean expert and veteran of back-channel regional negotiations remarked that Saakashvili had probably been deluded by his earlier successes, including the recovery of the less-noticed separatist enclave of Adzharia in south-east Georgia in his first months in office. The

Georgian president's pattern of rule, he went on, casts retrospective light on the overthrow of Eduard Shevardnadze in 2003–4: how much was this a 'revolution' and how much a near-accidental power-grab whose triumph deluded Saakashvili about the opportunities in store?

But my Armenian hosts were puzzled – even alarmed – by Russia's decision to recognise the full independence of the two breakaway entities. Yerevan's orientation (like the Central Asian republics allied to Moscow) may be pro-Russian, but it is not prepared to follow on this one. Armenia has its own interests to consider, one of which is the flow of remittances from its diaspora in Russia on which it so much depends. The accelerating capital flight from Russia – in part a consequence of the global fallout of the financial crash, but also a response to political sensitivities – has tough implications for a small trading economy.

In a longer-term perspective, however, the Russian–Georgian war has done little to alleviate, far less resolve the major problems Armenia faces. They centre on the power of the new elite and the dramatic effects of social inequality, poverty and exclusion. The enduring poverty of the country is evident to any visitor who leaves the central area of Yerevan with its modern buildings, restaurants and hotels. Much of the population lives in deprivation; corruption pervades all areas of government; and an astounding proportion of the population, almost half by some estimates (many from its most educated and enterprising groups), has left the country for Russia or the West.

Armenia is not a bloody dictatorship, but nor is it a democracy: like its two south Caucasian neighbours (with which it has much more in common, politically and culturally, than nationalist pride would admit), it is ruled by a post-communist elite, some of whose members operate in legal grey areas for purposes of enrichment and power accumulation. The appropriation of assets from two sources – those of the Soviet period and a significant part of the $1.3 billion sent back by Armenia's diaspora – plays a vital role in consolidating the elite's power and enhancing its lifestyle.

This elite is led by former president Robert Kocharian (still the country's strongman), and many members of it also come from Nagorno-Karabakh. They have shown that they are prepared to intimidate, censor and manipulate to suit their ends. The press and the media are controlled, when not by the state then by right-wing nationalists based in California. The penalties may not involve being arrested or shot, but they can be severe: if you criticise the government too overtly, you may lose your commercial licence (if you are in business) or your job (if you work for the government).

The ruling network is also prepared to resort to the gun: as in October 1999, when a gunman with some official protection assassinated the prime minister, the speaker and six other officials in parliament; in September 2001, when the president's bodyguards beat Poghos Poghosian to death in the Aragast (Poplavok) jazz cafe in Yerevan; and in March 2008, when the president sent police to beat up a crowd of opposition supporters protesting the election outcome, an assault in which nine were killed. No one will ever know exactly what happened on 1 March, but there are credible rumours that the police planted guns among the sleeping protesters. What does seem certain – and was confirmed to me by one Western diplomat who has attended the proceedings – is that the trials of the protesters have been rigged.

The unresolved conflict with Azerbaijan over Nagorno-Karabakh overshadows all the events, regional and domestic, in which Armenia is embroiled. Notwithstanding its ethnic Armenian majority, this contested region of around 140,000 was allocated to Azerbaijan by Moscow in the 1920s. a small part of the broader reassignment of peoples and territories across Europe after the Great War and the Bolshevik revolution.

The loosening of political controls during the Mikhail Gorbachev-era perestroika in the late 1980s enabled an immense nationalist mobilisation in Armenia and Nagorno-Karabakh itself in favour of the latter's incorporation into the former. The tensions with Azerbaijan grew; war erupted in 1992 between the by-then post-Soviet independent states of Armenia and Azerbaijan, which concluded in 1994 with the Armenians in control of Nagorno-Karabakh and a swathe of Azeri territory including the Lachin corridor. Since 1990 Yerevan has professed a belief that Nagorno-Karabakh should become an independent state rather than be annexed to Armenia; thus the region joins Abkhazia and South Ossetia in limbo-land, while Armenia's territorial gains provide it with a bargaining-chip in any negotiations.

Over the years, many international negotiators have sought to find a solution to this problem. Indeed, a negotiated settlement of the problem is the common aim of the United States and Europe in the Organisation for Security and Cooperation in Europe (OSCE's) Minsk Process; one shared by Armenia's close – if understated – ally, the Islamic Republic of Iran. On the ground and on both sides, however (the Azeri even more than the Armenian), nationalist rhetoric and intransigence prevail; though a readiness at least to meet at official level offers some grounds for belief that in time this may change.

In effect, the current Armenian political leadership, deeply influenced by its origins in Nagorno-Karabakh, and the powerful military and financial interests that have arisen from the war have sequestered Armenia as a whole; the inflow of money and the reinforcement of nationalist sentiment from the diaspora form the third leg of this unholy trinity. The results of the Moscow–Tbilisi war show every sign of confirming this ruling pattern.

There may, however, be another lesson which the events of this summer should draw to the attention of politicians and officials in Yerevan: namely that for all the advantages they now think they have in their dispute with Azerbaijan, and for all the nationalist sentiment attached to this issue, the danger of another war with Azerbaijan cannot be excluded. Azerbaijan is getting richer and stronger; its clearly fixed elections of 16 October 2008 are conducted with barely a peep of protest from its Western investors; and the new generation there, with no memory of coexistence with Armenian neighbours or fellow citizens, is in key respects more militant than its predecessors. A wise Armenian academic observer in Yerevan put it to me thus: 'The one thing you learn from living in the south Caucasus is that there are no such things as "frozen conflicts".'

6.   IN THE DARKEST PLACE:
A MORNING IN AUSCHWITZ
26 January 2007

Theodor Adorno famously said that there can be no poetry after Auschwitz; the great independent Marxist writer Isaac Deutscher (many of whose relatives died in these places) thought that any lessons would take centuries to offer themselves. Yet here in southern Poland, on a sunny morning sixty-one years later, the lessons do seem to flood in: inchoate yet powerful, in ways that make this citizen of the age, teacher and parent feel that all human beings should listen to and act on them.

The approaches to the Auschwitz complex – an extensive area that included forced labour and detention camps as well as places of extermination such as Birkenau – do not prepare the visitor for what is to come. The drive from the beautiful Polish city of Kraków, through attractive villages with flowers in bloom and churches newly painted, takes less than an hour. The only premonitory moment comes when stuck in a tunnel under a railway line; an old goods train, its wheels and connections clanking ominously above, evokes an echo of the transports of death.

Then, without warning, my driver points to some distant buildings: 'Now you can see Birkenau.' And suddenly, there it is. The all-too-familiar watchtower that stands over the main entrance, with the railway line running underneath; the ghastly forking of the railway lines where the transport trains came to a halt and the new arrivals were separated and despatched, sometimes within a few minutes, to their death.

From the watchtower itself, the expanse of a few acres is clear enough: the blockhouses, mathematically constructed so that even now you can peer from the window at one end and look right through the whole complex past the sections where individual groups – women, Czechs, Roma – were incarcerated. Upwards to the left are the remains of one of the several gas-chambers. The roof is broken where the SS sought to blow up the traces of their crime as they retreated, but the ramp down which the victims made their final descent makes it all too identifiable. Elsewhere are the sites where bodies were burnt, stolen goods collected and the ashes of the murdered scattered.

At 10.30 am, the tourist buses have not yet arrived. This space of evil is entirely empty, silent apart from the birdsong. I keep walking, past the gas-chambers to the post-Second World War memorial that urges the world never to forget these crimes; then through a small gate at the back and into the long grass of the field beyond, at the end of which my guide is waiting.

The experience of walking through and out of a place that took the lives of so many, and who never found a friendly guide waiting on the other side, is in its way the key to an initial response to Auschwitz. Life has gone on, it will go on, and we must never forget what happened here. My son visited this place at the age of nineteen; I feel that all people of the world – starting with the students of around the same age and older whom we teach at university – should be encouraged to do the same. This is not least because in the six decades since the Nazi genocide, other terrible and in their own way incomprehensible crimes have been committed: in Cambodia and Rwanda, at Sabra and Shatila, Halabja and Srebrenica, to name but a few. Humanity has evidently not progressed, and in the turmoil of the early twenty-first century would appear to be unlearning whatever the genocide might have taught it.

What happened here, and across the myriad sites of the Nazis' exterminatory project? It was not some providential or religious event, as the biblical term popularised in the 1960s, 'holocaust' (literally 'total burning') might imply. The descriptive secular Hebrew term *shoah* ('catastrophe' or 'disaster') is both more accurate and more enabling as a tool of humanity's self-education.

For there are indeed lessons to be learnt here, that remain true to the sufferings of those who died and the injunctions on the Birkenau memorial. The first is an insistence on the importance of universal human rights, and of those institutions set up to protect them, not least at a time when they are under attack from so many quarters. The starting point is the United Nations, the 1948 Universal Declaration of Human Rights, and all the other conventions and treaties that have followed from that – predominantly the Convention on Genocide.

The uniqueness or otherwise of the Nazi killings of more than 5 million Jews may absorb historians and moral philosophers, but there can be no question that the lessons are universal. This was recognised in the Nuremberg trials themselves, where the Nazis were prosecuted for crimes against humanity, and equally in the corpus of UN human rights law. The recent work of writers such as Michael Mann, Zygmunt Bauman and Mark Mazower has further tried to relate these specific events to the broader place of violence, extermination and coercive racism within modernity itself. Modernity may not necessarily be murderous but it has had more than a chance relationship to mass murder as well as to its subsequent denial.

A second lesson concerns the presentation of these events solely in terms of victimhood. Those killed in Birkenau and elsewhere were victims, in large measure unaware of what awaited them and powerless to prevent it. Yet there is a danger and a distortion involved in the general presentation of the *shoah* as one of passivity and fate.

Many Jews, the overwhelming majority of those killed in the camps, resisted before they met their fate. Doomed as it was, the uprising of the Jewish ghetto in Warsaw in 1943 inspired others to resist across Europe. Thousands of Jews fought in the armies that defeated Nazism: from the Red Army in the east, to the United States armed forces in the west, and in the French and Italian resistance movements. Many, and the large numbers of others who defied the Nazis, did so in the name of the countries of which they were a part and/or of humanity and its ideals as a whole.

This theme of resistance is one that is suggested, albeit in a largely unrecognised way, in the choice of 27 January – the day in 1945 when Auschwitz was liberated by the Soviet army – as 'Holocaust Memorial Day'. For late January was the moment of another significant wartime event: the first armed attacks on German troops by inhabitants of the Warsaw ghetto took place on 18 January 1943 (albeit the main uprising itself began only in April).

A third lesson is about solidarity. It can be approached by noting the way in which the *shoah* is portrayed in other memorials to these times. In Warsaw itself, there are several monuments to the 1943 uprising, most famously the large frieze by Nathan Rapoport (originally erected in 1948) portraying the heroic people on the front and the desperation that followed on the back. The message (in Polish, Hebrew and Yiddish) is simple, and without broader political connotation: 'To the Jewish people'. At the site in the former ghetto where Mordechai Anielewicz and his comrade made their last stand, there is a deliberate attempt to link the insurrection and its heroism to the broader cause of humanity. The Warsaw insurgents were a coalition: some Zionists, some Bundists and others considering themselves Polish nationalists.

In other memorials, themes of universalism and resistance also receive due recognition. In Berlin's Jewish Museum, the exhibit on the Second World War extermination is (at the request of its Israeli sculptor) explicitly dedicated to all victims of war. In Yad Vashem, the mountainside site in Jerusalem commemorating these events, there are several monuments to the Jews who fought, including one to an estimated 1.5 million Jews who served in the armies that defeated Hitler, thus recognising the place of resistance within the story as a whole.

These three broad, even universal, lessons carry a particular charge when seen in the light of contemporary debates and events, especially in the Middle East. Two currents are immediately apparent and ines-capable: on one side, the selective and instrumental usage of the *shoah* by the Israeli state to justify some of its actions and violations of inter-national law, and to convey some prior moral entitlement over land or sovereignty on the part of the Jewish people and at the expense of the Palestinians; on the other, a grotesque inversion of the same false link-age, whereby those opposed to Israeli policies, or to the very existence of an Israeli state (most recently Iran's president, Mahmoud Ahmadinejad), extend their argument to deny the very fact of the Jewish genocide itself.

The two currents share a disabling fallacy, namely that the *shoah* itself should serve as a legitimisation for Israel; whereas the case for an Israeli state rests not on some spurious ancient privilege, but on the same grounds as that of any other people in the world to their own state, namely their existence as a nation, with rights to territory and recogni-tion following from that.

About Auschwitz-Birkenau – and Sobibor, Treblinka, Dachau, Belsen and all the rest of a terrible litany – it is too soon for silence. Far from it: what took place here in the 1940s contains much that is neces-sary for shaping a vision for humanity's future. Indeed, it is perhaps only by revisiting and discussing these twentieth-century events that we will be able to purchase our entry-visa to the twenty-first. In so doing, we might even learn to free ourselves from their abuse in modern Europe and the Middle East, and begin to move on.

Conclusions

1. THE WORLD'S TWELVE WORST IDEAS
8 January 2007

In identifying error, two great models at either end of modern times exist. The first is part thirty-nine of Francis Bacon's *Novum Organum* (1620), with its four categories of idol: those of the cave (of individual men), the tribe (human nature), the marketplace (intercourse of men with each other) and the theatre (philosophical dogma). The second is Francis Wheen's *How Mumbo-Jumbo Conquered the World: A Short History of Modern Delusions* (Fourth Estate, 2004).

Some errors are products of the unchallenged, the routine, the conventional. Some are new, products of fashion, of novelty, even of globalisation. Everyone has his or her own selection, born of profession, personality and place. The list could be a long one but, like Christ and his disciples, twelve seems a comfortable figure, at once extensive and compact. Here, for 2007, is one suggested list, in ascending order:

Number twelve: Human behaviour can be predicted.
In the name of a supposedly 'scientific' criterion of knowledge, scholars are berated for not predicting the end of the Cold War, the rise of Islam, 9/11 and much else besides. Yet many natural sciences – seismology, evolutionary biology – cannot predict with accuracy either. Human affairs themselves, even leaving aside the matter of human intention and will, allow of too many variables for such calculation.

We will never be able to predict with certainty the outcome of a sports contest, the incidence of revolutions, the duration of passion or how long an individual will live.

Number eleven: The world is speeding up.
This, a favourite trope of globalisation theorists, confuses acceleration in some areas, such as the transmission of knowledge, with the fact that large areas of human life continue to demand the same time as before: to conceive and bear a child, to learn a language, to grow up, to digest a meal, to enjoy a joke, to read a poem. It takes the same time to fly from London to New York as it did forty years ago, ditto to boil an egg or publish a book. Some activities – such as driving around major Western cities, getting through an airport or dying – may take much longer.

Number ten: We have no need for history.
In recent decades, large areas of intellectual and academic life – political thought and analysis, economics, philosophy – have jettisoned a concern with history. Yet it remains true that those who ignore history repeat it; as the recycling of unacknowledged Cold War premises by the George W. Bush administration in Iraq has devastatingly shown.

Number nine: We live in a 'post-feminist' epoch.
The implication of this claim, supposedly analogous to such terms as 'post-industrial', is that we have no more need for feminism in politics, law or everyday life, because the major goals of that movement, articulated in the 1970s and 1980s, have been achieved. On all counts, this is a false claim: the 'post-feminist' label serves not to register achievement of reforming goals, but the delegitimisation of those goals themselves.

Number eight: Markets are a 'natural' phenomenon which allow for the efficient allocation of resources and preferences.
Markets are not 'natural' but are the product of particular societies, value systems and patterns of state relations to the economy. They are not efficient allocators of goods, since they ignore the large area of human activity and need that is not covered by monetary values – from education and the provision of public works to human happiness and fulfilment. In any case the pure market is a fantasy; the examples of the two most

traded commodities in the contemporary world, oil and drugs, show how political, social and cartel factors override and distort the workings of supply and demand.

Number seven: Religion should again be allowed, when not encouraged, to play a role in political and social life.
From the evangelicals of the United States and the followers of Popes John Paul II and Benedict XVI, to the Islamists of the Middle East, the claim about the benefits of religion is one of the great and too little challenged impostures of our time. For centuries, those aspiring to freedom and democracy, whether in Europe or the Middle East, fought to push back the influence of religion on public life. Secularism cannot guarantee freedom, but against the claims of tradition and superstition, and the uses to which religion is put in modern political life from California to Kuwait, it is an essential bulwark.

Number six: In the modern world, we do not need utopias.
Dreaming, the aspiration to a better world and the imagination thereof, is a necessary part of the human condition.

Number five: We should welcome the spread of English as a world language.
It is obviously of practical benefit that there is one common, functional language of trade or air-traffic control, but the actual domination of English in today's world has been accompanied by a tide of cultural arrogance that is itself debasing: a downgrading and neglect of other languages and cultures across the world, the general compounding of Anglo-Saxon political and social arrogance, and the introverted collapse of interest within English-speaking countries themselves in other peoples and languages; in sum, a triumph of banality over diversity. One small but universal example: the imposition on hotel staff across the world, with all its wonderful diversity of nomenclature, of name tags denoting the bearer as 'Mike', 'Johnny' or 'Steve'.

Number four: The world is divided into incomparable moral blocs or civilisations.
This view has aptly been termed by Ernest Gellner as 'liberalism for the liberals, cannibalism for the cannibals'. But a set of common values is indeed shared across the world: from democracy and human rights to

the defence of national sovereignty and a belief in the benefits of economic development. The implantation of these values is disputed in all countries, but not the values themselves. Most states in the world, whatever their cultural or religious character, have signed the universalist United Nations declarations on human rights, starting with the 1948 Universal Declaration.

Number three: Diasporas have a legitimate role to play in national and international politics.
The notion that emigrant or diaspora communities have a special insight into the problems of their homeland, or a special moral or political status in regard to them, is wholly unfounded. Emigrant ethnic communities almost always play a negative, backward, at once hysterical and obstructive, role in resolving the conflicts of their countries of origin: Armenians and Turks, Jews and Arabs, various strands of Irish, are all prime examples on the inter-ethnic front, as are exiles in the United States in regard to resolving the problems of Cuba or policy-making on Iran. English emigrants are less noted for any such political role, though their spasms of collective inebriation and conformist ghettoised lifestyles abroad do little to enhance the reputation of their home country.

Number two: The only thing 'they' understand is force.
This has been the guiding illusion of hegemonic and colonial thinking for several centuries. Oppressed peoples do not accept the imposition of solutions by force: they revolt. In the end it is the oppressors who have to accept the verdict of force, as European empires did in Latin America, Africa and Asia and as the United States is doing in Iraq today. The hubris of 'mission accomplished' in May 2003 has been followed by ignominy.

Number one: The world's population problems and the spread of AIDS can be solved by 'natural' means.
This is not only the most dangerous, but also the most criminal error of the modern world. Millions of people will suffer, and die premature and humiliating deaths, as a result of the policies pursued in this regard through the United Nations and related aid and public health programmes. Indeed, there is no need to ask where the first mass murderers of the twenty-first century are; we already know, and their addresses

besides: the Apostolic Palace, 0120 Vatican City, and 1600 Pennsylvania Avenue, Washington DC. Timely arrest and indictment would save many lives.

2. THE REVENGE OF IDEAS:
KARL POLANYI AND SUSAN STRANGE
24 September 2008

During the two decades or so that I taught International Relations as an academic discipline at the London School of Economics and Political Science, the most challenging and rewarding part of the job was giving core course lectures on political and social ideas – sometimes branded 'theory'– that are relevant to understanding the arena of relations between states and peoples. The heart of the postgraduate masters' course was a set of 'great books': not a tight or fixed canon but a body of works that introduced some shaping ideas (sovereignty, states and nation, for example) and which, above all, got the students thinking.

There were three books that gave me particular satisfaction in teaching, because each in its own way did what all education should do, namely challenge the assumptions of common sense. The first was E. H. Carr's classic, *The Twenty Years' Crisis: 1919–1939* (Macmillan, 1939), a work that combined an attack on the illusions and wishful thinking of much writing on international relations with a staunch defence of the need for utopia, dreams and distant aspirations in human affairs.

The second key book was Benedict Anderson's *Imagined Communities* (Verso, 1983), a study of how the sentiments and affinities of people who had no direct experience or contact with one could coalesce into a shared identity which they came to understand as national, and of the arbitrary and artificial (if often inexorable) nature of this emergent belonging. To tell a group of one hundred young people from all over the world that their own much-cherished nations were modern rather than ancient, little more grounded in objective fact than the loyalties of a club of football supporters, and that the very concept of 'nation' was analytically and morally questionable, was a rare professorial and cosmopolitan pleasure. If they remember nothing else of what I taught, I hope they remember that.

The third great and thought-provoking work was Karl Polanyi's *The Great Transformation: The Political and Economic Origins of Our Time* (1944). This is a book of imaginative and wide-ranging historical sociology that traces the rise of the modern capitalist market from the Industrial Revolution in England in the late eighteenth century (the 'great transformation' of the book's title) to the convulsions of the 1920s and 1930s and the outbreak of the Second World War. Polanyi's book begins in the unlikely setting of the Pelican Inn – a pub in Dorset, where agricultural labourers met in the 1790s to protect their living standards. It goes on to provide a compelling, if wilfully digressive, account of how modern markets work; in particular of the inbuilt instability and inexorable swings and oscillations that they embody. The author challenges the idea that there is anything 'natural' or universal about the modern market; Polanyi emphasises the cultural and political underpinnings of markets, and shows how this complex phenomenon – at once generating wealth and provoking instability and poverty – is the particular outcome of modern industrial society.

His conclusion is a product of the broad social-democratic and informed liberal opinion of the time; that is, in the aftermath of the great depression in the 1930s and during a global war: that markets are human and contingent entities that have to be regulated and managed by states. There is no such thing as a 'hidden hand'. A 'pure' market unanchored to other social institutions and practices cannot exist.

The argument that Karl Polanyi (1886–1964) makes about markets could be extended to other human practices and institutions for which the same universality and inexorable 'naturalness' is sometimes claimed: belief in God, the authority and indeed desirability of monarchs, the heterosexual and nuclear family, the inevitability of empires and other forms of inter-state inequality, the violent character of particular peoples or regions of the world, and the liberal-democratic order itself. In the face of such 'reification' – the resort to inevitability that defenders of all these institutions make – the prerequisite critical move is less to challenge the institutions' desirability (which may in some cases be strong) than to show how arbitrary, fragile and contingent they are. It is precisely this historicisation and demystification that critical thought is intended to achieve.

Polanyi himself led a nomadic existence. He fled his native Hungary in 1919; worked as an economic journalist in Austria until 1933; lived in England where he taught for the Workers' Educational Association through the Second World War; then moved to teach at Columbia University before being obliged to move residency to Canada because his wife Ilona Duczynska's communist affiliations meant she was denied an entry visa to the United States. Polanyi died in Canada in 1964 and is interred with his wife in his Hungarian homeland.

Throughout his life, in Austria as much as in the US, Polanyi criticised the lack of realism of orthodox economics. *The Great Transformation* has been subjected to criticism from a number of directions, while more recently the tradition that its author represented has been pushed to one side by financiers and speculators (in the world of practice) and the majority of economists (in the academic world). In the process, a raft of ubiquitous supportive words and phrases has been generated to perpetuate the idea of the naturalness of the market – among them 'market adjustments', 'natural self-correction', 'iron laws of trade and finance' and 'market forces'. But the greatest myth of all is that of the 'free market' itself, as if the modern market was ever free in any meaningful way of state guarantees, of security, international law, labour control and regulation; and as if a system in which power was allocated in a grotesquely unequal and unstable manner could be said to guarantee the 'freedom' of most people subject to it. For Polanyi, the market – and the economy generally – was (in the words of one of his most important papers) an 'institute process'; a perspective that opens lines of inquiry that still reverberate across several disciplines.

The high point of such neo-liberal glorification of markets came in waves: with the Reagan–Thatcher years of the 1980s; the fall of the socialist planned economies in the early 1990s; the IT boom and the rise of China in the 2000s. All seemed to confirm the trend. Yet throughout these years the message of Polanyi – and of others who had insisted on the need for the state to regulate markets, such as J. M. Keynes in Britain and J. K. Galbraith in the US – continued to inspire some people. Among them, and with a flamboyance born of her earlier years as a financial journalist on the *Observer* and *The Economist*, was my former colleague and patron, Susan Strange (1923–98). Susan was a pioneer of the reintegration of politics with economics in the discipline named 'international political economy'; together with a number of colleagues in the US, she sought to re-establish the analytic and public-policy linkage between states and markets.

Long before most, Susan recognised that the world of finance was growing in importance on a global scale and was not merely determined by the field of production. Her *Casino Capitalism* (Blackwell, 1986), a book of prophetic insight, was indeed about how a new world of global finance, independent of states and of industrial production, had begun to emerge. It had been made possible by Richard Nixon's cutting the link of the dollar to gold in 1971 and by new forms of global communications technology. The 'casino' in the title refers not to the role of speculation and gambling in world finance, but to the fact that for the first time in history, global markets were open twenty-four hours a day.

This conception of finance as an autonomous sphere of economic activity was presented alongside the argument that no economic system – industrial, financial or agricultural – could function without the active role of the state. Her theoretical aspiration was to echo the pioneering work of Adam Smith, David Ricardo and Karl Marx in bringing together the study of politics and the state with that of the economy and markets. The policy injunction that followed was that the modern state must promote and protect markets, just as it did security of travel and transport, the stability of currencies, the promotion of education and scientific research, and other often unacknowledged but essential supports.

This approach was developed in Susan's later book *Mad Money: When Markets Outgrow Governments* (Manchester University Press, 1998). This work anticipated the current hubris of financial leaders and policy-makers in their belief not just that one upon another set of bogus practices and inflated loan systems could be sustained, but in that what they had created somehow corresponded to a natural and hence implicitly eternal order. Such beliefs are above all rooted in ignorance of history. Now, amid the dramatic crisis of the financial system, the unprecedented intervention of the United States government and of its European counterparts in financial markets also confirms the validity of much of Karl Polanyi and Susan Strange's approach to the understanding of political and economic life and institutions.

I never met Karl Polanyi, though I did meet his daughter Kari Polanyi-Levitt (Professor of Economics at McGill University, Montreal). I did know and admire Susan Strange, a person of indomitable optimism, humour and mordant tongue. Her favourite slogan, one that from his experience as a financial journalist Polanyi would for sure have endorsed,

was: 'Always attack the economists!' I can only imagine her now, prop-
ping up a bar somewhere in southern England, a pint of beer in her hand
and a twinkle in her eye, pouring scorn on the placebo analyses of Alan
Greenspan and George Soros, on the conceits of her former employer,
The Economist, and on the folly of the captains of finance in the City of
London and Wall Street.

Yet both Susan Strange and Karl Polanyi would also affirm that if
the equilibrium-seeking self-corrective mechanism of markets was fic-
tive, moments of economic crisis and transformation were a challenge to
make their own ideas part of the self-understanding of the age. Perhaps,
then, the financial sector's unfolding implosion will – as well as teaching
market fetishists a sobering lesson – create further space for a revival of
interest in the work of these fine, relevant thinkers. In the meantime,
and with every day's news confirming the instinct, let there be no respite
for the economists.

3. A TIME IN BARCELONA
5 October 2009

> I have loved the Mediterranean with passion, no doubt because I am
> a northerner, like so many others in whose footsteps I have followed.
> I have joyfully dedicated long years of study to it – much more than
> all my youth. In return, I hope that a little of this joy and a great deal
> of Mediterranean sunlight will shine from the pages of this book.
> Ideally perhaps one should, like the novelist, have one's subject under
> control, never losing it from sight and constantly aware of its over-
> powering presence. Fortunately or unfortunately, the historian has not
> the novelist's freedom...
> (Fernand Braudel, Preface to the first edition, *The Mediterranean and
> the Mediterranean World in the Age of Philip II*, Collins, 1972)

A few weeks ago, I was invited by the veteran presenter and journalist Josep Cuní to appear in a debate, or *tertulia*, on Catalonia's TV3. In
my profession, of academic commentator on international affairs, something I have done for more than 40 years, you can quickly ascertain, in
15 seconds at the most, the quality and attentiveness of your interviewer:

in the case of Josep Cuní, I long ago realised I was in the presence of a professional of the highest quality, at once informed, well-organised and astute, and, somewhat of a surprise among veteran TV personalities anywhere, be it in the UK or Spain, someone who avoided digressive and self-referential interventions.

The topic of the *tertulia*, occasioned by controversy on hostile coverage in the British journal *The Economist*, was on the international image of the country, and, in particular, on what Catalonia, and the Catalan government, could do to improve this situation. By dint of my having lived and worked much of the past five years in Barcelona, and of intending to continue to do so, and also because, while speaking in Spanish, I can understand discussion in Catalan, I was invited to take part. A lively, perhaps somewhat fauvist, discussion soon followed: Pilar Rahola, one of Catalonia's most controversial and outspoken writers, an equivalent of Janet Daley or Melanie Phillips in the British context, dressed in an orange suit with large tigerskin lapels, and someone with whom I came immediately to feel a certain affinity, was in characteristic form, denouncing Catalan politicians for wasting money on 'embassies' in foreign cities, while others – wiser representatives of Catalan culture, business and journalism – offered their thoughts: Salvador Sala, the former TV3 Washington correspondent, Oriol Bartomeus, a political analyst, Ramón Bagó, president of the Barcelona Tourism Salon, Enric Pujadas, president of the Bassat Ogilvy group, and Enric Larruela, a specialist on Catalan language and literature. With much of what they said, I was in agreement, above all the insistence of Enric Larruela that 'Refusal to learn the language of another people is an insult to them.'

For my part, not being Catalan, being in legal terms as a university professor a functionary of the *Generalitat*, and having long decided to avoid involvement in internal Catalan debates, following the advice of my father, an Englishman who lived many years in Ireland ('Never forget you are in someone else's country'), I forwent the chance to comment on the issue of the *Generalitat*'s embassies: had I given it, my opinion would have been – and emphasising that on matters of apparently unique or particularist nationalist sensibility I always try to phrase matters in comparative terms – that there is nothing unusual about that. In dealing with other countries that have 'federal' political systems, and in this, for all the peculiarity of the Spanish/Catalan debate, Spain is one such country. London has no problem in having missions from the provinces of Canada and Australia, not to mention from the government of Iraqi Kurdistan. For myself, and not least in my capacity as Honorary President, along with my LSE colleague Professor Paul Preston, of the Catalan Society of the London School of Economics (established January 2008), I would welcome such an institution in the British capital.

My own contribution to the *tertulia* began with some obvious, perhaps banal, observations. While in the Catalan debate words and tempers can become heated, Catalans should not overreact to the article in *The Economist*, some of which was inaccurate, but some of which was, in English terms, 'fair comment'. The author of the article, its Latin American correspondent Michael Reid, was a sincere and professional writer, in his earlier years famous as leader of an anarchist *okupa* in central London, and had found it difficult to find Catalan politicians who agreed to be interviewed by him: hence Pilar's pertinent remark, in a newspaper article, that such a controversy would never have happened in the time of Pujol. In general, I suggested, it is a mistake for peoples, however strong their national pride, to become too agitated by chance observations made about them. Instead, I suggested, they should take note of the remark by Mahatma Gandhi: 'No one ever insulted me without first receiving my permission.' I am not sure how, or if, these phrases translate into Catalan, but in English we say: 'Take the rough with the smooth', or, in American colloquial, 'You win some, you lose some.'

On the basis of my time welcoming friends and conference guests from abroad, I also felt about to remark on something which causes me as much embarrassment and irritation as it does to any Catalan: that part of the responsibility for ignorance about Catalonia, and susceptibility to myths about the country, is the fault, not of the Catalans, but of the foreigners who visit and write about the country. The latter are, in fact, remarkably few: looking through books on the literary history of Barcelona (e.g. Sergio Vila-Sanjuán and Sergi Doria, *Paseos por la Barcelona Literaria*, Ediciones Península, 2005), it is striking how in the past two centuries so few foreign writers or travellers ever came here, in comparison to France, Italy or Greece, or, further afield, Egypt, Persia, India or China. The only book that most English-speakers of my generation know is that of George Orwell, *Homage to Catalonia* (Secker & Warburg, 1938), a courageous book in its critique of Stalinism, but a work of little use in understanding either the Spanish civil war or the politics, culture and history of Catalonia itself. As Paul Preston has, with characteristic irony, remarked: 'Orwell's *Homage to Catalonia* bears as much relation to understanding the Spanish Civil War as Spike Milligan's *Adolf Hitler, My Part in his Downfall* does to World War II'. Most people in London that I meet know only two other things about Catalonia and Barcelona: the Barca football club, and the character of Manuel, a Catalan waiter, in the 1970s TV series *Fawlty Towers* – which, when dubbed into Catalan, cast Manuel as a Mexican.

For sure, this lack of international knowledge about, and intellectual engagement with, Catalonia extends to ignorance and lack of informed curiosity about Spain as a whole, but in the case of Barcelona it has, in my view, been compounded by images of the city, and of Catalonia, which, for understandable reasons of tourist promotion, and the 1992 Olympics, have been promoted in recent years: the Costa Brava for mass tourism, the theme park of Gaudí and the guided tours of the novels of Carlos Ruiz Zafón, perhaps also of Manuel Vázquez Montalbán and Eduardo Mendoza for the more discerning. These works are of high literary quality, but tend to essentialise a city that is at once plural and ever-changing. And, of course, the tourist site most visited in Barcelona has nothing to do with history or culture, but is the Museo del Fútbol Club de Barcelona. That the second most-visited museum is that of 'Picasso', even though, in fact, the Malaga painter spent little time in the city before his 1900 move to Paris, perhaps compounds the artificiality of this history.

The silences, not to say evasions, associated with the post-1975 pacted transition have also had their effect. That many of the most attractive sights in Barcelona are of less than historic antiquity matters little. Every city, and every nation, is entitled to inventions and recuperations. That such now-established festivals as that of the Mercé, or the book day that falls on the festival of Sant Jordí of 23 April (so chosen as it is the day in 1616 when both Cervantes and Shakespeare died), let alone the national holiday, the Diada, of 11 September, are recent creations does not detract from their popular, and emotional, importance. Similarly, with the fact that the term *Barri Gòtic* was invented in the 1920s, that of the Rava' ditto, the apparently baroque when not medieval square of Sant Felip Neri is a concoction of architectural removals, hardly more ancient than the sandy beaches installed in the 1980s for the Olympics to replace the industrial port district. The same reconstruction, a sort of historical

Lego or Ikea, applies to the Plaça del Rei, site of the Museum of the City of Barcelona, a seventeenth-century merchant's house transplanted here in the 1930s and of the medieval banqueting hall, the Saló del Tinell. Ditto the mock-Venetian bridge straddling two buildings in the Carrer Bisbe. Of the 'Laietani' who are said to have inhabited these parts before the arrival of the Romans, and who give their name to the arterial road driven down to the sea in 1907, we know next to nothing. As for the claim, represented in the tower and statue erected for the 1889 World Fair that bear his name at the bottom of the Ramblas, that Christopher Columbus was Catalan, neither history nor common sense suggest that it has much foundation.

What matters more is the occlusion of important, and significant, modern history. While for European intellectuals of my generation the first associations of Barcelona and Catalonia are with the civil war of the 1930s, and the role of the International Brigades in that conflict, no guidebook on sale on the Ramblas or outside the most ugly edifice of La Sagrada Familia, an 'Expiatory Temple' as it nauseously chooses to call itself, will tell the visitor, or, for that matter, a younger genera-tion, where to find the monument erected after the transition to the International Brigadistas. And, when you finally do locate it, somewhat lost in the middle of a motorway in the northern hills (outside the Túnel de Rovina, Ramblas de Carmel), there is nothing on the sculpture to tell you what it commemorates, only a quote, eloquent but unsourced, from *La Pasionaria*. When I asked some men sitting nearby on a bench what the memorial represented, they had no idea – '*Por los caídos,*' said one. '*Cada año, viene gente de los Estados Unidos y hace mucho ruido,*'[1] this pre-sumably a reference to the music of the band of the Abraham Lincoln Brigade. And, for sure, and returning to the Sagrada Familia, few of those guides who visit or patrol the site tell visitors about the building's most intriguing detail, the elevated statue of a Catalan anarchist holding a bomb, on the left next to the entrance of the Claustre del Roser.

Finally, I suggested in the TV3 *tertulia*, one thing that could help to promote knowledge of Catalonia abroad would be a different literary and cultural image. Of Barcelona, two such images are readily available. The first is that of the foreign tourist, student and temporary visitor, of the Olympics and of Woody Allen's 2008 film, *Vicky Cristina Barcelona* a

---

1   'For the fallen. Every year people come from the USA and make a racket.'

city of beaches, music, wonderful food, spectacular architecture, for some also clubs and *botellón*, for sure one of the most interesting and stimulating (in my humble view, the most interesting) cities in the world: while Barcelona does not have the diversity, the size, of its competitors, London, Paris, Berlin, New York, it uniquely has a variety, climate, scale, location and style of life which, unlike any other of these others, permits someone, with at least sufficient money, to find a balance between work and leisure.

The second image is that of the capital city of Catalonia, a product of the enormous political, economic and cultural changes of the past century or more, international in aspiration and in its receipt of tourists. The Catalan people, and its political, architectural and civic elites, have, in Barcelona, created one of the truly greatest, most beautiful, most varied and most humane and creative cities, perhaps the most humane. The civic commitment, and the urban planning and aesthetic skill, evident in this city should be a model to the rest of the world – a million years from the cult of deathly tall buildings, empty boulevards and homogenised and alienated shopping malls that prevail in much of the rest of the world. But this urban wonder has a curious social counterpart, that of a remarkably inward-looking Catalan society, one rightly proud of its achievements, but at times rather too shut to the outside world, and strangely indifferent to those who visit and come to live in it. Barcelona is a city of bright colours but surprisingly introverted social and professional circles. Barcelona is a wonderful city to visit, a very tough city to make a career or build a social network in. The issue here is not that of the Catalan language – I like the fact that I get up every morning and know I will have to work that day in three languages – but of a remarkably closed society, curiously innocent of, and perhaps indifferent to, the courtesies, inquisitiveness and hospitality which are found in most other states and cultures around the world. Every summer I notice the impact of this introversion, social and professional, on the friends I have made and students I have taught, from all continents: a third of them leave.

While this unduly self-referential world is, of course, the Catalan world of the most famous Catalan writers, and, in my experience at least, of most Catalan journalists, politicians and academics I have met, with few exceptions, this second image misses something else, hence my third suggestion on TV3: the new Barcelona of immigrants, technical change, cultural pluralism, in effect, and in the best sense of the word, 'postmodern' and necessarily 'post-nationalist' Barcelona. For this,

Barcelona awaits its writer, a John Dos Passos, a James Joyce, a Salman Rushdie, a Walter Benjamin, a Joseph Roth, a Herodotus, someone who can capture the many faces and sounds of this city in a kaleidoscopic portrait, at once true to what is the capital of Catalonia and one of the great world cities of the twenty-first century. Of modern Spanish writers, only Juan Goytisolo has sought to encapsulate this diverse, unorthodox city: but he has for many years declined to write about Barcelona, preferring broader themes, and the challenges of the Muslim world, as a way of working through his heterodox, cosmopolitan ideas.

This is the Barcelona, above all, that I have come to know and to love: the Chilean waiter in Sant Gervasi who teaches me left-wing slogans justifying mass land seizures in Mapuche; the Moroccan family I met on the beach at Barceloneta, who speak only Berber and Catalan; a sprightly gentleman of some eighty or more years, sipping coffee with his wife in a bar next to the offices of *La Vanguardia*, who, when I drop my pen, immediately jumps down and picks it up, and then presents his card, identifying him as the president of the Catalan Association of Republican Aviators, a veteran not only of the civil war, but, in exile, of the French air force as well; an Australian co-author, long resident in Papua New Guinea, now a leading translator of Catalan literature, ensconced in her book-lined eighteenth-century flat in the Born, with the volumes of Joan Corominas as backdrop; a man in his shorts, alone on the Carrer de Comercio on a torrid Sunday afternoon, singing the 'Mediterráneo' of Joan Manuel Serrat; my Icelandic designer friend who brings a small bottle of Brennivin, a 40-percent proof northern liquor from her country; the Filipino waiter who, on advising me of the best meat dishes in his country, after indicating which can be taken with chicken, pork or beef, then whispers that, of course, the best is dog; an Italian student, expert in Romance languages, and now working on Occitanian poetry, who consults me on the possible Arabic roots of this vocabulary; and my Catalan language teacher, a Palestinian translator from Los Angeles, to whom I have awarded the nickname Abu Tarjoma, 'the father of translation', whom I meet once a week for coffee and an exchange of linguistic and intercultural anecdotes. And many more.

Of course, every city, like the moon, has its shining side and its darker other. Barcelona is no exception. The particular mix of 1990s financial globalisation, coastal building speculation and drugs trading with the older habits of smuggling, corruption and state cover-up of the Franco period has produced a special, at times, dangerous brew in Spain, and not least in Catalonia. Anyone at all familiar with the night life of the city, or who has the time to read the police and court reports in the back parts of the main newspapers, will know about corrupt passport officials, drug-running policemen, bent – often very bent and very rich – municipal functionaries, prostitute enslavement rackets and the like, not to mention counterfeit CDs (42 per cent of those sold in Catalonia in 2007, according to the police) and smuggled cigarettes. The Ukrainian mafia have ensconced themselves in Tarragona, the Russians further up the coast, the Colombian narco-traffickers are hard at work and have brought *sicarios* (hired assassins) to enforce their trade.

And, uneasily adjacent to, and not entirely disentangled from, this dark world, is the grey, but extensive and visible, world of documentation, papers, residence and work permits, all that is summed up in that most potent of Spanish words, *trámites*.[1] This is the world of the long and often inconclusive queues at police stations, government offices and the like. Of apparently endless, and unpredictable, lists of documents, duly stamped and notarised, that are required for registration. Of the marriages made by Spanish citizens with foreigners to give the latter papers – the going rate in 2008 being around €6,000, double that of a year or two ago. Of work permits for jobs that do not exist, of people who enter on the passports of look-alike siblings and parents, of networks that smuggle, rob, deceive those they promise to get into Europe, of routines whereby arrivals from Latin America, via Moscow or Italy, are hustled into the toilets prior to passport control and then spirited, in cleaners' uniforms, out of the back door, losing their bags and worldly possessions on the way. And, for some, a world of daily fear and avoidance of places, such as buses or metros, where the police may raid and, with perhaps a night's interval, deport people, often without any clothes, back to their home country, the hapless victims of the dreaded *Extranjería*. A world too of urban rumours, often conveyed at the school gate or in the ethereal transnational world of the *locutorio*, or internet cafe, where Caribbean immigrants gather at times of hurricane and tropical storm in their own countries to gather news, rumours about the latest harassment of immigrants in Berlusconi's Italy, or new restrictions on immigration, of how 'they' – it is never sure who – killed a Dominican, or Cuban, or an Ecuadorian in some other part of town, or Spain, a day or two before.

---

1   Literally 'procedures', hence official 'paperwork'.

In all of this Barcelona is no different from, and probably no harsher than, a dozen other such internationalised cities in the world. And this postmodern and newly pluralistic Barcelona of course incorporates the richness and the delights of the Catalan aesthetic and urban achievement. Here many sights, sounds and memories rush together: of the Plaça Catalunya and Ramblas crowded on 23 April, the 'Day of the Book', one when convention has it that men give women a red rose (several million of which are sold that day) and women give men a book; of the crowds, respectful, proud but good-humoured, gathering in the Ciutadella Park on 11 September for the annual commemoration of the Diada, Catalan national day; of the view at night of Barcelona glistening below from the square outside the La Venta restaurant, half-way up Tibidabo mountain; of the beaches of the Puerto Olímpico jammed with thousands of tanning and variously disrobed bodies on a summer weekend, Bob Marley resonating from the beach bars, or *chiringuitos*; of a flight of green parrots in full voice flying in formation low up a totally deserted Caller Balmes one Easter Sunday morning; of a group of twenty people on horseback accompanied by cheerful and noisy drummers, coming round the corner one morning, on 3 March, the feast of Sant Medir, an early fourth-century hermit who lived in the hills north of the city, and whose cult is celebrated just in the districts of Gràcia and Sant Gervasi, until the latter part of the nineteenth-century villages, like Sants, separate from Barcelona itself; of the stillness of the Catalan Gothic Monastery of Pedralbes, and in that most beautiful of churches, the tiny Romanesque Sant Pau del Campo on the edges of the Raval; of the endless flow of fresh and succulent *tapas*, slices of *jamón ibérico, pimientos del padrón*, fresh shrimps, clams, anchovies and mussels, and the varieties (up to 43 it is said) of *pa amb tomàquet* (bread with tomato paste and olive oil) that await the visitor to many hundreds of bars; of the live Cuban music and salsa dancing on a Sunday evening in the Bar Havana-Barcelona in Barceloneta; not to mention the 'Patio of the Orange Trees' just outside my office window in Caller Elisabets; the wonderful view of Barceloneta, the harbour, Montjuic and the city from the terrace of the Miranda del Museu restaurant, on the fourth floor of the Museum of the History of Catalonia, a place of delight that I discovered only because I was giving lectures for the History Department of the University of Barcelona, on of all subjects Latin American revolutions, in a lecture theatre on the same floor (and where one of the audience turned out to be the son of the Madrid CIA station chief during Franco's last years); and the sight that greets me every morning, of the Mediterranean light, the 'rosy-fingered dawn' breaking over the rooftops, balconies and hills I see from the back of my sixth-floor flat, just as Homer celebrated it over two and a half thousand years ago.

This third, cosmopolitan and 'postmodern', Barcelona is one that encompasses the city's many personalities, some of whom I have had the good fortune to encounter by chance, or design: former Catalan Prime Minister Jordi Pujol, as sharp-witted and perceptive as ever, in an office off the Paseo de Gracia bereft of any personal adornment or distraction; the Barça footballer Ronaldinho arriving unannounced one evening after a match at Camp Nou in Monchos, on Travessera de Gràcia, accompanied by his mother, to the explosive delight of everyone in the restaurant; the philosopher Josep Ramoneda, reflecting in his office in the CCCB on the follies of modern politics; the Infanta Cristina, in her role as director of social projects with the Fundación 'La Caixa', graciously receiving some Sudanese guests I had brought from London; Josep Carod-Rovira, leader of the left-wing and pro-independence ERC, visiting IBEI, our institute, in his capacity as *Generalitat* official responsible for both foreign affairs and higher educational matters, remarking with unexpected frankness, in regard to Catalonia's foreign policy, that there were sometimes advantages in not being an independent state; and one of the city's most famous politicians and public figures, to whom I have often had the pleasure of listening, who, after arguing that, without responsible American leadership in the world economy, the rest of the world will suffer, concludes his statement (up to then given in formal Spanish): '*Sin los americanos,*' he pauses, '*no futim res.*'[1]

This third Barcelona is also that of the people – wise, wry, humorous – it has been my privilege to know: the staff and owners of my two favourite bars; the young taxi driver going up Paseo de Gracia, on the day in 2005 when the London bombings occurred '*La alegría redonda, la pena cuadrada;*'[2] an older man on a radio programme, heard passing through Plaza de España on my way to the airport, '*A la iglesia no puedo,*

---

1   'Without the Americans ... we can't even fuck.'
2   'Happiness is round, sadness is square,' i.e. happiness rolls away, but sadness stays, perhaps a rough equivalent to the famous Brazilian song of the 1960s, 'Tristeza não tem fim, felicidade sim.'

porque soy cojo. Pero a la taverna sí, poco a poco;[1] the 70-year-old taxi driver who told me he came in 1954, travelling three days on a bus from a village in Galicia, because he had heard that in the cinema queues of Barcelona *se podría ligar*, you could chat up women. Also of the *taxista* who, in mocking the name changes imposed by Franco on the city, recalled that in one case they had changed the sex of the street: believing that Hercegovína was a Catalan women's name, they had hispanized and masculinized it as Erzegovín. And, above else, and to me the most universal, eternal and, in these precipitate modern '24/7' times, most pertinent saying, the philosophy of every Barcelona taxi driver: '*O se vive para trabajar, o se trabaja para vivir.*[2] This, more than any cascades of Cava, baubles of Gaudí, the 43 varieties of *pa amb tomàquet* or the more prickly but by no means unique Catalanista linguistic sensibilities, is the message which Barcelona offers to the world.

Long may it be so. And if, perchance, such a putative postmodern writer, no doubt up-to-speed on the latest literary and discursive fashions of our age and computer-literate to boot, should wish to find inspiration, then there is nowhere better to turn, for inspiration and confirmation, than to the words of the greatest of all pre-modern and at the same time postmodern writers who, in a word he justly made famous, 'picaresque', in Chapter 72 of Part 2 of his *Don Quixote*, wrote the following about this wonderful city, which he probably visited on his way to Italy in 1569 and again in 1610:

> *Y así me pasé de claro a Barcelona, archivo de la cortesía, albergue de los extranjeros, hospital de los pobres, patria de los valientes, venganza de los ofendidos y correspondencia grata de firmes amistades, y en un sitio y un belleza, única ...*

> And so I came to Barcelona, a font of politeness, refuge for strangers, guesthouse for the poor, homeland of the brave, revenge of the insulted, and with a generous offering of firm friendships, and with a setting and beauty that are truly unique ...

Messrs Joyce, Rushdie, Benjamin, beat that if you can.

---

1   'To the church I cannot walk, since I am lame; but to the pub, I can make it, step by step.'
2   'You either live to work, or work to live.'

Books by Fred Halliday

Deutscher, Isaac, *Russia, China and the West 1953–1966*, Oxford: OUP, 1969; London: Penguin, 1970. (Serbo-Croat and German translations)

Korsch, Karl, *Marxism and Philosophy*, London: NLB, 1970.

Arabia Without Sultans, London: Penguin, 1974; reprinted 1975, 1979. (Italian, Japanese, Persian, Arabic and Turkish translations)

Iran· Dictatorship and Development, London: Penguin, 1978; reprinted 1979 (twice). (Japanese, Norwegian, Swedish, German, Spanish, Turkish, Arabic, Persian and Chinese translations)

Mercenaries in the Persian Gulf, Nottingham: Russell Press, 1979. (Persian translation.)

Soviet Policy in the Arc of Crisis, Institute for Policy Studies, Washington, 1981: issued as *Threat from the East?*, London: Penguin, 1982. (Japanese, French and Arabic translations)

with Molyneux, Maxine, *The Ethiopian Revolution*, London: Verso, 1982.

The Making of the Second Cold War, London: Verso, 1983; reprinted 1984, 1986, 1988. (German, Persian, Spanish and Japanese translations)

with Alavi, Hamza (eds), *State and Ideology in the Middle East and Pakistan*, London: Macmillan, 1988.

Cold War, Third World, London: Radius/Hutchinson, 1989. Published in USA as *From Kabul to Managua*, New York: Pantheon, 1989. (Arabic and Japanese translations)

Revolution and Foreign Policy: the Case of South Yemen, 1967–1987, Cambridge: Cambridge University Press, 1990.

Arabs in Exile, The Yemeni Community in Britain, London: I.B. Tauris, 1992.

Rethinking International Relations, London: Macmillan, 1994. (Japanese, Spanish and Portuguese translations)

From Potsdam to Perestroika, Conversations with Cold Warriors, London: BBC News and Current Affairs Publications, 1995.

Islam and the Myth of Confrontation, London: I.B. Tauris, 1996. (Arabic, Persian, Turkish, Indonesian, Polish and Spanish translations)

Revolution and World Politics: The Rise and Fall of the Sixth Great Power, London: Macmillan, 1999. (Turkish translation)

Nation and Religion in the Middle East, London: Saqi Books, 2000. (Arabic translation)

The World at 2000: Perils and Promises, London: Palgrave, 2001. (Greek and Turkish translations)

Two Hours That Shook the World. September 11 2001, Causes and Consequences, London: Saqi Books, 2001. (Arabic and Swedish translations)

The Middle East in International Relations. Power, Politics and Ideology. Cambridge: Cambridge University Press, 2005. (Italian translation)

100 Myths About the Middle East, London: Saqi Books, 2005. (Arabic, French, Italian, Portuguese, Spanish and Turkish translations)

Shocked and Awed. How 9/11 and the War Against Terror Changed our Language, London: I.B. Tauris, 2010.

Caamaño in London: the Exile of a Latin American Revolutionary, London: Institute of the Americas, 2010.

Language and Politics in the Middle East, London: Saqi Books, 2011.

Index